P9-DWP-316

THE COMMUNICATION, CULTURE, AND RELIGION SERIES
SERIES EDITORS: PAUL SOUKUP, S.J., AND FRAN PLUDE

The **Communication, Culture, and Religion** series publishes books that explore the religious and theological implications of contemporary and popular culture, especially as manifest in mass or interactive media and media products. The series encourages a dialogue in which communication practices and products shed light on religion and, in turn, religious reflection deepens an understanding of communication studies.

Through a Catholic Lens

Religious Perspectives of Nineteen Film Directors from around the World

Edited by
PETER MALONE

Communication, Culture, and Religion Series

A SHEED & WARD BOOK

ROWMAN & LITTLEFIELD PUBLISHERS, INC.
Lanham • Boulder • New York • Toronto • Plymouth, UK

A SHEED & WARD BOOK

ROWMAN & LITTLEFIELD PUBLISHERS, INC.

Published in the United States of America
by Rowman & Littlefield Publishers, Inc.
A wholly owned subsidiary of The Rowman & Littlefield Publishing Group, Inc.
4501 Forbes Boulevard, Suite 200, Lanham, Maryland 20706
www.rowmanlittlefield.com

Estover Road
Plymouth PL6 7PY
United Kingdom

British Library Cataloguing in Publication Information Available

Library of Congress Cataloging-in-Publication Data
Through a Catholic lens : religious perspectives of nineteen film directors from around
the world / [edited by] Peter Malone.
    p. cm. — (The communication, culture, and religion series)
  Includes bibliographical references and index.
  ISBN-13: 978-0-7425-5230-2 (hardcover : alk. paper)
  ISBN-10: 0-7425-5230-6 (hardcover : alk. paper)
  ISBN-13: 978-0-7425-5231-9 (pbk. : alk. paper)
  ISBN-10: 0-7425-5231-4 (pbk. : alk. paper)
  1. Motion pictures—Religious aspects—Catholic Church. I. Malone, Peter, 1939–
PN1995.5.T47 2006
791.4302'33092273—dc22

                                                                    2006031490
Printed in the United States of America

⊖™ The paper used in this publication meets the minimum requirements of American
National Standard for Information Sciences—Permanence of Paper for Printed Library
Materials, ANSI/NISO Z39.48-1992.

Contents

Introduction

Peter Malone

When British director Ken Loach was asked what it was like to make five films with Catholic Scottish writer Paul Laverty, he stated that he had learned a great deal about the Catholic Church. It was not, as he had previously thought, monolithic. For a Catholic, it is often surprising to hear commentators from outside the church describing it. Some sweeping generalizations are often made by outsiders. Assertions are voiced about authority and allegiance that are not true at all. It is assumed that all Catholics think in the same way.

This is a necessary caution to state at the beginning of a book of essays about film directors who have a Catholic background. Catholicism is not monolithic.

The origins of this book began with interviews with film directors. Initially, it was surprising to hear their answers to questions about religion. Almost immediately they would state that they were not religious or at least had no church affiliation. But then they would add, almost too hurriedly, that they were *spiritual*. They were generally happy to speak at some length about this spirituality, about their values, and how these were important in their films. They seemed to be glad to be asked these questions—instead of questions about budgets or whether this or that star was temperamental and difficult to deal with.

This was true of directors with Catholic education, especially the questions about not having a church affiliation anymore. And yet, it seemed clear that their films reflected their religious education, especially when they wrote their own screenplays as well. The obvious question to ask was whether their Catholicism, accepted, rejected, or just simply let go, was a subtext of their work. Critics and students have no difficulty in searching for all kinds of subtext in films. Is there a cultural subtext in the films of Hong Kong's *Wong Kar Wai*? Is there an African American subtext in the films of Spike Lee? Is there a Scandinavian Reformation subtext in the films of Ingmar Bergman? The obvious answer seems to be yes. So why can a Catholic subtext not be discerned?

When I listened to a conference paper by Tom Aitken on Luis Buñuel, *Viridiana*, and Catholicism (included in this book), I was convinced that the subject was worth pursuing. Aitken is not a Catholic and was not trying to prove a

1

prior thesis. And Buñuel was no exemplary lifelong Catholic. His films contain many an image and plotline that could be construed as vigorously anti-Catholic. Yet, his Catholic sensibilities pervaded his films for almost half a century. It seemed, then, worth looking at the work of other directors. It also seemed worth looking beyond Europe and the United States, although that is where most of the directors come from. Essays on a wide range of directors were commissioned.

And then Richard Blake's important book, *AfterImage*, was published in mid-2000. Blake had been fascinated by the same questions about these directors. He developed the metaphor of the afterimage to illustrate his insights. When we look intensely at a light source, he says, and then shut our eyes, the afterimage of the light remains—even if the source of the light is darkened or removed. So it is with directors who have been exposed to the light of Catholic upbringing. It remains even if it has been rejected. This seems to be a useful image to indicate all kinds of subtexts in film.

Fortunately, for this project, Blake confined himself to six directors who were American or who had long careers in the United States. The Americans he chose were John Ford, Frank Capra, Martin Scorsese, Francis Ford Coppola, and Brian de Palma (some Irish heritage but predominantly Italian Americans). He also included Alfred Hitchcock, who was born in England but spent almost forty years in the United States.

The directors selected for this study include many European directors as well as Americans, but they also represent all continents. The Europeans are: Neil Jordan (Ireland), Terence Davies (England), Louis Malle (France), Roberto Benigni (Italy), Pedro Almodóvar (Spain), and Krzysztof Kieslowski and Andrzej Wajda, focusing on Catholic–Jewish issues (Poland). The Americans (United States) are John Sayles, Kevin Smith, and Nancy Savoca (reminding us how difficult it is to find Catholic directors who are women). Directors from beyond the United States are Denys Arcand (Canada), Gaston Kaboré (Burkina Faso), Lino Brocka (Philippines), Walter Salles (Brazil), Eliseo Subiela (Argentina), Carlos Carrera (Mexico), and Fred Schepisi (Australia). There are two other directors who have double homelands: Luis Buñuel, Spain and Mexico, and Mel Gibson, Australia and the United States. This group is obviously representative, not exhaustive.

Looking at this list reminds us again that the Catholic Church is not monolithic. Clearly, the differing cultural backgrounds (Hispanic compared with Anglo-Celtic) will shape quite different, in fact, vastly different Catholic styles and practice. Anglo-Celtic liturgy has a long way to go in persuading Mass-goers to sing, let alone with enthusiasm. In Africa, Mass-goers go singing and dancing up to the ministers holding the bag for the money offerings, and swaying rhythmically, they give generously.

To appreciate the different types of Catholicism, it is useful to examine a distinction made by St. Augustine (354–430) about faith: firstly, to believe God's truth and secondly, to commit oneself to God in action. He was able to use the more succinct phrases of Latin: *Credere Deum*, to believe God, and *Credere Deo*, to believe in God.

Credere Deum

For many Catholics, their faith can be a profound belief in the deepest mysteries of God, creation, incarnation, and redemption. The tenets of the creed summarize for a Catholic the religious experience of God's truth. But this is not always the case. For many who recite the creed, and regularly recite it, their faith is not really moved by these mysteries, and there is no felt need or conviction to try to understand them. They are, rather, a ritual formula that is required to belong to the Church. The formula is like any other formula of loyalty or belonging to a significant group. The creed is more an expression of a religious ideology than an expression of faith. It is the same for attendance at Mass and church services. This is required, so it is done—although far more loosely and less regularly in recent decades. This is a formal Catholicism, almost minimal, a code for acceptability and acceptance.

Credere Deo

This is a lived faith. It involves personal and communal commitment to faith, not simply fulfilling formal requirements of belonging to be able to place a census tick in the Catholic box. Committed Catholics take their religion and spirituality out of the church on Sunday to find ways of living it, especially in charity and prayer, and witnessing to it in their daily lives. Critics of the church, including those who leave it, have high expectations of what this lived faith should be like, even if they find they cannot do it themselves. This is what some authors call *the Catholic thing*, something that pervades and can inspire even those who have rebelled against it or rejected it. It is often admired by those outside the church and can be the driving force for those who remain.

Catholicism offers a worldview; it includes personal questions, like destiny, sin, guilt, and repentance, pervasive in such creative but struggling Catholics like Graham Greene who knew sin but looked for virtues to admire and to try to live by. It provides a sustaining story, history, and even mythology. As Maggie Roux suggests, a personalized responsibility in mature Catholicism can give a mandate for fine attitudes and deeds (although can sometimes be bastardized into guilt). Even a superficial adherence gives a language, a sense of ritual, and an opening to something transcendent.

Not living the commitment, merely paying lip service to belonging to the church, brings the frequent charge of hypocrisy. This is especially true if the charge is made, right or wrong, against those in leadership roles in the church who are judged not to practice what they preach. It is also true if the charge is made, right or wrong, against church people, official or not, who have offended, been cruel to, or who have abused—with the consequence that the victim, hurt or angry, has left the church. These are themes to be found in the films of many of the directors under consideration. Buñuel, and later Almodóvar, have reviled the Spanish church, especially its clergy. Schepisi experienced the hothouse regime of a 1950s Juniorate. Arcand went through the upheaval of the Quebec church throwing off perceived religious shackles. Davies was angry at his treatment by the church for being gay. Others found that the church they knew was empty and had nothing to offer them.

This means that in reading about these directors and discerning the sub-texts, we will be discovering different Catholicisms. They all have their roots in two thousand years of preaching of the Gospel of Jesus Christ and of his saving mission. They all have their roots in the history of the church, its grace and its sinfulness. They all have an experience of liturgy and worship, of religious education, of a moral foundation, and of a sense of worldwide communion. However, for some of the directors, the major influence was the cultural dimension of the church. For some, it is the piety, practice, and education that they experienced when young. For some, it is the power and truth of the church's teaching. The reader will be alert to this variety in Catholicism in appreciating how the writers have highlighted particular facets and found these in the text and subtext of their films.

The chapters were originally set in alphabetical order of surname. However, on reflection, it seemed more helpful to set up particular groupings and to write an introduction for each section indicating aspects of faith and church rather than leave it to a general introduction. The groupings highlight what the directors have in common: Jordan, Davies, and Schepisi come from the Anglo-Celtic tradition in Ireland, England, and Scotland and Australia; Sayles and Savoca come from the mainstream American tradition; from Spanish and Portuguese Iberian Catholicism in Europe or in Latin America, come Almodóvar, Subiela, Carrera, and Salles; there are three directors who saw themselves as agnostic or atheist ("thank God," said Buñuel), Buñuel, Arcand, and Kieslowski; the "missionary" Catholicism in colonies from European powers is found in Kaboré and Brocka; Jewish-Christian relations and tensions appear in Malle, Wajda, and Benigni. And how to finish? With two directors who live in the United States and see themselves as practicing Catholics, Gibson who looks to the past and to traditions, and Kevin Smith, the youngest of all the directors in this book (born 1971) who shows something of the Catholicism of the present (certainly not monolithic) and who looks to the future.

Each of our contributors was asked to select one film from their director so that readers could appreciate the background and type of Catholicism in that director's work. They locate the director in his or her culture, indicate aspects of faith and lack of faith, of belief and spirituality—whether the afterimage metaphor illuminates the film (how pervasive is the Catholicism, how explicit or implicit?) and whether the film illuminates aspects of Catholicism while challenging it.

That is why the title of this book includes the image of the lens. Film directors use many lenses in their work depending on their vision, the feeling they want to capture, particular angles, or a different focus. For the directors whose work is explored here, there is also a Catholic lens.

The reader will put together a Catholicism of the twentieth century, worldwide, strong or weak, as old as Buñuel and as young as Smith, revealing that with the history of film, a changing church is revealed, changing spirituality and belonging. And it will make the reader wonder, would Buñuel like *Dogma*?

Part 1

Anglo-Celtic Catholicism

Celtic Catholicism has one of the longest histories, dating, of course, back to St. Patrick in the fourth century. Patrick opposed the now-called Celtic spirituality, which derived from nature religions and the Druids. However, it was never far below the surface of Irish culture. This religious culture developed and spread across to Scotland and Northern England, a balance (and sometimes rival) to the Anglo Catholicism that was finally established by St. Augustine of Canterbury at the end of the sixth century. The two have interacted ever since; the British imposing themselves on Ireland in the Middle Ages and continuing to dominate while not eradicating the Celtic traditions.

Irish Catholicism, especially from the time of the Reformation and the rule of Oliver Cromwell in the seventeenth century, was often a survival Catholicism, faithful to what it thought that Rome required, pious with more than a touch of Jansenistic unworldliness, and dominated by the clergy. With the Reformation, the Anglo tradition of Catholicism was persecuted and went underground. Those faithful to Rome were called recusants who refused to submit to the new Church of England. In succeeding centuries until the repeal of anti-Catholic laws in 1829, clergy were trained in France and ministered to Catholics, often with the patronage of wealthy Catholic families.

The meeting of these two Catholicisms came about with Irish migration to England and to Australia in the nineteenth century. It has been noted that there are still traces of two Catholicisms in Britain; one the upper class, refined Catholicism seen in such novels as *Brideshead Revisited*, the other, the popular, pious Catholicism of the Irish working classes. With changing patterns of migration in recent decades, Catholics are composed of Africans, West Indians, and people from such European Catholic countries as Poland and Italy. While there was an Irish domination of Catholicism in Australia, this changed, especially after World War II with migrants coming in great numbers from Italy, Malta, Poland, and other European countries.

This Anglo-Celtic tradition in Ireland, Britain, and Australia has meant strong allegiance to the structures of the church, to formal professions of faith, to a devotional life, and a pride in being called Catholic. It was part faith, part ideology. The difficulty with these stances is that when the ideology is undermined and the faith is not a strong commitment, both can lapse. This has been the case with reactions against authoritarian education, questioning of moral positions, and a perceived excessive control of personal freedoms by Church authorities (some of whose status has been destroyed by abuse scandals).

Neil Jordan received a Catholic education up to university studies, where he met Michael Paul Gallagher, but moved away from the authoritarian Irish Church. His Catholic sensibilities can be seen especially in his version of Graham Greene's *The End of the Affair*. Terence Davies grew up in 1950s Liverpool, a city that received so many migrating Irish Catholics whose faith set the tone for Catholic life there. Davies has recreated the devotions and piety of that era, especially in *The Long Day Closes*, visualizing the prayers of his childhood. This kind of upbringing was shared by Maggie Roux in Glasgow who empathizes with Davies. Davies, however, has a more personal dispute with the Church. In an interview with Melvyn Bragg at the time of the release of *The Long Day Closes*, he quietly but angrily denounced the church's stances on homosexuality, distancing himself from belonging to the Catholic Church.

Fred Schepisi grew up in Melbourne (Australia), with both Irish and prewar Italian Catholic background. Peter Malone examines this Australian Catholic heritage. So devout was Schepisi that he entered the Juniorate of the Marist Brothers in Melbourne at the age of thirteen. It proved to be a time of disillusionment for him, a time of sexual tension leading to a criticism of his faith. However, his earliest films broke ground in Australian cinema by treating explicitly Catholic themes: the 1970s crisis in the priesthood as well as a recreation of his year in the Juniorate. In recent years, he has mellowed considerably toward the Church.

A Song That Will Not Die:
The Films of Terence Davies

Maggie Roux

> *"If there had been no suffering, there would be no films."*
> —Terence Davies[1]

> *Who made you?*
> *—God made me.*
> *Why did God make you?*
> *—God made me to know him, love him, and serve him in this world and be happy with him forever in the next. What is God?*
> *—God is Love.*

Anyone brought up in the 1950s in a British working-class Catholic household will instantly recognize these pivotal questions from the *Penny Catechism*. All Catholic schoolchildren were expected to know their catechism, and I remember well from a Scottish, Glaswegian childhood, "woe betide you" if you did not!

In the final part of *The Terence Davies Trilogy (Death and Transfiguration,* 1983) children are heard reciting these three catechism questions as Robert, dying from old age, flashes back to different stages in his life. It could be argued that Davies has spent his filmmaking years trying to make sense of everything the catechism questions are about—not just the meaning of the questions themselves but also his culture. Davies, like many other children of his time, was carefully imbued with a strong sense of personal sin. Understanding and assenting to the teachings in the catechism was an essential weapon in the battle against daily temptations leading children to hellfire and damnation. The sound of children reciting their catechism from these years stirs up images of church and school, and memories of feeling overwhelming guilt and even the fear imbued on the young that one was personally responsible for the suffering and death of the son of God.

It has been said that memory works by distilling raw experience into a few stories, a few set pieces. It is the set pieces that are remembered.[2] Remembering his childhood drives the work of Davies. His memory set pieces are placed firmly within the family, the school, and his Catholic culture. The essential props in his set pieces are drawn from music, the movies, and religious iconography, particularly that of the Pietà and of the cross. He also draws, to some extent, powerfully, though narrowly, on nature.

Born in Liverpool, England, in 1945, Davies was the youngest of ten children. He left school at fifteen and worked in accountancy until some years later in the early seventies when he began to study acting. He directed *Children*, the first film in his trilogy, in 1975, which went on to win a bronze Hugo at the Chicago Film Festival in the same year. His second film from the trilogy, *Madonna and Child*, was made in 1980 when he was studying at the National Film and Television School in Beaconsfield. He finished *Death and Transfiguration* in 1983 and released all three as *The Terence Davies Trilogy* in 1984.

Davies returned to the themes of his Catholic childhood in his acclaimed films, *Distant Voices, Still Lives* (1988) and *The Long Day Closes* (1992). *The Neon Bible* (1995), adapted from *Confederacy of Dunces*, a novel by John Kennedy O'Toole set in the American Bible Belt, hints at a similar emotional landscape of childhood powerlessness in the face of paternal violence, peer bullies, and religious dogmatism. *The House of Mirth* (2000) from Edith Wharton's novel also has a main character who lacks emotional and material security and is finally destroyed by her inability to fit into the straightjacket of the social expectations around her.

His early film tools became his trademark. Ingmar Bergman was an influence. The two men—one a Swedish Protestant and the other an English Catholic—share much in common in terms of attitudes to life and film. Much of Davies's filmmaking echoes Bergman's insights on "film as dream, film as music."[3] Davies and Bergman both insist on a measure of stillness in the viewer's gaze as the camera rests on ordinary, everyday items and infuses them with transcendent light and focus. Bergman tried to penetrate his long vanished emotions by studying photographs of his childhood, in particular his mother's face, not unlike the use of photographs in *Distant Voices, Still Lives*.

In his use of lighting and long still scenes (ensuring the persistence of our gaze so that we might reach out and touch the essence of misery or joy) Davies matches the best in Andrei Tarkovsky, who was described by Bergman as one who "moves with naturalness in the room of dreams."[4] Davies, too, moves us through his dream rooms "deep into the twilight room of the soul."[5] The glorious scene in *The Long Day Closes*, when we find ourselves in close examination of a carpet, brings to mind a scene in Tarkovsky's *Nostalghia* (1983) where our attention is focused on a drop of water, which becomes a puddle, which becomes the universe. Stark and transcendent use of lighting, varied camera angles, flashbacks, his preferred framing techniques, and his favorite tracking shots have earned him praise as the "British cinema's poet of memories." Davies is from Liverpool, which for many is a tough city, where survival is married to an acute sense of humor. He might demur therefore at being described as a lyrical film-maker, but he is one, nevertheless.

"When film is not a document it is a dream."   —Ingmar Berman[6]

Davies's work at times crosses the boundaries between document and dream and at times merges the forms together and at times makes clear distinctions between each.

Filmed in black and white in the style of social realism, *The Trilogy* is an exploration of Davies's childhood, school days, family life, and his emotional development as a homosexual. His father, a rag-and-bone man, was a drunkard, brutish, and terminally ill with stomach cancer during Davies's early childhood. All the family was subjected to his father's violence, but Davies was particularly distressed at the violence his mother experienced (in one terrible incident she was threatened with an axe). Davies was devoted to his mother throughout her life—a devotion movingly portrayed in *Madonna and Child*. In *The Trilogy*, Davies positions mother and son alone without his siblings. Neither could save the other from daily misery, but both found in each other a reason to endure. The Pietà appears in several scenes and serves as a heartbreaking metaphor for the suffering nature of their relationship—the broken mother lovingly, but powerlessly, cradling the broken son.

As the youngest of the children Davies seems to feel he, his mother, and his father were locked together in a fearful family trio, although he later explored the trials of the family as a whole in *Distant Voices, Still Lives*. Looking back at his life through the character, Robert Tucker, the final part of *The Trilogy*, *Death and Transfiguration*, takes him into a future as an old man waiting to die in bleak geriatric surroundings, flashing back through moments in the first two films *Children* and *Madonna and Child*.

The Trilogy, then, sets out to document a life which, perhaps, he needs to reexperience to defuse its power. Davies, though, denies the experience is therapeutic.[7] His father's violence, in particular, had a lasting effect—"the damage that is done when you are a child is so long lasting. I'm still acutely aware of atmosphere in a room. When I was a kid and if he didn't want anyone around he'd just kick me from one end of the house to the other."[8] The violence, particularly against his mother, was terrifying but also "the silences and the cruelty that was in the air. Then it would start all over again."[9]

The soundtracks are powerful in Davies's choice of music (another of his favorite tools), but his use of silence is effective, too. In *The Trilogy* silence is set within an echo, evoking a feeling of being watched and heard wherever one is, whatever one is doing. Thus a child lives with the fear of discovery and unloving judgment every day, every moment. The fear is all the worse as God can see into one's soul. Psalm 139 promises the authentic love of God who knows all our ways and seeks our safety within his presence. The reality for Robert is that there is no safety anywhere, not at home or at school. This is a horror in *The Trilogy*. There is aching loneliness but nowhere to be alone.

Throughout *The Trilogy* and throughout Davies's later films, the church portrayed is the male church of the schoolteachers. His sexuality aside, the adult male (and to some extent his male peers) was the great dragon for Davies as a child. His father was a bully but different only from the teachers in that the father's cruelty was hot tempered and unpredictable. The violence of the teachers was predictable, ideological, and ice cold. The scenes where the children have left a teacher's room after a caning are telling. The camera rests its gaze on the teachers who remain stiff with self-righteous fury at childish misdemeanors. There is no tenderness, no understanding; much worse, there is no justice. The biblical injunction to *suffer the little children to come to me* is a text that holds no sway in the teachers' behavior or understanding.

Davies sees more deeply. His camera shows the teachers as martinets betraying themselves and their vocations in the service of a lie. Their persuasion is that their violence is almost a saving grace bestowed on their charges. Sinfulness must be purged no matter at what cost for the sake of the children's souls. Bergman and Davies share similar memories of school and teaching methods in which "punishments were exemplary and often affected the offender for life" and "the implanting of a guilty conscience." Robert's nightmare from which he wakes up screaming is of himself dead in his coffin while the prayers for the dead are intoned over him. He hears the biblical warning, "The time is at hand. Thy judgment is come." The judgment of God is the stuff of terror. This permeates the attitude of the school toward the children. It is a place of the death of the spirit. But the camera's gaze is both warning and compassionate. The violence of the teachers violates them as surely as it violates the children, just as his father's violence earned him his family's approbation and hatred.

In one stunning scene the camera pans slowly over empty school desks and chairs while the soundtrack has children reciting the creed. This scene seems prophetic when read against the contemporary crisis in church attendance. Was the Catholic school system so busy saving the souls of children through liberal use of strap, cane, and contempt that it destroyed the safe future of the church itself? As one of a similar age to Davies and schooled in a similar environment, watching these films hooks me into painful reconstructions of my own. Davies has the power not just to portray memory but to make it *felt*.

Davies, however, displays a complete lack of self-pity in his *remembering*. As director he seems to place himself, rather, as a witness to the fact of the stories. He uses the device of cameos, short little bursts of storylines, to embrace the complexities of human behavior and of family life and relationships. Andrew Greeley describes the "Sacramental Imagination" as one who tends to see things not as black and white but rather in "grayer and problematic colours."[10] Davies is a master at probing the problematic using focus, lighting, and shadow exploratively and wonderingly. An incident in *The Trilogy*, which is clearly from his childhood, is when Robert and his mother are traveling home by bus. As the child gazes out through the bus window, the mother weeps silently in abject despair. Another from *The Trilogy* is of Robert (now an old man) breathing his last in an elongated, shattering silent scream while reaching toward the light (I remembered a similar device used to great power in Francis Ford Coppola's *Godfather: Part III* [1990] when Michael held his dying daughter in his arms—her death the result of his descent into evil).

Davies witnesses to brutality and to casual or institutional cruelty, but the key element in his storytelling is that of comforting love. He is a filmmaker who deals not in answers but who is, rather, seeking out moments of grace. He questions not what it is to be right, but rather, what it is to be loved. This is brought powerfully to bear in the scene where, after a beating, the mother comes into Robert's bedroom. Mother and son sit watching and loving each other in stillness, unable to reach out and hold each other in case they break down completely. The emotional framing is one of immense compassion.

The power of Davies's *Trilogy* leaves us in a terrible place. His filmmaking is not clinical, but it is sparse. The place these films inhabit is the place of dark memories, memories that eat at the self, the soul, and faith in God.

"Film-making is an agonizing struggle. It is in itself, a quest for truths, for understanding." —John Boorman[11]

Boorman's statement encompasses the importance of being a filmmaker to Davies. The search is for understanding, not just of self but, more essentially, of the self imposed on a small child who followed the beat of a different drum to those around him. Davies has gone on record as regarding his homosexuality as a curse. This is not to suggest he sees homosexuality as a curse in itself but for him in his background and experience it "ruined my life."[12] *The Trilogy* explores Robert's *felt* difference in sexual orientation, almost without comment. We are given no strictures from scripture, catechism, or sermon. That the boy, however, believes his growing sexual interest and desire is sinful is not in doubt. Almost in a pantomime gesture Davies cuts to a church scene with the choir singing as the adult Robert is heard on the telephone asking a tattooist for highly intimate, sexually uncompromising tattoos. As the phone conversation goes into lurid detail the camera marks the Stations of the Cross, the body of the church, and finally the high altar. The link between sensuality and the search for ecstasy, leading ultimately to suffering and death, is further drawn as the camera rests on the station where Jesus is brought down from the cross. At that moment the tattooist slams the phone down on Robert's request.

Homosexual activity is portrayed at one point almost as fun but generally as mechanical and cold. There is an appalling scene of fellatio—brutal, completely lacking in tenderness and relationship. There is no relationship either in the confessional. It is not the place of self-understanding (as it has since become in the Sacrament of Reconciliation) but only of bitter self-accusation.

Robert believes his sexuality, his sexual practice, and his desires are sinful. He cannot receive absolution without making, as the catechism used to say, a "firm purpose of amendment." Robert cannot be other than himself and therefore cannot fulfill the requirement. And so the religious trap is sprung. The only truth he can tell in the confessional is that he is guilty of the sin of despair. When Robert, later in his office, replays his "false" confession back in his mind and hears the words of absolution, he weeps. Having made a false confession, Robert is now in an even worse state of sin. Davies said that "on one occasion I prayed until my knees bled."[13]

But Davies does not quite leave it there. The most powerful church image in *The Trilogy* is just before the confession scene where Robert and his mother sit close to each other in church—the two figures foreground and frame the Pietà at the back of the church. The meditation on the thirteenth station, which leads to the Pietà, is of the body of Jesus being taken down from the cross and in the words of *A Simple Prayer Book* "placed in the arms of his afflicted Mother, who received him with unutterable tenderness, and pressed him to her bosom."

Robert (not Davies) believes it is the nature of his sexuality that is sinful. Few Catholics from his background and his time, however, no matter what their sexual orientation, would have felt otherwise. Sexuality itself was sinful. The body was the temple of soul, but its physical nature was problematic. The body should be hidden. Many Catholic children were instructed not to look on their own nudity while bathing in case of sinful thoughts. Catholic heterosexuals, homosexuals, and lesbians alike grew up believing that physical desire was entirely wrong despite the small print studied in theological colleges. Catholics were taught how to examine their conscience before going into the confessional. The sticking point for many was the question "have I been immodest or impure in thought, word, and deed with myself or with others?"

Girls were, often, not only ashamed of their desires but ashamed of their physical makeup. Menstruation was their first great dark secret. Some girls I knew from convent days even avoided the Eucharist at those times in case their "filth" contaminated the sacrament. The altar railings separated the laity from the clergy (the profane from the sacred), but women were clearly the worst profanity. That women were banned from the altar further impressed on young girls the undesirability of their physical selves—not to mention the hallowing of Mary's perpetual virginity.

Davies, who clearly believed that Catholicism compounded his sense of guilt, rejected the church at the age of twenty-two. Interestingly, his films concentrate on the effects of the Catholic school rather than that of the clergy. He has almost nothing to say on the priesthood in any of his work.

"Looking into your heart can be a very painful process. Being aware is a mug's game. An absolute mug's game."   —Terence Davies[14]

While homosexual contact in *The Trilogy* is shameful, brutal, unsatisfactory, and ultimately destructive of one's immortal soul, in *The Long Day Closes* the child's sexual awakening is placed in a different frame. The child (Bud), free from the malign effect of paternal violence, blossoms in the love of his mother, who is lit almost as an old master would use light to indicate the sacred (Davies particularly loves Vermeer). Bud is an innocent and as he gazes out from his room (in which at night he attempts to trace the night shadows on his wall, a theme continued in *Neon Bible*) he sees a beautiful youth, stripped to the waist, building a brick wall. The moment is transformational. Their eyes meet, casting for a moment a spell in which the boy becomes sexually awakened. He is mesmerized and shy. His reward for his frank admiration is an uncomplicated smile and wink from the young builder. It is a moment in Eden and a celebration of physical and sexual beauty. But he cannot hold the young man's openness; overwhelmed and confused he retreats behind the window.

The face of the young man comes back to Bud later in the film as he prays before the crucifix. At the words "deliver me from the misfortune of falling into mortal sin" he hears the sound of the nail being driven into Christ's hand. As he gazes on the crucified figure he sees the face of the young builder there on the cross looking up at him.

Davies speaks movingly about how we notice odd things at the most awful times of our lives.[15] A childhood spent in Catholic schools and churches initiates one into the iconography of suffering and horror from the start. The crucifixion is the great saving sacrificial death on behalf of us all, the price paid for our sins. The sheer horror of this juxtaposition of a sexual daydream while meditating before the cross might be lost on non-Catholics or even young contemporary Catholics, but in the Catholic environment of Davies's youth it would have a powerful and disturbing resonance.

Salvador Dali's painting of St. John of the Cross—merging Catholic iconography and homosexual eroticism—was perhaps too obvious a model for this scene, but it works well through Davies's distorting both view and sound. Bud suppresses the moment in the remainder of his prayer (still recited by many Catholics today at the end of each decade of the Rosary) ". . . do with me what thou wilt. Grant that I may love thee always."

"I want the truth of something and the real truth real truth of something is always small."   —Terence Davies[16]

Davies ventures into the same family and semiautobiographical territory as *The Trilogy* in the outstanding films *Distant Voices, Still Lives* and *The Long Day Closes*. Indeed one writer refers to *Distant Voices, Still Lives* as two films with *The Long Day Closes* forming the last in another trilogy. However, if the first trilogy is a cathartic telling in almost documentary form the second trilogy moves into *dream*.

The Long Day Closes opens with a still life—a vase of flowers that links it with its predecessor *Still Lives*. After the credits, the camera tracks down across the ancient rain-sodden street of his childhood memory with Nat King Cole singing Stardust in the background. *The Trilogy* had introduced us to Davies's techniques of framing his character through windows, doorways, stairwells flanked by railings, or stairways flanked by banisters (*Neon Bible* repeats such a shot of the boy on the train). *The Long Day Closes* evokes a boyhood bound within protective familial happiness against the religious, social, and sexual ideologies and mores threatening his emotional center. The stunning opening tracks into dark places and dark memories, but the lyrics of Stardust lull our fears—we are entering *the meadows* of the heart, *the stardust* of yesterday.

Davies is on different ground in *The Long Day Closes*. The father is dead, and Davies points to something heartbreaking but commonplace. There are parents so damaging that the family can survive only if that parent dies or disappears. This was clearly Davies's experience. His father's death set Davies, his siblings, and his mother free from fear. Years later Davies stated "I hated him and I still do. He was brutal. I can forgive what he did to my brothers and me, but I can't forgive what he did to my mother, who was so loving and gentle. He was never tender with me."[17]

Through the material of his own films, Davies almost celebrates himself as a film buff. Interlinked with his memories of church ritual, hymns, and school, movies are his main afterimage. Catholicism clearly shaped Davies, but the movies were the necessary counterpoint—particularly the musicals. Three of his favorite movies were *Singin' in the Rain* (1952), *Young at Heart* (1954), and *Meet Me in St. Louis* (1944). Indeed it is *Meet Me in St. Louis* that one might argue is closest to *The Long Day Closes* with its warm family life, giggling, feminine sisters with their young men, and the beautiful evening fairground scene. But a touch of gentle melancholy is overlaid on the piece by a moving rendition of the folk song *She Moved through the Fair*, a song about the death of love and hope. Bud's mother picks up the melody and tearfully sings it for him as they sit together in front of the fire.

The film writer, Jonathon Coe, points out the remoteness of Davies's beloved healing comedies and MGM musicals from the austerity of Davies's own work. "How," he asks of *The Neon Bible*, "did Davies get from there to here?"[18] Daniel

Taylor in his book *The Healing Power of Stories* points out that "we embrace those stories which create a world in which we find it possible, even desirable, to live. The stories we value the most reassure us that life is worth the pain . . ."[19] Davies said of the central scene in *Singin' in the Rain* that "[d]uring the big dance sequence I just cried and cried because this was such happiness, I'll never know such happiness again—it breaks my heart." He further described this pleasure as "one of the most transcendental experiences of my life."[20]

   The Long Day Closes has been criticized as a lesser work than *The Trilogy* and *Distant Voices, Still Lives*, because it lacks the "inexpressible rage and disappointment which erupts in *Still Lives*."[21] John Caughie detects in *The Long Day Closes* a "shadow of cynicism and detached reason"[22] over the whole film and accuses the scene where Bud's mother is at the washtub, singing a line from a well-known British World War II–era song, "If you were the only girl in the world" (reprised from *The Trilogy*) as exploitative in his use of lighting and composition. Caughie goes further, almost accusingly: "without wishing to make too much of biography it seems that 1956 [the years of Suez, Hungary, and the breakup of the left, which have no mention in Davies's work] for Davies represented only the rule of the father being replaced with the care of the mother."[23]

   However, viewing the film within the full opus, there is an argument that can be made that *The Long Day Closes* should be a different film experience than the previous works. What separates *Long Day* from *The Trilogy* and *Distant Voices, Still Lives* is an abrupt and amazing change in experience itself; the vale of tears has become a place of benediction. The film image that comes to mind is Dorothy stepping across the doorstep to find herself over the rainbow. We are now in a place of sheer wonder and grace. Bud/Robert/Davies knows that the wicked witch is "most sincerely dead."[24] A child emerging into the light from a brutal early childhood into a world in which ordinary pleasure, warm-heartedness— even exhilaration—is possible at all, let alone encouraged, knows he is now on sacred ground. For the first time in Bud's life the present moment does indeed become sacramental. Factual history in the making does not have an automatic right to a place in such memories.

"Types and shadows have their ending."   —*from* The Tantum Ergo Benediction Hymn by St. Thomas Aquinas

Long Day Closes is about family celebration, family gathering, family members giving each to the other their place with consideration, and love set against the long night of painful memory when such things were impossible. There is a powerful sense of innocent pleasure asserting itself with all that implies for safe emotional development. This is previously uncharted (even unimagined) territory set against the previous films. Davies avoids sentimentalizing this memory but rather through the production design of Christopher Hobbs *hyperrealizes* it, makes it larger than life. It is not "how it was" but rather a "re-creation of Terence's memory."[25] Questions raised about the nonlinearity of his work is answered in *The Long Day Closes*. "I'm not interested in what-happened next, I'm interested in what-happened-emotionally next."[26]

Bud still has to face his dragons. Davies himself is a sensitive man aware of the misery humming beneath everyday life: "I'll see something that in anybody else would not matter and it will make me feel so depressed, someone crossing the street or an old person not being helped or something and that's it—the veil falls from life and you see what lies behind it, and it's absolute horror."[27] Despite the movies, the music, and sunny washdays Bud has to withstand school bullying, the school system itself, and what Hannah Patterson has described as the intangible threatening male presence, which she sees pervading all Davies's films.[28] But his spirit and courage are replenished at home. The family is his real church. The home is the real shrine. His mother is the *Star of the Sea*, the mother most high in whom his wanderings will be safe. The three catechism questions are making sense at last as the family becomes a realization of the kingdom of God. Marital relationships are demonstrated as possible with the cameos of the neighbor who is a kindly and amusing drunk married to an affectionate, witty wife.

The many mansions within mother's house contain laughter, music, tenderness, and fellowship, too, with the wider community. In a blaze of delightful over-the-top kitsch, Davies stages a Christmas scene with the family Christmas meal. The candlelit interior, decorated and festooned with decorations and presents, merges with the snow-covered street outside. As Bud watches the scene, the family turns to the camera and wishes him a happy Christmas. The snow falls gently, magically, over all. It is sheer Hollywood excess, and Davies could be accused of overegging the nostalgic pudding.

Yet an alternative reading might be made. Davies's memories include school nativity pageants and children singing the celebratory twelfth night carol, "We Three Kings." Leonardo da Vinci's painting *The Last Supper* is a compelling image in many Catholic homes, and while it points to betrayal and the sacrificial nature of the meal, the promise inherent in the Eucharist is that of the great heavenly feast of life everlasting. Davies frames the family Christmas table as da Vinci does his last supper. This scene connects with the afterimage suggested by Richard Blake.[29] Davies's memory bank interlinks Hollywood movies and music with those parts of Catholic ritual, which promise the light after darkness. But another, perhaps deeper link can be explored between the table (with the mother as the central figure) as the heavenly feast in *The Long Day Closes* and the table of betrayal portrayed in *Distant Voices, Still Lives* where the father destroys the hope of the Christmas message with his violent destruction of the family Christmas meal.

Interestingly, *The Long Day Closes* echoes the voice-over from Stuart Walker's film, *Great Expectations* (1934), where another sacramental table, that of the wedding feast, has been turned into dust by the crumbling of hopes and family. As Miss Haversham intones her despair of the sharp teeth of regrets and her last hope for the light of life, "I have a fancy I should like to see someone play." *The Long Day Closes* on the sound of a great bell chiming (the bell often a symbolic referent of the voice of God) while Bud and his friend Albee gaze in wonder at the immensity of the night sky.

> "If you want to accomplish something in the arts, if you want to learn to make good films, don't be impersonal, don't be afraid of the pronoun I."
>
> —Andrei Tarkovsky[30]

Davies has said he does not wish his work to explore his life in the cathartic sense: "It's never catharsis because it's too painful."[31]

Nor would he, I think, describe himself as a Catholic director. In his films, the Catholic school is often a place of violence and denigration of others that he experienced and so much detests. He refers to Catholic ritual and hymns in his memory set pieces but does not explore dogmatics, the institutional church, or even the priesthood in any obvious way.

I would describe him so, however. His use of imagery is so compelling that the essence of the sacramental imagination is clearly demonstrated. His films are underpinned by a sensitivity to Paul Tillich's understanding of "The Ground of our Being"—an existentiality contextualized in universal love and relationship with the divine experienced through the overarching quality of nature, light, and music but also in the smallest things, such as the empire red lipstick and Evening in Paris perfume Bud was sent to buy for his sisters. Davies positions this scene after the children have sung "The Tantum Ergo" in church. Such mundane items encapsulate pleasure but more importantly possibilities and promise. Davies is awake to all such nuances. In simple things like a bike ride, swinging on a bar, or sitting in his mother's arms as she sings in front of the fire, Davies seems to point to something of the abundance of God through his imaging.

"The least you do undo these little ones you do unto me."[32] Davies cannot help but express the full meaning of the biblical injunction in his films from *The Trilogy* right through to *The House of Mirth*. Cruelty leads to the spiritual wasteland; kindness and understanding bestow eternal life. He has made it clear that for him the guilt implicated in his sexuality came from his Catholic roots; but Bergman, too, suffered horror and guilt in his own sexual awakening and sought release through spiritual exercises and prayers. Davies, though, grasps the essence of what Rosemary Haughton frequently names "the Catholic enterprise," "the Catholic Thing." His work demonstrates the understanding that seeds of the kingdom of God are in all things, perhaps hidden, but, once identified and celebrated, become transcendent.

Davies's favorite poet is T. S. Eliot, in particular Eliot's poem, *The Four Quartets*. With the loss of his faith and of his mother, Davies mourns "Oh dark, dark, dark, we all go into the dark."[33] But his films evoke not just grief but Eliot's wisdom that memory work is about "finding ourselves back in the place where we first started and understanding the place for the first time." Bergman struggled, too, with his faith in God. "I have struggled all my life with a tormented and joyless relationship with God. My prayers stank of anguish, entreaty, trust, loathing and despair. God Spoke, God said nothing. Do not turn from me Thy face."[34] Bergman's despair echoes Robert's despair in the confessional. Bergman came finally to an existentialist position that there was no meaning or purpose other than that living being its own meaning. Davies has said that he wishes he could believe that "we go into a greater life, but I think there's nothing out there."[35]

But while Davies denies the church and a belief in God, perhaps he continues to seek the possibility of grace. *The House of Mirth* ends with a beautiful scene—a still of Lily lying in her sleep of death. The music that plays out the film over this scene and into the credits is Aleksandr Porfirveyich Borodin's *String Quartet No. 2 in D*. Davies knows his music and his movies. Is he making a point here? The quartet was adapted for the musical *Kismet* (which means fate). It became the melody for the film's great love song "This Is My Beloved."

Whatever else *The Long Day Closes* is about, the gentle, generous, and loving nature of Davies's mother is the overarching theme of the film. Speaking of her death he said he "wanted to die. That's it, I thought there's nothing else to live for, there just isn't because she was the love of my life. I loved her with all my heart and I was able to tell her."[36] In the song "Libretto" (by Charles Lederer and Luther Davis) from *Kismet*, the beloved is the one perfect one who embodies all that is necessary for the heart lifting.

The lyrics continue:

and when she speaks, and when she talks with me—music, mystery!
And when she moves and when she walks with me
Paradise comes suddenly near.

Perhaps because Davies has tasted paradise in the relationship with his mother, in his delight in music, art, film, and poetry, and "the magical way that light falls on a window," it might be he has never quite given up on the possibility of divine love. Speaking of his love of music he wishes he could be like Joseph Anton Bruckner ". . . and just yield to God and think 'it's been hard but it's worth it and you think you can die quite happily now.'"[37] In *The House of Mirth* Lily commits suicide. Is Davies (who believes that suicide can be an act of courage) through his choice of lyrics indicating paradise for Lily?

He still feels the pain of separating from the church. "I really did believe that religion with my whole soul. . . . Now I'm an atheist and that's very hard because there's no comfort in it."[38] While that pain may be felt by Davies the man, his work is shot through with the transcendent envisioned within Catholic references. It's there in the final scene in *The Long Day Closes*. Bud and Albee gaze at the night sky, their imaginations stirred with the miraculous and the infinite. Bud tells

Albee that the light in those stars began "when Jesus was born." "How do you know?" asks Albee. Bud knows because that's what they told him in his Catholic school. Davies creates the scene clearly understanding and celebrating that the emotional truth in the story should override scientific facts. As his camera directs our gaze toward the stars we, like the boys, may wonder at a special child and a special star—astronomy lessons illuminated by faith.

Reviewing the Chapter

1. Is Davies's picture of Catholic life in Liverpool a particular portrait or the universal portrait of the church at that time? How much is Davies's memory and a nostalgia for the past?

2. *The Long Day Closes* shows many visual images of Catholic piety and links it especially through the crucifix. What is Davies saying about belief, piety, and prayer, the Catholic thing?

3. Davies also links Catholic imagery with sexuality, more particularly homosexuality. What is Davies saying about the Catholic Church, homosexuality, and repression?

Notes

1. John Caughie, "Halfway to Paradise," *Sight & Sound* (May 1992), 13.
2. George Johnson, *The Palaces of Memory: How We Build the Worlds Inside Our Heads* (New York: Grafton, 1992).
3. Ingmar Bergman, *The Magic Lantern* (London: Penguin, 1987), 73.
4. Bergman, *Magic Lantern*, 73.
5. Bergman, *Magic Lantern*, 73.
6. Bergman, *Magic Lantern*, 73.
7. Caughie, "Paradise," 11.
8. film.guardian.co.uk/interviewpages/0,6737,388979,00.html (accessed December 5, 2002).
9. film.guardian.co.uk/interviewpages/0,6737,388979,00.html (accessed December 5, 2002).
10. Andrew Greeley, *The Catholic Myth: The Behavior and Beliefs of American Catholics* (New York: Charles Scribner's Sons, 1990), 81.
11. John Boorman, *Money into Light. The Emerald Forest—A Diary* (London: Faber & Faber, 1985).
12. film.guardian.co.uk/interviewpages/0,6737,388979,00.html (accessed December 5, 2002).
13. film.guardian.co.uk/interviewpages/0,6737,388979,00.html (accessed December 5, 2002).
14. film.guardian.co.uk/interviewpages/0,6737,388979,00.html (accessed December 5, 2002).

15. film.guardian.co.uk/interviewpages/0,6737,388979,00.html (accessed December 5, 2002).

16. "Terence Davies: Some Thoughts on Acting," *Sight & Sound* (October 1995), 17.

17. "Terence Davies," *Sight & Sound*, 17.

18. Judy Stone, *Eye on the World: Conversations with International Filmmakers* (Los Angeles: Silman James Press, 1997), 305–7.

19. Daniel Taylor, *The Healing Power of Stories: Creating Yourself Through the Stories of Your Life* (New York: Gill & Macmillan, 1996), 85.

20. Caughie, "Paradise," 15.

21. Stone, *Eye on the World*, 305–7.

22. Caughie, "Paradise," 13.

23. Caughie, "Paradise," 13.

24. Caughie, "Paradise," 13.

25. *The Wizard of Oz* VHS, directed by Victor Fleming (Santa Monica, Calif.: MGM/CBS Home Video, 1980).

26. Pat Kirkham and Mike O'Shaghnessy, "Designing Desire," *Sight & Sound*, May 1992), 13–14.

27. film.guardian.co.uk/interviewpages/0,6737,388979,00.html (accessed December 5, 2002).

28. film.guardian.co.uk/interviewpages/0,6737,388979,00.html (accessed December 5, 2002).

29. Yoram Allon, Del Cullen, and Hannah Patterson, eds., *The Wallflower Critical Guide to Contemporary British and Irish Directors* (London: Wallflower Press, 2002), 72–74.

30. Richard Blake, *AfterImage: The Indelible Catholic Imagination of Six American Filmmakers* (Chicago: Loyola, 2000).

31. Leila Alexander, "Secrets and Sacraments of Andrei Tarkovsky" in *About Tarkovsky* (Moscow: Progress Publishers, 1990), 299.

32. Holy Bible, King James version, "Whoever gives only a cup of water to one of these little ones to drink because he is a disciple—amen, I say to you he will surely not lose his reward," Matthew 10:42.

33. Rosemary Haughton, *The Catholic Thing* (Dublin: Villa Books, 1979).

34. Stone, *Eye on the World*, 305–7.

35. Bergman, *Magic Lantern*, 73.

36. Stone, *Eye on the World*, 305–7.

37. Stone, *Eye on the World*, 305–7.

38. film.guardian.co.uk/interviewpages/0,6737,388979,00.html (accessed December 5, 2002).

Two Films of Neil Jordan: In an Irish Context

Michael Paul Gallagher

Ireland has changed so much. Such a refrain is heard in many circles and with varying tones. It can be an expression of surprise, voiced, for example, by visitors returning after a number of years and struck by the visibility of new wealth and its attendant lifestyles. It may be a statement of worry, possibly on middle-aged lips, implying that older values are in danger of being lost through the sheer speed of change. Or it can be a cry of victory, by those who fought for new approaches on various fronts and who are delighted to say good-bye to previously dominant assumptions. Among those in the latter category one can include many writers and artists of the generation to which Neil Jordan belongs.

Neil Jordan is undoubtedly Ireland's best-known film director, even though he is rivaled by some of his near contemporaries, such as Jim Sheridan, Peter Sheridan, or Gerry Stembridge. As it happens all of these were students of mine in the English department of University College, Dublin, and at that stage they were already leaders in the field of theater. I recall being shown one of Neil's earliest stories when he was about nineteen, and even then he was exploring zones of ambivalence and how these were regarded with hostility and prejudice from the perspective of the normal world.

Two Cultural Revolutions

It is important to situate this group of filmmakers and their companion novelists, such as Joseph O'Connor, Roddy Doyle, Aidan Mathews, Colm Toibin, Emma Donoghue, and Niall Williams among others, as part of an unusual explosion of talent in the relatively small world that is Ireland. (In fact all of those mentioned studied in that same English department, though not at the same time). Having known most of them personally, my own oversimple comment would be that they were born in the old culture and spent their childhood in a highly traditional

Catholic Ireland. Then came the first cultural revolution of the seventies when many of these were students, and it was a time of exciting awakening for them. This was a period when a creative minority was forging new horizons. I recall a Jim Sheridan production of *Oedipus Rex* in the old *aula magna* of Newman House, where the audience had to climb up on uncomfortable scaffolding and act the role of the citizens, except that the city was not Thebes but Derry; these were the early years of the Northern troubles, the time of Bloody Sunday, and the South also experienced a new drive for liberation from old molds.

Pushing this insight further, Albert Camus once wrote that people write tragedy when they are changing their gods. This new generation of Irish artistic talent had all experienced "on their own skin" (as they say in Italian) the shift from one Ireland to another. It was a time of anger and of critique of all authorities, including of course the Catholic Church. Many of this creative galaxy now look back on their Catholic upbringing with more nostalgia than bitterness. It had its securities despite all the narrowness, a theme evoked in Seamus Heaney's poem *In Illo Tempore*. (Of course Heaney belongs to an older generation than any of those mentioned here.) As Jordan himself has said in an interview with Adrian Wootton, it was easy to abandon the outer aspects of a religion learned as a child, but "they never leave your sensibility." Even though I have lost contact with Neil in the last decade or so (because I now live in Rome), I was reliably informed that he was delighted to know that a priest in Dublin commented positively on *The Crying Game* as part of his Sunday sermon. He is also on record as saying that although he does not count himself as a believer, he actually likes churches. Concerning *The End of the Affair*, Jordan quipped that "I'm not as tortured about religion as Greene," but that he wanted to confront something that could not be explained. Again, he would surely have been pleased that this film was listed among the best ten of 1999 by the U.S. Catholic Bishops' Conference.

Before coming to discuss two of Jordan's films from a somewhat religious perspective, one has to mention Ireland's second cultural revolution, which happened in the nineties. These were years of much more visible change than in the seventies. Newspaper headlines can sum up the main strands: "Celtic Tiger" (unprecedented economic success, now in some decline); "Artistic Renaissance" (the emergence of that new generation to international success, including U2 and other musical names); "Church Disgraced" (from the point of view of the Catholic Church these have been terrible years, mainly on account of the scandals of sexual abuse among clergy). In short, within the last decade the Catholic strand in Irish life entered an unforeseen desolation, whereas creative and economic Ireland was experiencing an equally unexpected boom.

This more recent wave of cultural change certainly affects that generation of creative artists now largely in their forties or early fifties. Jordan was born in 1950. But I would argue that the main forces shaping his (and others') imagination came earlier. The exploratory and rebellious sensibility of a Neil Jordan is testimony to a transition from one world to another. Indeed, as I want to propose here, a recurring and central concern in his work is with frontiers of strangeness. J. R. R. Tolkien once remarked that he wanted to retrieve an "arresting strangeness" that seemed lost or suppressed in modern culture. Jordan's focus is more on a disturbing and entangling strangeness. He wants his audiences to be drawn beyond safe normality and to encounter something of the fear and the attraction of the unfamiliar.

Film as Audience Rhetoric

In this light I want to argue that religious commentary on film is often blind in one eye. It sees mainly the content of the story and tends to undervalue the process of the viewer's experience. I am not saying that Jordan is didactic or anything of a preacher, but I am proposing that he wants his audience to undergo a conversion of consciousness. Moreover, if we focus on the aesthetic experience of the spectator rather than on the surface plot or technical structure of the work, it is easier to discover in Jordan's work hints of a concern with religious frontiers.

Perhaps one of the principal differences between commercial films and what we can call quality films lies precisely in this area. The typical commercial product has no ambition to transform the viewer's horizon except during the fleeting hour or two of attention to the screen. An action movie offers temporary excitement but few lasting fruits. An art movie aims higher, seeking in various ways the transformation of the viewer's perspective. Indeed the poverty of much commercial cinema often lies in its cowardice to challenge the prejudices of the viewer. It simply reinforces the typical assumptions and priorities of his or her culture rather than enlarging into new territory. However, Jordan's films have the courage to challenge viewers to transcend their cultural blinkers and to lead them into regions of wonder and surprise beyond routine judgments. To repeat, I make this suggestion, not concentrating on the content, but from the more subtle point of view of "response criticism" (*Recepzionskritik*). Perhaps we can best discern the spiritual value of cinema through this emphasis on process rather than by attending to surface plot.

Companion Films of 1991–1992

To come more specifically to two of Jordan's films, I want to present him as a rhetorician of cinema, persuading his audience to cross thresholds of sympathy into worlds that initially seem alienating and incredible. He has directed thirteen films since *Angel* in 1982. For this short chapter I want to focus on two films that come from the years 1991 to 1992, sixth and seventh in his career. The first, titled *The Miracle*, is not well known, and yet it was said to be Jordan's own favorite film. It is an attractively playful story set in Bray (near Dublin) where he grew up, although he was born in my hometown of Sligo. It concerns two teenagers, Rose and Jimmy, who walk around inventing stories about the hidden lives of the people they see around them. Then at a certain stage, fantasy becomes painful and complex reality when a tourist woman, whom they decide is a French film star and about whom Jimmy entertains romantic hopes, turns out to be the boy's real mother. This is one of the many twists in the tale, but in Jordan there is always another level of mystery. As the title indicates, he also wants to evoke quasi-religious horizons. A crucial scene at the end of the film finds the boy praying in church for a sign from God and a comic miracle happens: All the circus animals are liberated to wander around the town. Leaving aside many details, my purpose, as already mentioned, is to stress that the film rhetoric of Jordan is one of conversion of horizon in his viewers. There are surprises not only of plot but of wavelength of communication; hence what I am calling the rhetoric, or persuasive, impact of the film on its receivers, which leads its audience away from predictable levels of consciousness to a sense of wonder and of cultural otherness quite rare in contemporary cinema. But it also is one of the hallmarks of Jordan's work. If this expansion of consciousness is gentle and attractive in *The Miracle*, some years later it was to be more violent and agonizing in *The Butcher Boy*. Even here, Jordan works something of a rhetorical miracle, in retaining empathy for the boy in the midst of his appalling revenge on the world.

The Crying Game is also a film of surprises (one that concerned gender identity and was initially kept secret at the request of the distributors). It received six Oscar nominations and was awarded one for best screenplay. The film critic Roger Ebert has introduced it in these words: "Some movies keep you guessing. Some movies make you care. Once in a long while a movie comes along that does both things at the same time. . . . Jordan's wonderful film . . . involves us deeply in its story, and then it reveals that the story is really about something else altogether . . . we have to follow [the central character] through a crisis of the heart but the journey is worth it."

What are the areas where this film leads its audience into what D. H. Lawrence would call new fields of "sympathetic consciousness"? It tackles two of the most predictable themes of cinema—violence and sexuality—and it succeeds in surprising its audience, leading them beyond their expectations in both areas. It does not simply tell a story: It involves a process whereby the viewer is invited into what we can call transcendence, a double transcendence in fact. The film starts with the kidnapping of a black soldier serving with the British Army in the North of Ireland. He is held by the Irish Republican Army (IRA) to force the authorities to release one of their leaders. If not, he will be shot within three days. Jordan relishes in tempting the viewer to think that this is a normal action movie. Initially it has all the rhythm of a political thriller, with elements of danger and violence. But a strange friendship is born between Fergus, one of the IRA guards and Jody, the captured British soldier. On at least three occasions during this initial part of the film the strategy of music signals to the audience that there is a change of wavelength happening here.

This film has two main movements. The first undermines, even deconstructs, expectations of political violence to establish a human friendship that transcends differences—differences between Irish and English, between white and black, between terrorist guard and imprisoned enemy. The second part repeats this transformation of sympathy in the field of sexuality. Once again the challenge to the previous horizons of Fergus is experienced by the audience as an expansion of its own sympathetic consciousness. An initially physical attraction with Dil, the dead soldier's wife (that was the original title, *Soldier's Wife*) runs into surprises and ambiguities that force both protagonists and audience toward a metamorphosis of Eros.

With great delicacy Jordan creates this second story of conflict where Fergus learns another level of love that goes beyond predictable physical expressions. In this way the audience undergoes two conversions of horizon. The first part undermines the conventional political film of violence. The second part repeats this process in the field of sexual assumptions. Jordan himself commented that *The Crying Game* was mainly a love story but one that delved into political, sexual, and racial paradoxes. In a quietly postmodern way he offered his audience the challenge of recognizing and accepting diversity.

Christian Echoes

To support the interpretative emphasis I am suggesting, let me look at a two significant moments in the film. In the first part when Jody, the black soldier, is a prisoner of the IRA and when Fergus is his guard, a surprising friendship develops between them. At a crucial moment in their conversation the soldier narrates a parable (which, I am told, was used by Orson Welles in his 1955 film *Mr. Ardakin*). The story goes as follows, as told by Jody from under his hood:

> Scorpion wants to cross a river, but he can't swim. Goes to the frog, who can, and asks for a ride. Frog says, "If I give you a ride on my back, you'll go and sting me." Scorpion replies, "It would not be in my interest to sting you since as I'll be on your back we both would drown." Frog thinks about this logic for a while and accepts the deal. Takes the scorpion on his back. Braves the waters. Halfway over feels a burning spear in his side and realizes the scorpion has stung him after all. And as they both sink beneath the waves the frog cries out, "Why did you sting me, Mr. Scorpion, for now we both will drown?" Scorpion replies, "I can't help it, it's in my nature."

It seems obvious that the whole of the film is designed to undermine the fatalism of this parable. The rest of the action evokes an alternative faith, where transformation is possible, and where Fergus (and the audience) can be drawn beyond prisons of prejudice—imaginatively but concretely. A final confirmation of this comes in the closing moments of the film when Fergus is himself a prisoner in a British jail, in fact by his own choice, doing time for a killing actually carried out by Dil. By so doing he has also saved Dil from suicide. In terms of the parable, the nature of the terrorist has undergone more than one conversion and experienced more than one version of redemption. The crowning moment comes when Dil (whom we of course now know to be male) arrives to visit, dressed to kill, one might say, in a leather mini coat and sporting large earrings. In a tone of tenderness Dil says "You're doing time for me. No greater love, as the man says. Wish you'd tell me why." And Fergus replies enigmatically "As the man said, it's in my nature." When Dil asks what that means, Fergus begins to retell Jody's story of the scorpion, but the camera retreats, the music increases (Lyle Lovett singing *Stand by Your Man*) and thus the film ends.

The casual reference to the New Testament in the words "No greater love" is not the only one in the course of the film. In the first part, Jody at one stage has been crying under his hood and asks Fergus to tell him a story, any story, something like the scorpion one. With the underlining music in the background, Fergus begins "When I was a child," which seems like the perfect opening for a story. However he continues "I thought as a child. But when I became a man I put away childish things." Jody interrupts with "What does that mean?" and Fergus replies "Nothing." Are we to interpret this as a moment of emptiness, where the old language of St. Paul on love has collapsed into a rootless echo? Or in the wider perspective of hope that is the thrust of this movie, can we not see here again a core vision of Christianity as religiously faded but humanly alive? Once again the fragment of a story recounted by Fergus is destined to be transformed by the emotional rhetoric of the film as a whole. His helpless nothing is not the note on which *The Crying Game* closes. The whole dynamic of its plot has incarnated, however shyly or ironically or humanistically, something of Christian conversion toward the self-giving called agape.

It is striking that in a highly professional study of the film written by Jane Giles and published by the British Film Institute, it is argued that "*The Crying Game* is the story of the redemption of its protagonist." It would clearly be wrong to claim that it is a religious film in the normal or explicit sense of that term. However, as Karl Rahner insisted on more than one occasion, even an image that does not have a specifically religious theme can be a religious image through its "sensory experience of transcendence." Perhaps Jordan himself was not far from the same intuition when in his Oscar acceptance speech he commented: "the way audiences have responded to this film has taught me that they have it in their hearts to embrace any range of characters and any range of points of view."

Reviewing the Chapter

1.   What kinds of cultural change seem to provoke an explosion of artistic energy?

2.   In what sense can Jordan's movies be termed religious?

3.   How would you describe the film rhetoric of *The Crying Game*—in the sense of how it transforms the horizons of its audience?

3

Revisiting the *Devil's Playground*: The Films of Fred Schepisi

Peter Malone

A Catholic Past

It is 1993, and it has been forty years since Fred Schepisi's time in the Marist Brothers' Juniorate as a thirteen-year-old boy. Schepisi is directing Donald Sutherland and Stockard Channing in *Six Degrees of Separation*. His company is making a documentary about him, and they have taken time off from the New York locations.[1] Schepisi is back in Australia. He is visiting Kilmore in country Victoria, Assumption College, where he went to school as a boarder in the 1950s and where he once thought he had a vocation to join his teachers and become a Marist Brother. Wandering around the grounds of the college, all rugged up on a glum wintry day, he reminisces about those long-ago school days, about the movies that he saw at Assumption, and the love for the movies that this generated in him as well as about vocation and the life of a Marist Brother.

Devotees of Schepisi's films—the three and a quarter made in Australia and the eleven and a half[2] in the United States and the United Kingdom—especially his semiautobiographical *The Devil's Playground*, might well have expected a tirade against religion or the Catholic Church or the narrowness of the Brothers' outlook. But this does not happen. In fact, Schepisi tells a funny story about the statue of Marcellin Champagnat in the college grounds, how the boys put a copy of *Man*, considered a salacious magazine in Australia in the early 1950s, into the hand of the Marist Brothers' founder instead of his Bible or his prayer book. (And, with the aid of special effects, this little joke now appears before our eyes.)

Schepisi goes further in being genial. He refers to the priest who used to come round to schools and give the boys a retreat: "He'd call you out of class and treat you as a special friend; you'd feel pretty good about that." Author and collaborator with Schepisi, Thomas Kenneally, played this kind of Franciscan in *The*

Devil's Playground. The retreat stirred up the boys' religious sentiments. Schepisi says that they saw the priest "as a good bloke" and "before you knew it . . . this isn't a bad life . . . I can live a decent life with good moral values . . . I can come out and teach children . . . you think you've got a vocation." The brothers seemed to be doing something worthwhile with their lives, so why not give it a try? Schepisi did. At the age of thirteen, he opted to try his vocation at the Marist Brothers' secondary school for aspirants to the order, their Juniorate at Mount Macedon, outside Melbourne, not far, in fact, from Hanging Rock.

What emerged was not Brother Schepisi, but a film twenty years later, which had enormous impact on the nascent Australian film industry. This film, which brought specific Catholic issues to the screen, some controversial and questioning issues, enabled later Australian films to tackle these subjects with frankness as well as artistic skill.[3]

Schepisi was born in December 1939, is of Irish Italian background, and is especially proud of the Italian, "more than anything, it's in the blood, in the passions." Yet, he was educated, as were Catholic children of the 1940s and 1950s, in Catholic schools in the Irish tradition. Director Philip Noyce, not a Catholic himself, sees this Irish Catholic influence as a strong cultural factor:

> The most interesting thing about Australia is Irish Catholicism—I mean, it's the basis of the country. I think that it is the basis of the value system and has had much more effect—or at least it has produced the unique Australian character— much more than the English, in my opinion, simply because of its strength.
>
> I think that Australia and the Australian character have been formed through the confrontation between Irish Catholicism and Anglicanism, and of course, these are, at least in part, seemingly irreconcilable philosophies.
>
> In my interpretation, the one philosophy, the Irish Catholic philosophy born out of the combination of the Irish experience and Catholic doctrine, is that you should not expect to inherit the earth while you're on the earth but you will later, whereas English and Scottish Protestantism says you will inherit it now and you should do everything you can to get it because it's yours.[4]

This blend of faith and a determination to overcome one's origins is called by poet Les Murray and his friend, writer-director Bob Ellis a "country of the mind":

> There was a point in Australian history when half the population were Irish and that must mean that something close to half the population is of Irish or part Irish descent. I mean, they multiply so thoroughly. It's not till I got to Ireland itself and saw Australian faces staring from behind every bar and down every street corner and all these names which I thought were restricted to Australian politicians up and down the streets that I realised how Irish we are. I think it's probably true to say that Australia is something close to being the first agnostic society on earth, with the exception of Catholicism which was, as it were, the loyal

opposition to the agnosticism which prevailed. It's a country of the mind that—
it's a country in the way that Australia never was.[5]

It is in *The Devil's Playground* that Schepisi presents his interpretation of Australian Catholicism, country of the mind, a country of great devotion and faith combined with authoritarianism and repression, which Schepisi, remembering his experience from the vantage point of his mid-thirties and in the more open climate of the 1970s, dramatizes at a time when the old Catholicism was crumbling. Bob Ellis notes:

> I've got the highest esteem for *The Devil's Playground*, which I thought a formidable act of bravery. I think, Schepisi got it about right, that mixture of absolute affection and absolute terror that was felt by the central character for the overarching authority figures of that school.[6]

Released in 1976, *The Devil's Playground* was a critical and commercial success, screening in Melbourne, for instance, for nine months. It was selected for the Director's Fortnight at Cannes and was nominated for many Australian Film Institute awards, winning out over Peter Weir's *Picnic at Hanging Rock* for Best Film and Best Director. Simon Bourke as Schepisi's alter ego, Tom Allen, shared the Best Actor award with Nick Tate as Brother Victor.

Libido: The Priest

However, before Schepisi filmed *The Devil's Playground*, he seized an opportunity to explore some aspects of Australian Catholicism in the short film, *The Priest*, for the portmanteau movie, *Libido* (1973). *Libido* was part of a project by the Producers and Directors Guild in Melbourne to collaborate with respected writers, including Kenneally, in making some short films. Schepisi chose the Kenneally script, because he was in the process of writing *The Devil's Playground* and wanted the novelist to read and comment on it.

The Priest (made over twenty years before the fine, controversial British film, *Priest*, written by Jimmy McGovern and directed by Antonia Bird) was inspired by the life and vocational crisis as well as psychological and LSD treatment of an actual priest. Kenneally himself had studied for the priesthood in Sydney but withdrew from the seminary a week before his planned diaconate ordination in 1959.[7]

The Priest is a short story about the contemporary vocational crisis (which, in fact, was in its earliest and uncertain years in Australia when the film was made). A Melbourne priest, Stephen Burn (Arthur Dignam) is in therapy. He also plans to marry a nun (Robyn Nevin). She, however, is a practical and commonsense teacher. He is unable to cope with the role of priest and his official ministry. This is suggested by flashbacks of prim convent-parlor discussions about children's confessions and "what the Bishop would say." Schepisi calls this aspect of church "politeness or the polite veneer." He declares he has lost his faith, although he continuously recites words from the creed in his delirium. He is in rebellion against the laws and discipline of compulsory celibacy for clergy but dreams of and fantasizes about his sexual liaison with Sister Caroline.[8]

She, on the other hand, wants to act with integrity. While she loves Stephen, she wants to wait several months until her temporary vows lapse, and she is free to leave her congregation. She expresses an awareness of responsibilities in the school, what she owes to parents, and of people's opinions and feelings. She refers to old bigoted stories about tunnels between convents and presbyteries and nuns being "priests' whores." She is prepared to live with Stephen until he receives an official dispensation from Rome to marry, but she still wants to be married as a Catholic and in a church.

Robyn Nevin's Caroline is gentle, reasonable, asking Stephen to meet her requests in compromise. But Dignam's somewhat theatrical Stephen is gripped by the church he wants to be free from and rebels against. He will not give in and damns Caroline's superior when Caroline refuses to leave.

Visually and verbally, Schepisi and Kenneally, respectively, capture convent and presbytery atmosphere and the language and nuances of Catholic behavior. Despite the melodrama, it was—and is—an authentic reflection of what was happening in the crisis for clergy all over the world.[9]

Australian Catholicism

Schepisi sees the Australian experience of this kind of crisis in church, in priesthood, and in morality as having national and cultural importance, in writing and filming with greater depth:

> I think it's rather significant, by the way—I don't think this is true now, but it was true then—that many of the people doing things, writing books, plays, getting into film, were Catholics or ex-Catholics or traumatised Catholics, and it was all strictly railing against that Irish Catholic severity and obsessiveness that I think most of us saw was counterproductive to what religion really should be doing. And I don't think it's any accident. As Philip Adams and various people have written, while not a lot of great cinema, or anything, was coming out of Australia, it was a fairly complacent society and there was not a lot to rail against.
>
> But since there is little to rail against other than, say, mental torpidity or spiritual barrenness, then there's not a lot of great work happening. Great work, unfortunately, seems to come out of oppression or deprivation. So I think at that time that area, oddly enough, was religion.[10]

Schepisi himself has a view on how Australian Catholicism developed. He sees a popular mindset in Australian culture as anti-British. This is particularly difficult for representations of the Anglican Church in literature and cinema, as it is still seen as The Church of England. The anti-British culture was encouraged by the strong feelings of such groups as the predominantly Roman Catholic working-class Irish dissidents. These feelings were strengthened by such matters as the ascendancy of British settlers, the landed gentry, inequality in property ownership, and in favored trading arrangements. Whether consciously or otherwise, there was evidently a need to forge an identity free from such a negative colonial past.

This attitude was strengthened in Victoria, Schepisi's home state, by the dominating presence of Archbishop Daniel Mannix of Melbourne (as bishop from 1912 to 1963), a vocal dissident on conscription for World War I, and himself interned on board ship on a voyage to Ireland. Mannix personified for a half century this staunch Irish Catholicism.

The Devil's Playground

But Schepisi's particular view of Catholicism derives principally from his school days, particularly those in the Juniorate at Mt. Macedon, the devil's playground. His central character, fourteen-year-old Tom Allen, played by Simon Bourke, is a more or less autobiographical portrait.

By focusing on the Catholic tradition with its sometimes severe Irish heritage and its Roman organization and legislation, Schepisi was inviting audiences to look at an important influence on Australian culture: the strict Catholic tradition of morality and education and the contribution of religious orders to propagating and maintaining this. Schepisi's point of view is clear. The seminary was repressive. Boys were trained by men who were too strict, too prudish, too cut off in their masculine world, and too committed to their interpretation of the tenets and rules of their religion to help the boys grow into mature, balanced men. Some of the brothers were able to manage their lives well; others collapsed, opted out, or drifted within the order.

Dignam appears again, this time as a neurotic teacher, Brother Francine, with the same tensions but with no outlet except voyeuristic behavior and emotional and mental collapse. In its presentation of the Brothers, *The Devil's Playground* shows a range of religious men, an unexpected cross-section: old Sebastian, who has lived a fruitful life; zestful Arthur, who chases basketballs and teaches well and professionally; Celian, the headmaster, who encourages his community to talk about the institute and the need for change (but is not in touch with the boys' sexual preoccupations); James, who is young and trying to cope with his studies and work; Victor, who manages his life reasonably well, likes the kids, sees need for change, drinks a bit, likes football, and flirts with some girls in a pub; and Francine, who has so suppressed his personality that he spies on the boys, upbraids them prudishly, and is a voyeur of women at the city baths.

There were some good people around—some very good people around, good
brothers too—and they were there with the sick buggers, and the rest of it was
just like misguided religious zeal.[11]

Two priests appear: the over-severe Irish chaplain, with the obligatory grim
confessional sequence, and the jolly priest who comes to preach (echoing James
Joyce's *Portrait of the Artist*) with a mixture of sympathy and damnation.

The sequence most frequently shown in documentaries about Schepisi's
work is the shower sequence in *The Devil's Playground*. For those who lived
through those times, it is startlingly real. The boys, mainly thirteen- and fourteen-
year-olds, are in the shower block drying off. Brother Francine, in his religious
habit, is supervising. The boys shower wearing trunks. Francine opens a cubicle
door and finds Tom not wearing any trunks. The dialogue which follows is a
resume of the severe Jansenistic spirituality that marked many of the French and
Irish traditions of religious life in Australia.

> BROTHER FRANCINE: It's disgusting. . . . Where's your modesty, Allen? Exposing
> yourself . . . learn your body is your worst enemy . . . if you are to become a lit-
> tle Brother of Mary. Avert your eyes, you lot. . . . The eyes are the window of
> the soul and must be protected. Be on your guard against all your senses at all
> times . . . stringent vows, chastity, poverty, obedience, do you hear that, Allen,
> chastity. . . . Self-denial, self-examination, self-discipline.[12]

Tom's departure from the Marist Brothers' Juniorate represents breaking free
of a restricted systematized faith, one which in many ways denies personhood.
All of this had a kind of mesmerizing appeal for Catholic audiences, especially
on the film's release in 1976, who remembered the past and who, in watching the
film, had an opportunity for reassessing this past. It also had a fascination for
younger audiences for whom the world portrayed seemed so unreal that they
found it hard to believe that it had really existed and only twenty years before.
For some commentators who remembered the church culture of the early 1950s,
Schepisi's screenplay seemed too knowing in the boys' experience of their developing sexuality. They remembered boys at boarding schools and minor seminaries as more sheltered, at times, ignorant. The explicit language and swearing of
the film were not so widespread in the early 1950s. Schepisi disagrees, "No, I
held back, believe me. Believe me, I held back."[13]

Schepisi says that many who had a troubled childhood identified with the
film. He also says that he is embarrassed about how much of himself is up there
on the screen. He cringes. His life outside the movies has been complicated, "I've
been married—three times to be exact." He asks himself why he still does things
when "I've solved it up there on the screen." He believes in "absolute passion,
integrity and energy," which, in *The Devil's Playground*, overrides everything,
including the technicalities, and that got across to people.[14]

On the issue of sexuality, celibacy, and vocation, Schepisi still has strong ideas:

There were a few priests who used to visit me because they had worked in aboriginal missions. These awful situations that they were put in. They were out there seeing the aborigine living in the life that is so particular to them, setting up a conflict in the priest trying to take them out of this world into another world, and then questioning "Why are we really doing this?" They were absolutely conflicted by this, that their celibacy was preventing them from doing the right job if, in fact, it was the right job in the first place.

One of the things I always thought was strange was that there was a lot of pressure on the missionary role of a person in religious life. It was always held up as one of the great things, you know, to go off to Africa or to go to New Guinea, somewhere like that, when right round the corner was a problem larger and more important than travelling to distant places. I was always unsettled by that lack of attention to the needs of the neighbourhood, if you like.[15]

The Chant Of Jimmie Blacksmith

Schepisi continued to work with Kenneally in the adaptation of his novel, *The Chant of Jimmie Blacksmith* (1978), and it can lay claim to be one of the best Australian films. Its widescreen panoramas of the Australian bush are breathtaking. It tackles a subject that Australians are not comfortable with in reality, let alone on the screen, the treatment of the Aborigines who have been spiritually and culturally displaced. Kenneally drew on the true story of Jimmy Governor who went on a rampage in 1900 at the time that the six colonies were being federally united as the Commonwealth of Australia. In the new constitution, Aborigines would not have the vote—this did not happen until a referendum in 1967—and the immigration stance was a "White Australia Policy." The issues in the film were socially and politically significant. However, the film was not a commercial success (and Schepisi went to learn more about his craft in Hollywood).

The principal focus of church attention in *The Chant of Jimmie Blacksmith* is the Methodist Church and the contrast of its style and expectations with those of aboriginal religion. Where the Catholic Church appears is in the convent where Jimmie is finally captured. The nuns are shown living their religious life devoutly and performing its ritual. It is an official way of living religion that knows almost nothing of what goes on inside Jimmie's mind and heart. With an ironic touch, it is pointed out that in hiding, Jimmie has occupied (desecrated?) the Bishop's room. It is only a small sequence (which Schepisi on being asked about it confessed that he did not remember), but it continues the critical perspective of *The Priest* and *The Devil's Playground*.

Evil Angels

Schepisi has not explored any specifically Catholic themes since his films of the 1970s. However, he did return to Australian religion in the form of Seventh Day Adventism in his adaptation of John Bryson's study of the Chamberlain case, *Evil Angels* (1988). The disappearance of Azariah Chamberlain at Ayers Rock in Central Australia became one of Australia's most controversial court cases for more than five years. While Lindy Chamberlain claimed her baby Azariah had been taken by a dingo, many Australians believed she was lying and that she had killed her daughter. *Evil Angels* is an indictment of the Australian public, their too-easy acceptance of media prejudice and of gossip as well as their being uncomfortable with what they see as eccentric fringe churches. Given Chamberlain's seeming disregard for her media image and her religious beliefs, many Australians could not believe her. It is to the credit of Schepisi (aided by the outstanding performances by Meryl Streep and Sam Neill as the Chamberlains), that the film contributed to a deeper examination of conscience by Australians who saw it.

> [T]here's such a misapprehension about Seventh Day Adventists and their cultish behaviour and rituals. We think they're cultish. People think they're like Jehovah's Witnesses or Scientologists. And they get all that off-to-the-side religion misunderstanding. And what are the differences with Seventh Day Adventists? Well, their main difference is that Saturday is the holy day, not Sunday. Is that worth fighting about? Because when it's Saturday here it's Sunday over there or vice versa. So number one is that it's a basically decent religion.
>
> But the thing I hope comes out of it is that Lindy Chamberlain's faith is very real. She still truly believes that God will help her. Michael, who went around doing death counselling and all that stuff—he's the minister—his belief was more a hope than a belief, and so even though he went round doing the right thing, he wasn't as convinced or as deeply convinced as she was that it was all right. He was very easily shaken.[16]

and Since . . .

To listen to Schepisi speak, even conversationally, about filmmaking is to listen to a genial and ingenious master class. Schepisi went to the United States in the early 1980s and enjoyed a successful career there for ten years. His films in the early to mid-1990s, like *Mr. Baseball* and *IQ*, were not within his full control. Since then, his career has faltered. He spent a great deal of time and energy, reworking the British comedy, *Fierce Creatures*. His personal preferences were for projects that were values-oriented as well as entertainments. After three months, he left the production of *The Shipping News*, feeling that the casting of

John Travolta and his wife, Kelly Preston, was detrimental to his vision of Annie Proulx's novel. For years, he worked on a screenplay for Peter Carey's imaginative tale of what happened to the convict Magwitch from Dickens' *Great Expectations* during his time in Australia, but it has not found financial backing.

Schepisi did have a chance to make a worthwhile film in Britain in 2001, a version of Graham Swift's *Last Orders*, a comic glimpse of farewell rituals among a group of East End Londoners after the death of a friend.

One can experience something of Schepisi's feel for the world of values in the documentary, *Right . . . Said Fred* with which this chapter opened. As he has aged and come to terms with so much of his life, he can invest a scene with a transcendent feeling.

There's a lovely scene at the end of *Six Degrees of Separation* after Stockard Channing has talked about the experience with the young man who had entered her life claiming to be Sidney Poitier's son. He had conned them, but he also transformed them. She laments that people often reduce experience to anecdotes. For her this encounter was much more than an anecdote. Previously she had visited Rome and been invited to go up a ladder to look more closely at the roof of the Sistine Chapel, which was being cleaned. She touched Michelangelo's picture of God reaching out to give life to Adam. Now, as she's walking down the New York street, she almost leaps, stretching her arm upward as she did in the Sistine Chapel—meeting people is like touching God.

As Schepisi himself said, "Slapping the hand of God, doing the high-five."

Reviewing the Chapter

1.   Did *The Devil's Playground* help you to understand the Catholic Church of the 1950s, the church before the Second Vatican Council, including beliefs, practices, vocations to religious life and training, tensions, and aberrations?

2.   The film was made in the 1970s, ten years after the end of the Second Vatican Council. How was Schepisi's critique of his experience in the Juniorate and of the Brothers and their way of running the school influenced by the changes and openness of attitude after the Council?

3.   What did the film reveal about Schepisi's experience of Catholicism and his attitudes toward the church in Australia during the 1940s and 1950s? Was his experience the same as that for other countries and cultures?

Notes

1.   *Right . . . Said Fred: Fred Schepisi*, directed by Don Featherstone, 1993. All Schepisi quotes not attributed to another source in this chapter are from this documentary.

2.   In Australia, *The Priest*, half-hour segment—a quarter—in *Libido* (1973), *The Devil's Playground* (1976), *The Chant of Jimmie Blacksmith* (1978), *Evil Angels*, aka *A*

Cry in the Dark (1988); in the United States and the United Kingdom, *Barbarossa* (1982), *Iceman* (1984), *Plenty* (1985), *Roxanne* (1987), *The Russia House* (1990), *Mr. Baseball* (1992), *Six Degrees of Separation* (1993), *IQ* (1995), the reshooting and new material for *Fierce Creatures* (1997), which constitutes the "half," *Last Orders* (2001), *It Runs in the Family* (2002), and *Empire Falls* (2005).

3.   Schepisi himself developed religious themes in *The Chant of Jimmie Blacksmith* (1978) and *Evil Angels* (1988), but the principal dramatization of the Catholic Church and life in religious orders was Ken Cameron's miniseries for ABC (and its highest series ratings' achiever), *Brides of Christ* (1991). This is a miniseries of six episodes, with continuous plot while focussing on six different characters and issues of the Catholic Church between 1962 and 1968, including the time of the Vatican Council (1962–1965). The screenplay by John Alsop and Sue Smith is frank and insightful about the church, religious orders, and moral dilemmas. Alsop and Smith also wrote the screenplay for *The Leaving of Liverpool* (1992, directed by Michael Jenkins), based on the experiences of British children sent to Australia after World War II, many of who have, during the 1990s, raised issues of physical and sexual abuse by caregivers, especially the Christian Brothers in Western Australia who are the center of this miniseries.

4.   Peter Malone, interview with Phillip Noyce, in *Myth and Meaning, Australian Directors in their Own Words* (Redfern, New South Wales: Currency Press, 2001), 93.

5.   Peter Malone, unpublished interview with Bob Ellis, Sydney, August 1996.

6.   Malone interview with Ellis, 1996.

7.   Thomas Kenneally (1935–) became one of Australia's leading novelists, his early work, *The Place at Whitton* (1964) and *Three Cheers for the Paraclete* (1968), being based on his experiences in the seminary and going on to win the Booker Prize for *Schindler's Ark* (1983). A leading member of the Australian Republican movement during the 1990s, he has also chronicled the Irish influence in Australia in *The Great Shame*: "It's always the writer that makes the material, and that came deeply from Tom's experiences, although it wasn't autobiographical. One of Tom's best books by far is *Three Cheers for the Paraclete*. It's those things that are formed by personal experiences, not necessarily being them, that probably produce the truest work. His wife was a theatre sister and a nun and Tom went right through almost to the end of the seminary course, so I think they were his deeply personal observations. And they happened to dovetail with my experiences and the questions that one comes up with," Malone interview with Schepisi, *Myth*, 112.

8.   Four Australian directors, Tim Burstall, John B. Murray, Schepisi, and David Baker, explore different angles of libido, in the movie by the same name (*Libido*, 1973). Schepisi directed the segment *The Priest*, and quotes here are taken from the movie.

9.   Drawn from Peter Malone, "Catholics, Hostile, Lapsed and Faithful," in *From Front Pews to Back Stalls* (Sydney: Chevalier Press, 1996), 18–19.

10.   Malone interview with Schepisi, *Myth*, 113.

11.   Malone interview with Schepisi, *Myth*, 115.

12.   *The Devil's Playground*, directed by Fred Schepisi, 1976.

13.   Malone interview with Schepisi, *Myth*, 114.

14.   Malone, unpublished interview with Schepisi.

15.   Malone interview with Schepisi, *Myth*, 116.

16.   Malone interview with Schepisi, *Myth*, 119.

Part 2

Catholicism, Mainstream American

The United States has a history of religious immigration. Nonconformists sailed from England in the seventeenth century seeking religious freedom. Groups from Germany and other European countries arrived during the eighteenth century. The nineteenth century and early twentieth century saw the coming of the Catholics, especially poor immigrants from Ireland and Italy.

This means that American Catholicism has a history of mission activity, especially in the Louisiana area and in the Spanish missions of California with their saints' and angels' names. The Church became established in the east in the eighteenth century and came into its own with the Irish and Italians as well as Poles and Ukrainians from Eastern Europe. In all churches, Americans are more comfortable in being up front and open about religion than their counterparts in other English-speaking countries, England itself, Canada, and Australia. Americans are practical and pragmatic in most things, and their Catholicism is pragmatic as well as hands-on in action, financial support, plans, and programs.

The American Church experienced an upheaval after the Second Vatican Council, and it is often said, after Paul VI's Encyclical Letter, *Humanae Vitae*, in 1968 on human life with its condemnation of artificial contraception and controversies about dissent. There was also a large exodus of priests from the priesthood and nuns and brothers from religious life.

Both Nancy Savoca and John Sayles grew up in this atmosphere of a strong church and a church in turmoil. While both have let go of practice, they retain significant memories that pervade their sensitivities, Savoca reflecting on her Italian American sensibility and Sayles on a more mainstream Catholic life. Sayles attributes his passion for storytelling to listening to Jesus's parables at Mass and admiring his way of narrative teaching, and Savoca's passion is for stories of women.

4

Her *Household Saints*: Nancy Savoca's Saints

Gaye W. Ortiz

Filmmaker Nancy Savoca's work in contemporary American cinema has been described variously as "defying expectations and stereotypes,"[1] displaying an "attention to detail and keen sense of ethnic ambience,"[2] and as bringing a "sharply observed women's reality"[3] to her films. A review of her directing credits shows a steady development of her career, which has been encouraged and supported along the way by directors Jonathan Demme and John Sayles. For many years, Savoca has also collaborated in screenwriting with her partner Richard Guay, who also has been involved in producing some of her films.

Beginning with her early student filmmaking days at New York University, where she received the Haig P. Manoogian Award for overall excellence in making two short films, *Renata* and *Bad Timing*, Savoca steadily earned critical praise for her directing and screenwriting skills. In 1989 she won the Grand Prize at the Sundance Film Festival and was nominated for a Spirit Award as Best Director for her debut feature, *True Love*, starring Annabella Sciorra. A shrewd, serio-comic look at courtship and marriage in an Italian American community, this film was included in the 50 Greatest Independent Films of All Time by *Entertainment Weekly*.[4] The film received a major studio release after its purchase by MGM/UA.

Savoca's next film, *Dogfight*, with Lili Taylor and River Phoenix, was directed for Warner Brothers and released in 1991 to a disappointing box office reception. It was a romantic but challenging portrayal of a relationship between a waitress and a Vietnam-bound Marine in the early 1960s; out of the corpus of American films set in the Vietnam War era, this one stands out for its female perspective. Her 1993 independent film *Household Saints*, adapted from the novel by Francine Prose, received many admiring reviews and fared much better at the box office. Savoca and Guay received a Spirit award nomination for Best Screenplay for the film, in which the stories of three generations of Italian American women unfold. Savoca then directed in the medium of television between her third and fourth feature films, including two segments of the HBO movie *If These Walls Could Talk* (1997). This drama, exploring the issue of abortion rights, was the highest rated original movie in HBO history and was nominated for both Emmy and Golden Globe awards for Best Television Drama and Best Performance by actress Demi Moore.[5]

The 24 Hour Woman, starring Rosie Perez, was Savoca's next film, and it premiered at the Sundance Film Festival in 1999. It earned Savoca a nomination for an American Latin Media Arts (ALMA) award for Outstanding Director. In this satirical comedy Perez portrays a career woman who attempts to "have it all" but must deal with issues of parenting and stress, social expectations, and role-juggling. The next film from Savoca, *Reno: Rebel without a Pause*, was a departure in terms of her previous style; it is a documentary portrait of the comedienne Reno and premiered at the Toronto Film Festival in 2002. Savoca's most recent work, *Dirt* (2003), is an unsentimental drama about undocumented immigrants eking out a precarious living in contemporary New York City.

Although consistently offering her films to the studios before releasing them independently, few of Savoca's films have received much attention or financial commitment from Hollywood, despite a solid record of directing strong performances from up-and-coming actors, such as River Phoenix, Lili Taylor, Rosie Perez, and Vincent D'Onofrio. Some reviewers have dismissed Savoca's films as thematically narrow, in that they return to personal issues of family, community, and the changes to and challenges of modern culture and society.

Within this frame of reference, however, lies a rich seam of attitudes, beliefs, and behaviors that give meaning to everyday life. Savoca observes, often through the lens of her own life experiences, how relationships are defined, maintained, and strengthened. Growing up in the Bronx as a child of Argentinean and Sicilian immigrants, Savoca set her film *True Love* in that lower-middle-class Italian American community. Inspired by the lives of her parents, she created a screenplay that reflects an authentic interaction between the main characters within a tight-knit community. It is not a rose-tinted nostalgic portrayal of happily ever after, and Savoca and Guay deal honestly with the doubts that arise within the bride and groom as to the level of commitment that marriage requires. A *Newsday* reviewer approved of this approach by remarking, "Nancy Savoca's picture of two people sacrificing a variety of freedoms for the uncertain joys of marriage is a beauty—hilarious, moving, brilliant, involving."[6]

The "Afterimage" of a Catholic Upbringing: Influences on Savoca's Work

Jesuit writer Richard Blake is a noted film critic and professor of fine arts at Boston College.[7] His book, *AfterImage: the Indelible Catholic Imagination of Six American Filmmakers* (2000), theorizes about the discernible influence of Catholicism on directors and their films. Drawing on the work of theologian

David Tracy and priest-sociologist Andrew Greeley (on analogical and Catholic imaginations, respectively), Blake proposes that a characteristically Catholic view of the world comes from a "common core of Catholic belief,"[8] which people brought up within the faith experience. This Catholic worldview, even if Catholics grow up to reject their faith and fail to practice it, remains as an afterimage—hence the "religious influences in film that lurk beneath the surface [are] undetected even by the filmmakers themselves."[9] In analyzing how the Catholic afterimage operates in the disparate work of filmmakers such as Alfred Hitchcock, Martin Scorsese, Brian De Palma, and Francis Ford Coppola, Blake states:

> [Catholic filmmakers] are likely to carry with them the "stories" of their childhood through which they have learned to situate questions of the ultimate meaning of life, and these in turn tend to shape the meaning of events in daily life, like love, community, loyalty, death, family, sex, conflict, violence and sacrifice.[10]

He goes on to present a list of concrete connections between the afterimage of Catholicism and things remaining in the imagination for which Catholics have a fondness: Saints and devotional activities still are familiar and much-loved presences in many (especially ethnic) Catholic homes. Saints are role models, and it may seem that the more they perform fantastic miracles and achieve unattainable sanctity, the more they are venerated. They also serve to protect children who are named after them at baptism or confirmation.

Saints offer the example of an ideal life through narratives of moral growth, another thing Blake contends that Catholics are fond of. Blake comments that although there have been films about saints, there are many more films about sinners, who "exhibit the same kinds of strong personalities as the saints . . . saint and sinner alike point the way" to mythic stature.[11] To illustrate this point Blake presents the example of Scorsese's *Godfather* trilogy. However, stories of people who struggle and overcome adversity, like those in Frank Capra films, appeal to Catholics who try to be good in their daily lives.

When Blake states that Catholics are fond of "the ordinary," it is often because they recognize that many saints were men and women like themselves who rose to the challenge of living a life serving God. As Alfred Hitchcock and John Ford demonstrate time and again in their films, ordinary people faced with evil can find strength to fight or even defeat it.

Catholics appreciate the physicality of life and its worth, Blake argues: "They are comfortable with the physical because they tend to see it as the manifestation of God's presence in the world."[12] This is a direct link with sacramentality, a trait of the Catholic imagination, according to Tracy and Greeley, which posits God as present and immanent in—rather than other and apart from—humanity. Blake says that for a Catholic filmmaker, things will have a spiritual meaning that point beyond their material worth. He suggests that Catholic filmmakers are so influenced by their Catholic imaginations that God's grace and redemption can be detected in the ordinary, even in Blake's words "from a most unlikely, ungodlike savior, like Travis Bickle" in Scorsese's *Taxi Driver*.[13]

One other observation that Blake makes is that Catholic directors rarely feature women as strong or heroic characters in their films; this may of course be applicable to many of the directors he analyses in *AfterImage*, but this is most certainly not true of Savoca. Her films offer a wealth of women characters, who drive the plot and who offer a sometimes different and refreshing perspective on familiar themes (as in *Dogfight*).

Everyday Saints and Sinners: Household Saints

The film *Household Saints* is a much more personal project for Savoca than some of her other films, in that the original novel appealed to Savoca's own confusion about her Catholic identity; coming from a religious family, she questioned Catholicism only when she became a teenager:

> [The book] reflected the way I feel as a lapsed Catholic who did not stop thinking about it. There's so much ritual and beauty to Catholicism, that even if you turn away because of all the stuff there is to dislike about it, there are so many things you still carry with you.[14]

Savoca felt that making a film from the novel gave her permission "to start asking all the questions of myself that I had become embarrassed to ask because it wasn't hip anymore to do so."[15] As a filmmaker she met many people who had no faith and who were comfortable with their unbelief, but for someone who still had unresolved feelings the opportunity to work through them while making a film was a valuable one: "This movie works for many of us because we are confused. If we knew exactly what we were doing there would be no need to make it or to see it or to read it or to write it."[16]

The film uses a storytelling scenario to situate the action during the San Gennaro feast day in a New York City Italian American neighborhood in 1949; it is observed that "the grace of God" caused the young butcher Joseph Santangelo to win his wife Catherine at a pinochle game. In fact, the metaphor of living life as playing a game is prevalent throughout the film; in another segment, it is said that "man deals and God stacks the deck."[17] The regularity of the men's card games is as ritualistic as family meals (although this Italian American custom is subverted later in the film by the youngest character, Joseph and Catherine's daughter, Teresa). The ritual of making sausage to sell at the butcher's shop is passed down from Joseph's mother Carmela to Catherine in the same ritualistic manner.

However, all that the old generation holds dear in terms of the "old country," whether it is the devotion to household saints or the superstitions that guide everyday decisions and actions, is shown in the film to be swept away with the following generation. The lack of Catholic identity in the naming of babies by young couples is a sore point with Carmela—"who's going to protect them," she asks contemptuously, "Saint Stacey or Saint Scott?" The changes in religious traditions and practices, as emigrant communities attempt to assimilate into the American way of life, is an important factor in the film. It seems that, for Catherine, superstition, religion, and even spirituality have hindered the process of becoming Italian American. After her mother-in-law's death, Catherine begins to wear the latest fashions and to decorate her home in bold new colors, packing away Carmela's holy pictures and palm crosses stuck behind them. It could be said that the ideology of American consumerism is the new authoritative voice for Catherine. However, this rejection of most, if not all, elements of Italian American Catholic tradition (she continues to use Carmela's recipe for sausage, hearing Carmela's voice as she combines the ingredients) is upturned by Teresa's religious fervor. She replaces the decorations in her bedroom with her grandmother's religious artifacts and throws herself into devotional practices. She becomes terribly distressed about the secrets of the letter of Fatima, believing that the Pope's silence about its contents is somehow linked to her own lack of sanctity. Her desire to become a Carmelite, fueled by her obsession with St. Therese of Lisieux, is crushed by parental refusal to allow her to enter the convent. Teresa attempts to pressure her parents into letting her become a nun by refusing food, but her lengthy fast eventually is broken by helpless gorging on some of the family sausage.

The honored tradition of Catholic families to have at least one child take up the religious life is cast aside by her parents. Joseph says "Nuns are sick women, and my daughter isn't sick." Eventually accepting that her fate is to remain in the world, Teresa tries instead to discern the purpose of her life and prays to God asking for help to "bend" herself to God's will. She has a revelation shortly afterward that God is everywhere. With this in mind, she finds that performing the smallest chores—cleaning the floor, doing laundry—is how she can worship God. Despite (or because of) Joseph's derision of the religious life (because his daughter is not sick) Teresa does in fact become ill. She is confined to a mental institution, shortly after she has a vision of Jesus. This event is described by Catherine as the day when her daughter "went crazy ironing shirts in her boyfriend's apartment." When Teresa inexplicably dies, Catherine and Joseph have different reactions. No longer skeptical of his daughter's faith, Joseph suddenly smells roses in the room and sees wounds in Teresa's hands resembling stigmata. His sudden conviction that Teresa was a saint is confirmed by the film's narrator, who recounts the news that at Teresa's funeral all prayer requests were answered, and all inmates at the institution were cured. Moreover, Catherine's sausage suddenly began to cure sickness. So was Teresa a saint? The ending of the film is ambiguous, with the storytellers who began the film concluding with a shrug that Teresa "saw God in her work—how many of us can say that?"

Household Saints is remarkable not only because, as one reviewer put it, it "may well be the first American movie about three generations of an Italian-American family that doesn't have a criminal as a main character,"[18] but because the storyline seems so plausible despite its fantastic nature. *Variety* critic Todd McCarthy has used the paradoxical juxtaposition of the terms "strange" and "unexceptional" in describing *Household Saints*, "Spanning more than 20 years and embracing three generations of strange women, this is, among other things, a look at different kinds of faith within the context of otherwise unexceptional lives."[19] In doing so, Aaron Baker and Juliann Vitullo claim that McCarthy is tapping into the vein of female mysticism that has operated through centuries for women whose ordinary lives of domestic and patriarchal constraint contained liberating experiences of exceptional devotion and mysticism. They quote Simone de Beauvoir on mysticism as "adopting the social role that patriarchy expects the woman to play in a romantic relationship," that is, the mystic mimics in her role as bride of Christ the subservient role a wife undertakes.[20] But they also point to the problematic reverse, that a woman who undertakes a mystical role is also resisting patriarchal control by directly connecting to the divine without recourse to men (or the male Church hierarchy).

Savoca could easily have portrayed the novel's characters in a stereotypical manner of Italian Americans, all hand gestures and "Mama mia!" clichés, but these are real, complex people who have tragedy and happiness in their lives. The most tragic character is Joseph's brother, Nicky, whose obsession with opera drives him to suicide in his longing for a geisha like Madame Butterfly. This straightforward style of representation is seen from the start; it is a real story about real people, according to the old Italian American couple who are recounting it over an al fresco lunch. There are no cheap laughs with the story of the pinochle prize, and the unorthodox marriage of Joseph and Catherine is subsequently shown through tender scenes of lovemaking to be a good match. These are rendered somewhat surreal by Savoca's cinematic style; while Carmela sleeps deeply in the next room, Joseph and Catherine's vigorous lovemaking rattles the bedstead. Savoca visualizes this with Carmela floating peacefully on her bed through the couple's bedroom. In another scene, Catherine's first pregnancy ends tragically with the death of a newborn son, and a hushed discussion of infants in limbo is overheard while a surreal rail of tiny white coffins drifts across the screen.

Savoca makes directorial choices for other scenes that might be expected to call on more fantastic cinematic devices but that are actually presented quite conventionally. Savoca once remarked that her cinematic approach was to make "anything that was ordinary—cooking, eating, or making love or having a baby . . . extraordinary. And vice versa . . . if Jesus shows up while you're ironing, then those things have to be very normal."[21] When Teresa sees Jesus she has entered into a relationship with Leonard, a young student, and is ironing his red-checked shirt while he is out. Jesus appears and sits in a chair across from the ironing board, wearing a filthy white robe; he complains to Teresa that it has not been washed in two thousand years. A blond, smilingly affable Jesus, he then laughingly turns all the shirts in the closet into red-checked copies of the one Teresa is ironing. When Leonard comes in, Teresa tells him about this wondrous miracle and shows him the closet, which is filled with the regular assortment of clothes and not with a multitude of red-checked shirts.

Later, confined to bed with her illness, Teresa tells her parents that she has been playing pinochle with God, Jesus, and St. Therese (girls against boys, and not surprisingly the boys, being divine and all-powerful, win every hand). This is a scene that would be challenging to recreate cinematically, however surrealistically, and the temptation must surely have been there for Savoca to attempt to recreate the image of God placing bets at a card table. But the scene goes on to offer a disturbing description of God that could not so easily be visualized. Teresa reveals to her parents that God cheats at cards, just as Joseph has been seen elsewhere in the film cheating his customers by pushing on the meat scales with his thumb. Is this a picture of God that we are comfortable with—would such a saintly girl dream up such a deceitful God?

After Teresa's death the film asks the viewer to reevaluate Catherine's perception that Teresa was crazy or, as the psychiatrist puts it, suffering an acute hallucinatory psychosis due to religious obsession. Teresa's appreciation of faith as an ordinary and everyday observance is enhanced by Savoca's understated style, which asks viewers to make up their own minds about the miraculous nature of Teresa's life. Because of a strong performance by Savoca favorite Lili Taylor, Teresa is undoubtedly the main character of *Household Saints*. It is unusual for the main character to be introduced halfway through the story, but Teresa appears an hour into the film. Our perceptions of her importance are complicated even more when the viewer sees how balanced and leisurely paced the story is between the three generations. Apart from not anticipating the outcome of the story, the viewer spends the entire film immersed in a community of everyday saints and sinners where "the questions of sanctity and sanity are given . . . complex treatment."[22]

Savoca's confusion about her own faith, tempered with her admiration for the beauty of its traditions, perhaps is given space to assert itself in a story where there is no neat conclusion. The grandmother's question: "Teresa saw God in her work—how many of us can say that" is swiftly countered by her daughter's retort, "I could name a list of women as long as my arm who went crazy cooking and cleaning and trying to please everybody."

Conclusion

Richard Blake's theory of a Catholic afterimage seems to be well suited for the most part to Nancy Savoca's filmmaking influences, particularly when offering a reading of *Household Saints*. The novel was written by an author who is not even Catholic (or Italian), and in creating the screenplay Savoca and Guay strove to reproduce what David Schwartz calls "a novelistic texture and atmosphere."[23] The film is not an apologia for religion, yet pictures its practices and traditions with undisguised affection tinged with skepticism. If anything, the afterimage on display in Savoca's work has to do more with the search for extraordinary meaning in the ordinary; "Many of us have that yearning [for perfection and beauty], you just keep looking for it and that's what you live your life for."[24]

Reviewing the Chapter

1.   Do you think there is such a thing as a "sacramental" perception that Catholics might have that imbues material things with spiritual value beyond their worth? Explain your answer.

2.   Discuss the perspective that a filmmaker might have if he or she "uses life experiences to explore in film how relationships are defined, strengthened, and maintained."

3.   What would you identify as the difficulties filmmakers run into when they attempt to portray divinity (such as images of God) onscreen?

Notes

1.   David Schwartz, "Household Saints," Nancy Savoca Retrospective, January 1999, available at: www.ammi.org/calendar/ProgramNotes/ProgNotesSavoca%201-31.html (accessed November 12, 2002).

2.   "Nancy Savoca, Artist Biography," available at: www.blockbuster.com/bb/person/details/0,7621,BIO-P110007,00.html (accessed November 12, 2002).

3.   Marjorie Baumgarten, "The Twenty Four Hour Woman," *Austin Chronicle*, available at: www.filmvault.com/filmvault/austin/h/hourwomanthe1.html (accessed March 12, 2004).

4.   Biography for Nancy Savoca, available at: us.imdb.com/Bio?Savoca+Nancy (accessed October 31, 2002; hereafter cited as Biography).

5.   Biography.

6.   "True Love," Italian-American Film Festival Schedule, available at: www.cinemaartscentre.org/italianfestival/italianshows3.htm (accessed November 12, 2002).

7.   Blake's published works include *Woody Allen: Profane and Sacred* (Lanham, MD: Scarecrow Press, 1995) and *Screening America: Reflections on Five Classic Films* (Mahwah, NJ: Paulist Press, 1991).

8.   Richard Blake, *AfterImage: The Indelible Catholic Imagination of Six American Filmmakers* (Chicago: Loyola Press, 2000), xiv.

9.   Blake *AfterImage*, xvi.

10. Blake, *AfterImage*, 11–12.

11. Blake, *AfterImage*, 15.

12. Blake, *AfterImage*, 16.

13. Blake, *AfterImage*, 17.

14. From remarks made at a press conference, Toronto Festival of Festivals; "Nancy

Savoca, Household Saints," Mondo Video, December 2002, available at: www.mondofausto .com/interview-nancysavoca.htm (accessed November 12, 2002; hereafter cited as Press conference, Toronto).

15. Press conference, Toronto.

16. Press conference, Toronto.

17. *Household Saints,* directed by Nancy Savoca, First Line Features, 1993. All quotes in this chapter not attributed to another source come from the movie.

18. Schwartz, "Household Saints."

19. Quoted by Aaron Baker and Juliann Vitullo, *Mysticism and the Household Saints of Everyday Life,* available at: academic.brooklyn.cuny.edu/modlang/carasi /via/ViaVol7-2BakerandVitullo.htm (accessed November 12, 2002).

20. Baker and Vitullo, *Mysticism.*

21. Schwartz, "Household Saints."

22. Theresa Sanders, *Celluloid Saints* (Macon, GA: Mercer University Press, 2002), 203.

23. Schwartz, "Household Saints."

24. Press Conference, Toronto.

Parables on Screen:
John Sayles and *Men with Guns*

Greg Friedman

> *"A sower went out to sow . . ."*[1]
> *"There was a landowner who planted a vineyard . . ."*[2]
> *"A man was going down from Jerusalem to Jericho, and fell into the hands of robbers . . ."*[3]

Readers of the Christian scriptures, the New Testament, will immediately recognize these opening lines of three of Jesus's parables. Students of cinema will probably as quickly recognize the following thumbnail movie descriptions:

- Seven former activists from the '60s meet for a weekend reunion.
- A group of baseball players conspire with gamblers to throw the World Series.
- A union organizer arrives in a West Virginia coal town.

All three of these films (*Return of the Secaucus Seven, Eight Men Out*, and *Matewan*) come from the writing and directing genius of John Sayles. Since his first film in 1979, he has sought the freedom to tell his stories as he feels they need to be told. That commitment has resulted in a unique body of work both on the screen and in print.

Catholic Roots

Many of Sayles's fans may be surprised to find him in the company of directors with Catholic roots. While one of his films does flow from a Catholic concept (*Limbo*) and another, *Men with Guns*, includes a fallen-away priest, there is little in most of Sayles's films that would betray a Catholic upbringing. However, a study of Sayles's interviews over the past two decades, and a closer look at his movies, reveal how his storytelling abilities were awakened as a boy in

Schenectady, New York, when he heard the parables and stories of Jesus read each Sunday at Mass.

Born in 1950, John is the son of teachers Don and Mary Sayles. Mary was Catholic; her husband was a former-Lutheran-turned-atheist who nonetheless agreed to allow John and his older brother Doug to be raised Catholic.[4] John's brother Doug told Sayles's biographer Gerry Molyneaux that the boys' traditional upbringing meant they were not known among their peers for wild behavior. And Doug attested, "We had the added factor of growing up Catholic. We went to church every Sunday of our lives. We were raised old-fashioned, not modern Catholics, wooden kneelers, the whole thing."[5] John remembers his altar boy preparation:

> I studied to be an altar boy but I never actually served—it was the first time I had to learn lines and I actually have a good short-term memory for that kind of thing. I learned all the Latin for the Catholic Mass in one night, got a hundred on the test the next day and forgot it within a week, I'm sure.[6]

When Sayles left home for college, he also left the practice of his Catholic faith behind. In the 1990s, he listed his religion as "Catholic atheist" in his entry in Contemporary Theatre, Film and Television[7]—a description that reportedly upset his mother.[8] But unlike some filmmakers with Catholic roots, his movies do not betray outward antagonism toward the religion of his youth. Sayles continues to claim it as part of his identity and acknowledge its role in his life: "We were raised Catholic, which is definitely an influence. We went to church every Sunday. It's a belief system, a mythology that you're given. . . . I still think of myself as Catholic, as an ethnicity."[9]

Sayles remains interested in how religion functions as part of the fabric of life. He peopled his 1987 film *Matewan* with "hard-shell" and "soft-shell" Baptist miners, whose grassroots faith justifies an Old Testament, "eye for an eye" approach to violence:

> The hard-shell preacher I played really believes that his reading of Scripture tells him that union people are in league with the anti-Christ—he's an absolute believer. But that's one of the things that is tough about it all—there can be wonderful stuff in religion, but it can be used to chop people's heads off. And the same thing with any political belief; you can pervert it, just in the way you read it and interpret it.[10]

The "absolute believer," Sayles says, "can cause as much trouble as cynics. You might like the believers a little bit more, but whether they're Shi'ites, union men, or pro-lifers, they cause trouble because they absolutely believe."[11]

He says another character from *Matewan*, young Danny Radnor, is "a boy preacher who has both the Old Testament values of righteousness and retribution and the New Testament dreams of peace and justice,"[12] indicating the director's familiarity with the scriptures.

Parables

Sayles has attested to the influence of the scriptural stories he heard in church as a boy. In a 1981 *New York Times* interview he recalled, "I liked listening to the gospel at Catholic mass . . . Christ's progress to the cross was what I had instead of Buck Rogers serials, and the parables made me aware of metaphors and allegory."[13] In *Sayles on Sayles* he says much the same:

> Every Sunday there's a sermon based on the Gospel of that week. . . . You're constantly being given simile and metaphor. Christ is always talking in parables and the punchline is always a simile or an allegory.[14]

A parable is a familiar concept in both the Jewish and Christian traditions. Rabbis used parables, as did Jesus in the Gospels.[15] Gospel parables are usually extended similes; a fictitious story, drawn from life, completes the comparison: "The Kingdom of heaven is like . . ." The Greek term *parabol*, as used in the Gospels of Matthew, Mark, and Luke, may include proverbs, metaphors, and allegories. Thus, the description parable may fit a wide set of examples to the readers of those texts.[16]

One of the key twentieth-century scholars of the Gospel parable was British theologian C. H. Dodd, whose definition of parable is often cited: At its simplest the parable is a metaphor or simile drawn from nature or common life, arresting the hearer by its vividness or strangeness, and leaving the mind in sufficient doubt about its precise application to tease it into active thought.[17]

Dodd notes that even when the more symbolic dimensions of the parables emerge, they nevertheless preserve a "dramatic realism," a unified story. In describing the Kingdom of God, Dodd notes, Jesus wished to stress its "intrinsic" connectedness to both "the processes of nature and of the daily life of men."[18]

John R. Donohue, Society of Jesus (S.J.), says that the parables give us a "glimpse of the everyday life of first-century Galilee: the world of farming and fishing, of weddings and feasts, of landed gentry and restive tenants, of travelers knocking in the night, and of a widow standing up to a callous judge . . . where even the hero of the parable can be a pragmatic schemer . . . or a seemingly capricious landowner."[19]

In creating the situations and characters in his films, John Sayles also draws on a cross-section of everyday life, including his own wide work and travel experiences—factory worker, nursing home attendant, and hitchhiker, to name a few.

He also makes use of his interest in history, culture, and sociology. The results echo the themes described by Barbara Reid, Order of Preachers (O.P.), as characteristic of Jesus's parables, which "often identify with those on the margins of contemporary Jewish society; they portray a God who takes the side of the poor and oppressed; they stress a communal dimension of religious values."[20] Sayles's films likewise depict people on the margins of society (*Lianna* and *Brother from Another Planet*); those who struggle against oppression (*Matewan* and *Men with Guns*); and those seeking to form community, often amidst complex and contradictory forces (*City of Hope*, *Lone Star*, and *Sunshine State*).

As noted previously, Sayles's films contain little that is explicitly *Catholic*. In fact, he calls the films of Martin Scorsese "more Catholic than mine."[21]

One Sayles film, *Limbo* (1999), did emerge from a traditional Catholic concept—the place where unbaptized infants, unable to choose good or evil, remained in a state of natural happiness but without seeing God face-to-face. Contemporary Catholic teaching no longer refers to limbo but rather emphasizes that such infants are in God's care, presuming that God somehow embraces them fully.[22]

But Sayles, like most Catholics born prior to the 1970s, was taught the more traditional concept. In an interview on the Independent Film Channel, he explains how the concept became the movie's central metaphor: "I was raised Catholic and there was the Catholic fine definition of limbo which is, it's where the souls of people who weren't baptized go, who didn't get the chance to be officially good or bad. . . . Limbo is infinite; you're there forever."

In the film, Alaska fisherman Joe Gastineau is in a metaphoric limbo at the film's beginning. Years before, Joe lost his boat in an accident at sea. In the twenty-five years since then he has not taken a major emotional or physical risk. For Sayles, limbo can refer to any person or society that's trapped, unable to take a risk: "The thought of the hell that you could fall into . . . is so frightening that you don't try for heaven, so you just stay there. And you're not in hell, but you're not in heaven either."[23]

Sayles and Storytelling

Sayles has chosen to make movies with serious themes, a choice that often limits their appeal and rules out collaboration with mainstream Hollywood. Believing that "independent filmmakers do what they do because there's a story they want to tell,"[24] Sayles makes movies "because there are things and people happening out there that I see in life that I don't see on screen. I'm interested in them. . . . I want to go beyond the two-dimensional feel of most contemporary movies."[25] Like the parables, Sayles wants to touch his audience at a profound level:

> To me storytelling is about making some sense out of stuff, making some kind of connection. The movies I've made and the books and plays I've written have always been about things that I feel I need to know more about and want to figure out. I want to make films that I haven't seen before, whether it is in the com-

plexity that they're dealt with, or that I just feel like this is something that needs to be made. Even if making a movie that doesn't show in a thousand theaters . . . is not exactly touching popular culture, . . . There's at least that chance to get into the conversation.[26]

Engaging the audience is Sayles's primary goal in filmmaking: "[W]hen people leave the theater, I want them to be talking about human beings, about their own lives and the lives of other people they know or could know. . . ."[27] Here he echoes the contention of Donohue, S.J., that in Jesus's parables, ordinary people and events are "told in such a way that people from every age and culture have seen their own life with its hopes and challenges replayed. . . ."[28] In addition, many parables end with unforeseen outcomes, prompting listeners to radically rethink their values, as Reid, O.P., points out:

> Jesus'[s] parables do not stay on the level of the familiar. Always there is a catch. They were not pleasant stories that entertained people or that confirmed the status quo. They were startling and confusing, usually having an unexpected twist that left the hearers pondering what the story meant and what it demanded. As John Dominic Crossan puts it, "You can usually recognize a parable because your immediate reaction will be self-contradictory: 'I don't know what you mean by that story but I'm certain I don't like it.' "[29]

In 1991, after the release of *City of Hope*, his film in which characters wrestle with personal and societal choices in an urban setting, Sayles noted that some moviegoers asked, " 'So what was your point with this movie?' I think that's because they're used to: 'The moral of this story is blank.' I just want people to be thinking about these things when they leave, and the difficulty of them, and possibly having some sympathy for the people who have to make those hard decisions. . . ."[30] And making moral choices is a theme Sayles connects to his Catholic background:

> [I] think that seeing the world clearly and figuring out what you're going to do about either the world's limitations in regards to you or your limitations in regards to the world is a huge part of life. . . . I think when you're talking about character, many of the themes . . . are about characters presented with these moral choices, or moments where they get to show a lot of character or crap out on themselves. And that's the victory. So it's an area of drama that interests me more than who shot who and whether the hero escapes at the end.[31]

Our choices, he says, help to create who we are: "What do you choose to belong to? Have you chosen. . . . [T]here are choices that are more responsible and more personal, where you actually take care of somebody else and have to deal with somebody else and have to affect and be affected by the world."[32] Many of the characters Sayles creates face such choices:

- The ballplayers in *Eight Men Out* consort with gamblers and discover their families threatened with violence.
- In *Lianna,* when central character, Lianna, discovers her sexual identity, her established relationships are threatened.
- Wynn, a politician in *City of Hope*, wrestles with compromises that threaten his values.
- In *Passion Fish*, paralyzed actress May Alice must choose between anger and the risk of new relationships.
- In *Matewan* union organizer Joe Kenehan and the miners confront the issue of violence to gain justice.

The consequences of the choices faced by Sayles's characters often resemble the unexpected twists in parables that Reid and Crossan described. In *Lone Star*, sheriff Sam Deeds learns of his blood ties to the woman with whom he has fallen in love, a relationship whose next stage is left ambiguous to the audience. In *Limbo*, the characters' fates literally are left in "cinematic limbo" at the film's abrupt end.

The connection to the parables of Jesus is also evident in the way John Sayles tells his stories. In a 1997 interview in DGA Magazine, he traces the birth of his career as a storyteller:

> You might say that it began at Catholic Mass when I was a boy. I'd hear the story of Jesus over and over. I got to know every detail. It was much like seeing a film on tape, playing it back and forth, scene by scene, over and over. I came to understand the techniques used by [storytellers]. When I started writing short stories in the fourth or fifth grade, I knew how to use those techniques. They gave a story interesting nuances. I could write from differing points of view.[33]

Early in life Sayles learned to visualize his stories. The title of his book about making the film *Matewan* says it all: *Thinking in Pictures*. In the opening chapter, he describes his first novel, *Pride of the Bimbos*, as "originally a movie in my head. I started with a couple of scenes that I saw dramatically, saw the setting, imagined a certain graininess to the image, heard a country-western soundtrack compressed through a tinny juke box speaker."[34] Later in *Thinking in Pictures*, Sayles highlights the difference between writing fiction and writing movies:

> Fiction is words describing images, where in movies you have the images themselves. Fiction relies more on the imagination of the reader, while movies often seem to be imagination made solid. . . . Thinking in pictures is a way to inhabit the bodies of characters as well as their minds. Trying to bring those pictures, those feelings, to other people is a lot of what movie-making is all about.[35]

Sayles's storytelling technique, then, seems clearly to parallel what Dodd says about the Gospel parables Sayles heard as a boy at Sunday Mass:

> [A]ll is true to nature and to life. Each similitude or story is a perfect picture of

something that can be observed in our experience. The processes of natures are accurately observed and recorded; the actions of persons in the stories are in character; they are either such as anyone would recognize as natural in the circumstances, or, if they are surprising, the point of the parable is that such actions are surprising.[36]

In the Independent Film Channel interview, Sayles is asked if his film, *Men with Guns*, is about the ascension to heaven. Sayles's reply hints at the film's "parabolic" character when he says that "it's the ascension to a heaven that may not be there."[37]

Men with Guns

Men with Guns among all of John Sayles's films perhaps best demonstrates a relationship to the Gospel parables learned in his Catholic youth. In addition to references to heaven, Catholic sacraments, and priesthood, the film "feels" like a parable. One reviewer called it a "profound parable about a doctor's journey from ignorance to perilous knowledge."[38] Another pointed to the "parable-like wayfarers, each with a tale to tell" who travel with the film's central character.[39]

Sayles seems to have crafted *Men with Guns* as a parable. He wanted it to "have some of that generic, universal feeling." Its setting is deliberately unspecified, and the title, he says, could apply to "half the movies or books ever written."[40] He based the story on real-life experiences of people in Latin America caught between governments and guerilla movements, on the receiving end of violence from the ever-present "men with guns" depicted in the film.

The film's central figure is Doctor Fuentes, a prosperous doctor in an unnamed Latin American country. As the movie opens, the doctor decides to take a vacation to visit some of his former medical students who were part of an ambitious program he had started, to bring medical care to indigenous Indian tribes living in remote areas. It was, he says, his "legacy." Despite the concerns of family and friends and a heart problem, the doctor begins his journey.

Doctor Fuentes' ignorance and naïveté is signaled early on as he treats an army official. "You think like a child," the general says. The doctor replies, "ignorance . . . nobody is immune to this disease." In the city, one of his former medical students—now a drug dealer—tells him, "Dr. Fuentes, you're the most learned man I ever met. But also the most ignorant."

The theme of ignorance is central to the film. When two Americans ask the doctor about tortures and murders they have heard about, he assures them, "That happens in other countries, not here." Eventually, the doctor's naïve ignorance will give way to understanding. But he must first undertake a spiritual journey as well.

The doctor's physical journey through a constantly changing landscape is Sayles's attempt to create a symbolic geographical movement.[41] Along the way, the doctor becomes more and more personally involved with people and events.

"At first," Sayles says, "it's a story that's told to him and you imagine things. Then it's a story that's told to him and then illustrated. And he starts meeting the people themselves and finally it's a story that's happening to him."[42] The doctor's car is robbed; he loses his camera. His tires are stolen; eventually he faces the loss of his life at gunpoint. The physical journey begins to take its toll on his weakened heart.

Spiritually, the doctor moves from ignorance to understanding. As Sayles describes it, Dr. Fuentes:

> has avoided those tough moral choices by being ignorant on purpose. And in his case, it would take some work to know what was going on. Dr. Fuentes probably lives in a place where the government controls the newspapers, where the official story is not the whole story, not even much of the real story. But he could know if he wanted to. He probably had suspicions, he heard rumors. He even talks about rumors. But he didn't follow up because he didn't really want to. And that can happen in a family. It can be somebody who says, "No, your father didn't molest you. Come on." "Well, what about that time you found him in bed?" "Oh, come on, that didn't happen. I never found that." [S]aying the words, admitting it, changes your life forever. . . . But ignorance allows you not to carry the burden of that knowledge.[43]

Such a confrontation with complexity is contained in most of Jesus's parables: The elder brother of the prodigal son must decide whether to accept his father's forgiveness of the younger brother; the story of the Good Samaritan answers the question, "who is my neighbor"; and the parable of the vineyard workers dramatizes God's extravagant generosity.

In each, listeners are also forced to choose—by the power of the stories themselves. Like the parables, *Men with Guns* communicates its truths through the characters Dr. Fuentes encounters. The Indians he meets are identified only by the product of their labors: the "Salt People," the "Sugar People," the "Banana People," the "Gum People," the "Corn People." The names reinforce the film's metaphorical feeling. When individuals are named, it is mostly Dr. Fuentes' students, as he inquires about them from place to place.

In one village, no one speaks to him except for a woman who is blind. Ironically, she is the only one who "sees" everything. In another village, he meets Conejo, a young boy who guides him to a field strewn with human bones, and tells him, "This is where they take you when you graduate." In an abandoned village school, prisoners were either "educated," (i.e., confessed) or "graduated," (i.e., killed). Ironically, the school, a place to acquire knowledge, dramatically challenges the doctor's ignorance.

As Conejo and Dr. Fuentes return to his carryall (now stripped of its tires), Domingo, an army deserter, accosts them at gunpoint. He robs Dr. Fuentes of his money and takes the two coins the doctor gave to Conejo. (Later, Conejo asks the doctor if he has more money. When the doctor assures him he does, in the bank,

Conejo retorts, "He took everything I had in the world," showing the doctor another side of reality.)

Hours later, Domingo returns in another vehicle, bringing tires to replace those stolen from the doctor. But Domingo has been shot; he forces the doctor to treat the wound and to help Domingo escape his pursuers. We learn he was an army medic. When the doctor asks, "Where are we going?" Domingo tells him, "Further on." This recurring phrase reinforces the film's generic sense of place and suggests a rootlessness symbolic of losing one's soul, one of the key spiritual themes in the film.

The dialogue between Dr. Fuentes and the next character to join the band of "wayfarers" especially illustrates this theme. He is Padre Portillo, a fallen-away priest who calls himself "the Ghost." When asked, "Where are you headed?" he too replies, "Further on."

Dr. Fuentes asks the priest, "Are you lost?" Padre Portillo replies, "Yes, for a long time now." He tells the doctor he lives "neither here nor there," and explains how he originally taught religion through theater, but "stopped believing in my role and lost my faith." The doctor counters that "a man should believe in something." As a man of science, he believes in progress, but Padre Portillo tells him, "These days, I just believe in moving. Never mind which direction." Dr. Fuentes admits that his own faith has been shaken as his naïveté was tested, to which Padre Portillo replies, "I was a good priest until I was tested. . . . . I was tested and I was weak."

Testing—or temptation—is an element Sayles draws directly from his Catholic background. In *Sayles on Sayles*, in commenting on the theme of redemption, he says, "In the Catholic religion, and I think you see it in Scorsese's movies sometimes, . . . you need temptation and occasions of sin in order for you to be a good person. If everything was fine and there were no temptations, you wouldn't sin, but it wouldn't count for anything. You have to be tested."[44]

Both the doctor and the ex-priest are still being tested, and perhaps Domingo as well—as the doctor comments, "A priest without faith is like a soldier without a rifle," and turns to look at the deserter.

The conversation turns to talk about death. The doctor speaks of leaving his "legacy—something practical to be passed on from person to person." Padre Portillo's dream was to save souls, but he tells the doctor: "how much better to save a life. I dreamed your dream and you dreamed mine." The doctor sadly concludes, "and we both ended up a total failure."

But something is changing. The doctor says he should have known his students were in danger; perhaps he could have warned them. The priest is not so sure the doctor is responsible for their deaths but admits, "maybe ignorance is a sin."

In a marvelous storytelling scene around a campfire, Padre Portillo unfolds the ghost story of his failure. He tells in the third person how the army came to his village, demanding that he and five men be executed as the price for the village's survival. The priest fled, aware that his cowardice would doom the entire village. They accept his flight stoically and proceed to kill the other five men, hoping they will not be punished for the priest's lack of faith. When the doctor asks about the village's fate, the priest replies, "I've been to where it was. I obviously don't believe in heaven, Doctor. But I can give you a tour of hell." When his other listeners ask what became of the priest in his story, Padre Portillo replies, "I told you it was a ghost story. The priest wanders the roads and pathways of the country, never sleeping in the same place. He is neither here nor there—a ghost."

For Sayles, "spirituality and the loss of spirituality and the definition of people's spirituality is something that all of the characters have to deal with in some way."[45] Padre Portillo, Sayles says, possesses a spirituality common to Western religions; he had a "portable God." When his romantic notion of martyrdom comes face to face with the real thing, he flees, taking his God with him, and hoping—as Sayles speculates—that "maybe I can still be a Catholic and be good but why do I have to stay? Martyrdom is overrated."

But for the villagers, spirituality is not portable, Sayles maintains:

> If you leave that land and that way of life, if you stop growing corn, if you stop dressing a certain way, if you stop your customs of marriage and birth and how you address each other and how you respect each other and how you make decisions together, you're not a person any more. You don't have a spirit any more, you don't have a soul any more. . . . But it's not martyrdom to these people. It's survival to say . . . that five of us have to go. Our survival is the survival of our spirits, the spirits of our children.[46]

How does one who has lost his soul regain it? To answer this question, Sayles has his characters explore the notions of sin and redemption. Domingo wants to confess the atrocities he committed as a soldier, but Padre Portillo refuses to absolve him, claiming he is no longer a priest.

On the road, the men discuss the nature of sin. Dr. Fuentes asks, "Are sins only things that you do? Or can they be things that you don't do?" Padre Portillo gives the traditional Catholic teaching Sayles might recall from his catechism: "There are sins of commission and sins of omission. And then there's Original Sin. We're all born guilty in the eyes of the Lord." But what if someone unintentionally has injured another, the doctor asks. Then he's probably not a sinner, the priest replies. Domingo adds, "He's an idiot for sure." The priest agrees, "Of course. An idiot or a coward. But if God kept such people out of Heaven, He'd be very lonely."

They encounter an army roadblock near a detention camp. There, the priest allows himself to be led away by the guards. But he first turns back and tells Domingo, "I absolve you." In effect, Padre Portillo is a priest again, having reversed his betrayal in a moment of personal redemption and sacrifice.

One last character joins the group from the detention camp. She is Graciela, a rape victim who has not spoken in two years. She wants to go with them to

"Cerca del Cielo," a village supposedly higher up in the mountains, where refugees are hiding along with a woman doctor, who may be Fuentes' last surviving student, Dr. Montoya. Domingo is skeptical, believing the army would have discovered such a place. The boy Conejo tells him,

> "Just because you haven't seen it doesn't mean it isn't there."
> "You can believe in heaven if you want to, kid," Domingo says, "see where it gets you."

Apparently Doctor Fuentes is beginning to believe. When Graciela steals Domingo's gun to shoot herself, the doctor tries to give her faith that Cerca del Cielo does exist. He quotes words overheard earlier in the film when two tourists in the hotel were reading a brochure about Bali:

> There is a place . . . where your burdens are lifted from your shoulder on wings of peace . . . a place to forget, a place to grow, a place where each day is a gift and each person is reborn. Where is this paradise on earth, this heaven, this safe harbor?
> "And it's not far from here," Doctor Fuentes assures Graciela, "just a little further on."

They leave the road and begin to climb, encountering a band of guerillas on the way—more men with guns—who threaten to kill Domingo, but the doctor lies to protect him, and they continue to climb.

In a forest on the mountaintop, we see an Indian woman and her daughter—characters who have appeared earlier in scenes with a mythic quality. The woman seems to be expecting Doctor Fuentes. When the group arrives, she tells her daughter, "There's no hurry. He's come to stay." The doctor, whose heart condition has now worsened, is welcomed by a man who tells him there's no other doctor here, and says, "This is where rumors come to die." Dr. Fuentes slumps to the ground, dying. He says to himself: "This is my legacy. Every man should leave a legacy, something he built, something he left in the world, someone he passed his knowledge to, who'll carry on for him." He chuckles. "This is what I leave. At least, I don't have to climb anymore."

Domingo sees that the doctor has died, and wants to go "somewhere further on." But the young Indian girl comes to ask for help for her mother, whose leg was injured by shrapnel from an army land mine. Domingo first says he's not a doctor and tosses down the medical bag. Graciela hands the bag back to him, and he looks down at the doctor. "OK," he says, "where is your mother?" He leaves to help her. Graciela looks at Dr. Fuentes, walks into the forest, and gazes out at the next, higher mountaintop further on . . . and smiles, as the film ends.

For John Sayles, the question of whether the film is a "spiritual allegory" comes back to the reality of life: "Whether the movie is spiritual or not, it deals with people who are wrestling with that themselves—what is there that's practical and what is there that's spiritual and do I believe in spiritual things? . . .

Generally, only the people who are most committed to some kind of spiritual life are willing to go all the way, like the Indians."

The doctor, Sayles suggests, has learned—through his journey—the price of true knowledge: "he takes risks just to know and by the end of the movie he takes responsibility."[47]

Domingo, too, seems to have made a choice. For Graciela and Conejo, the story will apparently continue—in true fashion of a parable. And for Sayles's audience, questions remain open as well, another function of the parable.

Visions of the World

In the end, he has taught us in this masterful film-parable that "we have to all hold ourselves responsible, and that's a tough thing to do. It's hard to know all that stuff and then act according to it. The world is a complex place. Certainly the difficulty of our movies, and they are difficult to a certain extent, is that they're complex. And the whole point of most movies is to make things less complex."[48]

For those willing to encounter the complex kind of movies John Sayles has chosen to make, the rewards are evident. Challenging visions of the world unfold. It is a world of storytelling similar to that revealed in the Gospel parables Sayles learned as a boy, listening to the stories told at Sunday Mass. The gift of story-telling nurtured in his Catholic youth has matured according to his own unique and complex vision, forged in the tough choices faced by a truly independent filmmaker.

Reviewing the Chapter

1. How do films like *Men with Guns* help us understand the complexity of life?

2. How do our human choices help create who we are: the choices of the young doctors who went into the mountains, the priest, and the final choices of Dr. Fuentes?

3. What other films would you choose as contemporary parables to compare with those of Sayles?

Notes

1. Matthew 13:3–4, cited from The Holy Bible: New Revised Standard Version, Catholic Edition (Oxford: 1999).

2. Matthew 21:33, cited from The Holy Bible: New Revised Standard Version, Catholic Edition (Oxford: 1999).

3. Luke 10:29, cited from The Holy Bible: New Revised Standard Version, Catholic Edition (Oxford: 1999).

4. Gerard Molyneaux, *John Sayles: An Unauthorized Biography of the Pioneering Indie Filmmaker* (Los Angeles: Renaissance, 2000), 43.

5. Molyneaux, 43.

6. John Sayles and Gavin Smith, *Sayles on Sayles* (London: Faber and Faber, 1998), 1.

7. Sayles and Smith, x.

8. Molyneaux, 61.

9. Sayles and Smith, 1.

10. Sayles and Smith, 128–29.

11. Sayles and Smith, 123.

12. Kathy Huffhines, "Director John Sayles Makes Films with Convictions," in *John Sayles Interviews*, ed. Diane Carson (Jackson: University Press of Mississipi, 1999), 101.

13. Quoted in Molyneaux, 45.

14. Sayles and Smith, 1.

15. Barbara Reid, O.P., *Parables for Preachers: The Gospel of Mark, Year B* (Collegeville, Minnesota: Liturgical Press, 1999), 5.

16. Raymond E. Brown, S.S., Joseph A. Fitzmeyer, S.J, and Roland E. Murphy, O.Carm., eds., *The New Jerome Biblical Commentary* (Englewood Cliffs, New Jersey: Prentice Hall, 1990), 1364.

17. C. H. Dodd, *The Parables of the Kingdom* (New York: Harper and Row, 1961), 5.

18. Dodd, 9–10.

19. John R. Donohue, S.J., *The Gospel in Parable* (Philadelphia: Fortress Press, 1998), 13.

20. Reid, 9–10.

21. Sayles and Smith, 206.

22. Patrick McCloskey, O.F.M., "Ask a Franciscan," *St. Anthony Messenger* (July 2002).

23. "Independent Focus," (Television interview), Independent Film Channel.

24. Sayles and Smith, 250.

25. Eleanor O'Sullivan, "Director's Humanism Keeps Him away from Mainstream Movies," in Carson, *John Sayles Interviews*, 88.

26. Sayles and Smith, 27.

27. Sayles and Smith, 52.

28. Sayles and Smith, 14.

29. Reid, 7.

30. Nancy Scott, "Independent Sayles-Man," in Carson, *John Sayles Interviews*, 130.

31. Sayles and Smith, 206.

32. Sayles and Smith, 226.

33. Eliot Asinof, "John Sayles," *DGA Magazine*, December 1997–January 1998, www.dga.org/news/mag_acrchives/v22-5/john_sayles.htm.

34. John Sayles, *Thinking in Pictures: The Making of the Movie* Matewan (Boston: Da Capo Press, 1987), 4.

35. Sayles, 8.

36. Dodd, 9.

37. Dodd, 9.

38. Anthony Kaufman, "Lone Gun: A Conversation With John Sayles," *IndieWire*, www.indiewire.com/people/int_Sayles_John_980306.html.

39. Molyneaux, 243.
40. Sayles and Smith, 234.
41. Sayles and Smith, 241.
42. Sayles and Smith, 241.
43. Diane Carson, "John Sayles: Filmmaker," in Carson, *John Sayles Interviews*, 230–31.
44. Sayles and Smith, 206.
45. Carson, 224.
46. Carson, 224.
47. Sayles and Smith, 243.
48. Carson, 230–31.

Part 3

Catholicism and the Iberian Peninsula

There was a time when the Iberian Peninsula was the center of Catholic culture. Italy may have had Florence, Venice, Naples, Rome, and the Vatican itself, but the Spanish and Portuguese kingdoms of the fifteenth and sixteenth centuries combined religious and secular authority and power, Renaissance leadership, and an extensive coastline, which enabled them to conquer the lands they found in the Caribbean and through them, the whole of Latin America. Eventually, the Pope would divide the southern American continent between them.

They came confident in the rightness and righteousness of their cause. The quest was for gold. They held theological debates as to whether the indigenous peoples they conquered had souls and were truly human or not.

They came from sunny Mediterranean lands. They were hot-blooded and passionate, with outgoing sentiment and feeling, with exuberant and colorful piety, which soon linked with local religions and practices to form exotic beliefs and superstitions like Santeria.

Later Spain and Portugal declined in power and prestige. In the nineteenth century, the countries of Latin America were involved in uprisings against the colonial powers. In the twentieth century, both Spain and Portugal experienced new Leftist movements as well as revolutions and for Spain, a dire civil war. World sympathy tended to be anti-Franco's fascist forces while the Catholic Church supported him and his forty-year regime.

Latin America experienced social upheaval, coups, dictatorships, and social and religious repression as well as freedom movements, liberation theology, and Catholic action. Yet, the five hundred years of Catholic tradition still permeate the cultures.

Pedro Almodóvar led the Spanish cinema revival after the death of Franco in 1976. He is an uninhibited writer and director, who flaunts his flamboyance on and off screen. He is a world figure, winner of two Oscars, a vocal critic of government and Church but, as Rob Rix highlights, his movies rely on Catholic iconography, piety, and liturgy.

In Italy and in South American countries, the question whether a particular director is a Catholic or not is met with a bemused look. What else would the director be? Walter Salles stands in the Portuguese tradition that shaped Brazil. Jose Tavares de Barros analyzes *Central Station* in this taken-for-granted religious culture. He portrays and questions the devout piety of Brazilians. His own social justice concerns are also seen in his most recent movie, his version of the young Ernesto Guevara's 1952 journey around the continent and his awakening to justice issues, *The Motorcycle Diaries*, which was the winner of the Ecumenical Jury prize in Cannes, 2004.

Mexico, with its long Catholic tradition, has a number of significant directors on the world scene: Alfonso Cuarón, Guillermo del Toro, and Alejandro González Iñárritu. Luis Garcia Orso reflects on the work of Carlos Carrera, whose *El Crimen del Padre Amaro* deals specifically with the Catholic Church, priesthood, and moral dilemmas.

The spiritual journey of Argentinean Eliseo Subiela is the opposite of that of Almodóvar. His Spanish family was not religious, aligning themselves with left-wing politics. It was the adult Subiela, as Ricardo Yáñez highlights, who began to search more fully into the Hispanic religious tradition to discover who Jesus was and the spirituality of the Gospels. This spiritual search pervades his films, with some of his key characters being portrayed as Christ-figures like the man facing southeast.

6

The Mother of All Redemptions: Almodóvar's *All About My Mother*

Rob Rix

The most famous Spanish film director of recent times, double Oscar winner Pedro Almodóvar is paradoxically rated for his innovative, taboo-breaking images and narratives, while at the same time he appears to dwell on the most traditional obsessions of the Spanish cultural imagination: sex, death, bullfighting, and religion. In a postfeminist world, he is also renowned for his portraits of thoroughly modern women, yet often seems fixated by the most profoundly Spanish notions of the sacredness of motherhood. This is manifested in the *"madre sólo hay una"* ("you only have one mother") reverence for the Marian protectress, advocate, comforter, and object of absolute devotion, which Spanish males traditionally associate with both their own biological mother and with those ornate, spectacularly beautiful statues of the Virgin, which are paraded through towns and villages at Easter time, borne aloft on the shoulders of male penitents.

Images of the Virgin/Mother

Responding to a Spanish newspaper question about 9/11 one year later, Almodóvar revealed that it was while filming in the shrine of the Virgin of Araceli at Lucena that "beneath the gaze of the Virgin, beside the altar," he first heard the news of the attack on the twin towers.[1] For someone who claims to have lost his faith at the age of twelve, Spain's greatest living filmmaker has a remarkable predilection for images of the Virgin Mary. They appear in his films as a combination of kitsch décor and objects of genuine devotion, icons of Spanish popular religious culture, which seem to hold a lasting fascination for the prince-of-camp-turned-dramatist of the heart-rending. The frontispiece of the published filmscript of *All About My Mother* (1999) shows the director photographing himself before a picture of the Immaculate Heart, with the caption "First day of film-

5

ing. 21 September 1998"; the suggestion is surely that the Mother of God watches over the making of the film.[2] His "absolutely Andalusian" virgins form part of
the paraphernalia of hope for characters, such as the little girl Ada in *The Law of
Desire* (1985), who prays for purely profane favors at Our Lady's altar and Cross
of May in film director Pablo's home. The flames that engulf this domestic shrine
at the end of the film symbolize the destructive power of the passions that con-
sume the protagonists played by Eusebio Poncela and Antonio Banderas. The
Virgin seems to bless and suffer in her own effigy the intense homoerotic love
that has devoured their lives. Such an interpretation, however outrageous and
even blasphemous it might seem to some religious sensibilities, nevertheless
identifies a typical Almodóvarian use of Spanish Catholic statuary. The Virgin
represents the Mother who looks down on her abject sons with understanding and
compassion, revindicating their sacrifice despite their deviant (in the context of
official Spanish Catholic values) sexuality.

Spanish Mothers

Images of the Virgin (and occasionally those of Christ) appear in scenarios of
self-sacrificing passion and hope driven by innocence, with the apparent intent
of harnessing religious icons to Almodóvar's own extremely broad and unself-
conscious understanding of the spectrum of human sexuality. This is not done
in a satirical manner and not with the wicked delight taken by Luis Buñuel in
juxtaposing spirituality and carnality but in a way that accepts and even celebrates the topsy-turvy reality that could often be seen to contradict the eternal
values of traditional Catholic Spain. In *Labyrinth of Passions* (1982), Queti
(Marta Fernández Muro) submits to repeated rape by her deluded father
beneath the crucifix above her bed.[3] If Almodóvar is not in any sense disre-
spectful toward these images of popular religiosity, which he uses decoratively
but not indecorously, the institutional church and the Catholic faith in general
receive less than reverential treatment in his films. The clergy as such are rarely
portrayed; although choirmaster Father Constantino in *The Law of Desire*,
berated by transsexual Tina (Carmen Maura) for his nefarious effect on her life,
is emblematic of the tormented child molester often hinted at, if not directly
denounced by the director when recalling his schooling at the hands of the
Salesians in Cáceres. *La Mala educación* (*Bad Manners* [*Bad Education*],
2004), is avowedly anticlerical, and reflects his own childhood experiences in
the "Salesian brothel" or "Salesian hell" of a school where he excelled as a
choirboy and received what he called a "spectacular" religious education.[4]

Perhaps surprisingly, however, his most venomous critique of religion is
reserved not for the clergy but for "a certain type of Spanish mother," the castrat-
ing, bigoted Opus Dei supporter played by Julieta Serrano in *Matador* (1986).
Nuria Vidal identifies two images of Spain in the two contrasting mothers of this

film: the tyrannical repression of the past and the new, more tolerant and unprejudiced mother figure played by Chus Lampreave. Almodóvar's devotion to his own mother, Francisca Caballero, who appeared in cameo roles in several of his pictures before her death in 1999, did not prevent him from expressing his horror of typical Spanish mothers. Intolerance, authoritarianism, and hypocrisy are not portrayed as essentially maternal traits in his films; rather there are certain types of obviously dysfunctional mothers who embody one or more of these characteristics, often to the point of caricature (the stepmother and the mother of a test-tube baby in *Labyrinth of Passions*; Juani, mother of telekinetic Vanesa in *What Have I Done to Deserve This?* [1984]; and the self-centered Becky in *High Heels* [1991]). In the early films the first fully realized portrait of a mother comes in *What Have I Done to Deserve This?* in which the suffering, stifled Gloria (Carmen Maura) is unable to hold her family together in the face of poverty and depression in the urban jungle of 1980s Madrid, although in a last resort she is reconciled with a son she had previously sold to a pedophile dentist. The theme of motherhood as a positive role and even a vocation has taken time to evolve and embed itself in his cinema, albeit problematically.

All About My Mother

It is only with *All About My Mother* that a truly caring, nurturing, and protective mother is seen to prevail despite life's tragic betrayals. Dedicated intriguingly, "To my mother, to all mothers, and to all men who want to be mothers," Almodóvar's Oscar-winning box-office hit features Cecilia Roth as Manuela, a woman devastated by the loss of her son, who was run down by a car on his seventeenth birthday. Manuela, who works in the organ transplant unit of a Madrid hospital, is shown from the opening scenes as a woman who empathizes with those who suffer the loss of loved ones, a kind of virgin of sorrows who also acts a bereaved woman in a role-play videoed for hospital training purposes. She therefore assumes the mantle both of caring and of enacting the pain of loss, which soon, in a ghastly twist of irony, will turn from professional roles to personal experience when Esteban lies dying in the road. Her kneeling figure calling out for her son is a terrible, despairing Pietà. She then has to endure the moment, which she has rehearsed and lived from the other side, in her professional capacity, when doctors tell her that her son is dead and request her permission for the donation of his heart to save another life. Taken and recycled from a scene in *The Flower of My Secret* (1995), this melodramatic hospital setting roots Manuela's tragedy in the everyday world. Almodóvar seems fascinated by the casualty ward and by the tenuousness of life as it is seen to slip into the straight line and cold shrill tone of the electroencephalogram monitor. The mysteries of life and death are not surrounded by the trappings of religion and spirituality but by the instruments of contemporary clinical medicine and treatment.

If his latest films, and especially *Talk to Her* (2002), often include scenes or episodes involving the medical profession, the much earlier *Dark Habits* (1983) explored in bizarre fashion the goings-on in a convent of caring nuns, belonging to the fictitious order of the Sisters of the Community of Humiliated Redeemers. Dedicated ostensibly to the redemption of lost souls, they are led by a jealous, lovesick Mother Superior (Julieta Serrano) who conducts lesbian affairs with the prostitutes and drug addicts to whom they offer sanctuary. While as Mark Allinson points out, religion acts as a sublimation of desire for the nuns, the convent location and the rituals within it constitute merely a spoof scenario.[5] Almodóvar is interested not in any kind of spiritual life of the sisters, but rather in their interactions as women enclosed together in a privileged space, where female fantasies and emotions prevail. As such the nuns prefigure other groupings such as those *Women on the Edge of a Nervous Breakdown* (1988) who congregate in Pepa's penthouse flat and in *All About My Mother* the threesome who gather around Manuela's nurturing influence. For after the death of her son, Manuela returns to Barcelona after an eighteen-year absence, in search of her erstwhile husband and father of Esteban, the transsexual Lola. During her quest she encounters Agrado (Antonia San Juan), another transsexual, whose name reflects her desire to give pleasure to all comers, the young nun Rosa (Penelope Cruz), who is pregnant by the promiscuous Lola, and the actress Huma Rojo (Marisa Paredes), who was unwittingly involved in the accident that killed Esteban. In relation to each woman, Manuela is respectively rescuer and nurse (for Agrado), nurse and protector (for Rosa), and dresser/factotum (for Huma). She immerses her own sorrow as bereaved mother in the ups and downs of the three women who are linked to her through a perverse kind of destiny.

Manuela's initial return to Barcelona has her scouring the low-life zones of prostitution where, rushing to the aid of a prostitute being attacked by a client on waste ground, she discovers Agrado, a bosom-friend from her past, and the two pair up to find work (so that Agrado can quit the game) and to track down the elusive Lola. Checking out a rehabilitation clinic run by nuns, they talk to Rosa, who subsequently takes Manuela to her mother (Rosa María Sardà) who is in need of a maid but who rejects the offer, believing Manuela to be one of the prostitutes Rosa has devoted herself to helping. Far from the extravagant characters of the nuns in *Dark Habits*, Rosa is a naïve but earnest young woman in search of good causes. Her immediate plans to go out to El Salvador as a volunteer aid worker are scuppered by her discovery that she is pregnant and that she is HIV-positive. Alienated from her mother, she attaches herself to Manuela, who has meanwhile started working for Huma Rojo. Having visited the actress in her dressing room, piteously searching for all and any connections to her dead son, Manuela uses her knowledge of the drug scene in Barcelona to take Huma to her lover Nina (Candela Peña), who has run off to find a fix. From her bereaved solitude in Madrid she thus moves, albeit semi-reluctantly, into a melee of attachments to other women, all of whom come to depend on her to some degree.

As the film traces Manuela's slow recovery from the shock of bereavement to new and renewed caring friendships, the quest for Lola seems to be suspended, although we learn a little more of their past life together when Manuela tells Rosa all that she had promised to tell Esteban the night that he was killed (i.e., all about his father). Her story of a young couple in love with each other and with the theater in Buenos Aires, of her husband's move to Barcelona and subsequent sexual transformation, and of her desertion of this promiscuous macho transsexual when she discovered she was pregnant are the key facts that she had denied her son. She had always told him that his father was dead and would reveal nothing else, leaving him feeling only half a person, with an identity like the photos he found from which one-half had been torn away. Esteban's curiosity about his paternity and his expressed desire to write about his mother had perturbed Manuela during the opening scenes (on his fateful birthday). With his death, however, she no longer has anything to hide, and in her relations with Agrado, Rosa, and Huma she is quite candid, although she prefers to avoid talking overmuch about the loss of her son. Allinson maintains that all of these characters have a secret which testifies to their strength, as Almodóvar shows his admiration for women once again.⁶ This claim does not quite ring true, as it is mainly Manuela who has an apparent inner strength based on the secrets she has borne and that have to be revealed to release her from the pain of bereavement. This is why her mission to find ex-husband Lola is so important to her yet is postponed once she takes on the mothering of Rosa.

Mothers And Sons

Manuela rediscovers and reenacts (literally when she performs Nina's role as Stella in *A Streetcar Named Desire*) scenes and moments from the distant past when she was with Esteban's father in Buenos Aires and Barcelona; thus she returns to her son's origins and conception. At Rosa's funeral after her death in childbirth, the elusive Lola appears, surrounded by crosses like an angel of death (or a new Dracula, in Almodóvar's words), descending the great stone stairway of Montjuic Cemetery toward the uplifted face of Manuela. For a brief moment there is glimpsed the former camp glory of Almodóvar's special invention in his early films: the sexual ambiguity of the fashionable lifestyle and cultural revival in early 1980s Madrid known as *la movida* (the movement). In the eyes of Lola/Esteban we see the ruins of that youthful liberation, which spilled over into all manner of excess. Manuela reveals her secret of the son Lola never knew and will never know and then takes Rosa's baby to his father, who is dying of AIDS, to hold in his arms just once. She has taken on the mothering role with the newborn Esteban, firstly in the home of Rosa's parents but later returning to Madrid when she can no longer bear the shameful attitude of Rosa's mother toward the HIV-positive infant. The "miraculous" recovery of Esteban leaves the film's ending with an almost matter-of-fact messianic optimism, as Manuela has a son restored to her through this second coming, which brings the promise of a cure for AIDS.

Esteban's is not the first portentous birth in Almodóvar's cinema. *Live Flesh* (1997) begins with a momentously abject nativity on a Madrid bus, where a young prostitute (also played by Penelope Cruz, Almodóvar's choice for his own brand of *redemptoris mater*) is delivered of a son at Christmas. Víctor, at once the troubled protagonist of a thriller/melodrama based on obsessive crossed desires, is also, unwittingly, a harbinger of the democratic freedoms, which the filmmaker celebrates in the film's final scene and without which his work would not have been possible. As Víctor's child is about to be born, the erstwhile loser who has finally found his place in life reflects on the change in Spain during his lifetime, from a fear-ridden dictatorship to a land where people are out on the street, living without fear of repression. Whether in praise of democracy or in hope of an AIDS cure, Almodóvar seems to present procreation as a talisman of change for the better in this world.

Almodóvar and Women

Often praised for his ability to understand, portray, and direct women, for his "special intuitive gift for seeing into the lives of women," he once remarked that this was "a grace that God gave me." Seemingly never happier than when filming groups of women in intimate conversation, harking back to the world of his childhood surrounded by the voices of his mother and sisters and other village women, his portrayals can be frivolous as well as serious but never mocking. Neither does he display the almost paranoid fear of the matriarch, which informed many anti-Francoist films: his Opus Dei mother in *Matador* is the only character who could be identified clearly with the values and character of the dictatorship. The incestuous tyrant of José Luis Borau's *Furtivos* (1975), the authoritarian matriarch of Carlos Saura's *Mamá cumple cien años* (*Mother Celebrated One Hundred Years*, 1975), or the manipulative, draconian grandmother in Manuel Gutiérrez Aragón's *Demonios en el jardín* (*Demons in the Garden*, 1982) all symbolize the violence and repression of the Franco regime. The archetype partly derives from Federico García Lorca's eponymous matriarch in his play *The House of Bernarda Alba*, but even in the conventual setting of *Dark Habits*, potentially another enclosed house ruled by an iron-handed mother, the breath of desire keeps hope and illusion alive until its eventual closure and the dispersal of its inmates. Almodóvar's women are not living in a closeted or cloistered past, even if they still inhabit a society in which vestiges of authoritarianism and traditional machismo linger on doggedly.

Starting with the first scene of his first released feature, *Pepi, Luci, Bom* (1980), the director who has proclaimed himself to be "one of the least *machista* and most authentically feminist men in the world," has included scenes of women suffering abuse and rape at the hands of men in almost all of his films. When Pepi (Carmen Maura) offers sex to the policeman who has discovered her marijuana plants, she begs him to take her anally, as she wants to keep her virginity as a lucrative investment for the future. His insistence on vaginal penetration and his surprise at discovering she really was a virgin set off the action as Pepi swears revenge on him for stealing this valuable commodity (rather than for the rape as act of violence). Luci the masochistic housewife ends the film in hospital, happy that she has been beaten up by the same policeman/rapist, her husband. Virginity, machismo, domestic violence, and rape are tossed into the maelstrom narrative with lesbianism, golden shower, a General Erection competition, and all the pop/punk rebelliousness of Almodóvar's alternative aesthetic, casually satirical view in a comic-book style. Gay liberated postdictatorship Madrid coexisted with the traditional values and vices of the patriarchal past, and the young man from La Mancha was there to register, celebrate, and expose the culture shock waves rippling through Spanish society.

Subsequent films featured routine domestic abuse (*What Have I Done to Deserve This?*), incestuous abuse and rape (*Labyrinth of Passions* and *Law of Desire*) and priestly pedophilia (suggested in *Law of Desire*), but it was with *Tie Me Up, Tie Me Down* (1990) and *Kika* (1993) that Almodóvar courted the most controversy. Kidnapped in her own home by recently discharged mental patient, Ricki (Antonio Banderas), heroin addict and former porn star Marina (Victoria Abril) falls in love with her captor, submitting to his desire not in a masochistic response to violence, but in tender appreciation of his innocent need for a normality, which has been denied him in his marginal life as an orphan. Given an X rating in the United States on the grounds that it might encourage certain types of stalking and kidnappings, *Tie Me Up, Tie Me Down* was in truth a tale of two damaged people finding love and passion in a situation of extreme vulnerability and emotional nakedness, both on the edge of despair. While the film presents this newfound love movingly and sensitively, the plot in the abstract was less than politically correct, and it is here that Almodóvar challenges conventionality. Incensed at the decision of the Motion Picture Association of America (MPAA) to classify the film as pornographic for the sex scene between Banderas and Abril, the director defended the depiction of their lovemaking and accused the U.S. authorities of hypocrisy and protectionism.

In the extended rape scene from *Kika*, male violence against women was presented with a banality and absurdity that challenges the voyeurism and morbidity of a supposed "male gaze," but which outraged many on the grounds that making fun of rape is to further offend against the victims of sexual crimes. Gratuitously long and discomforting as the sequence is, the point of the episode, perhaps lost in the ensuing outcry, is that Kika is violated a second time, and if anything more damagingly, by the media invasion of her privacy (expressed in Spanish literally as "invasion of intimacy"). Kika's aggressor is a caricature of macho obsession with sexual performance; porn star and ex-jailbird Paul Bazzo (playing on the slang word *polvazo* denoting "great fuck" in Spanish) is portrayed as little more than a penis on legs. If the scene attempts (perhaps unsuccessfully) to demystify rape in the movies, its real purpose is to denounce the tacky intrusiveness of Spanish television's "reality shows." Deliberately parodying the gross sensationalism, which he wanted to denounce, Almodóvar provoked a mixed reaction among fans who had considered him to be a "women's director," and his feminist credentials were somewhat tarnished.

This digression into the world of women abused by men (a notorious social issue in contemporary Spain) is not intended as an examination of Almodóvar's moral stance on male violence against women. The dilemma for his audience is often based on the fact that his films neither denounce unequivocally nor justify such acts, although *Talk to Her* (2002), presents another taboo subject, the rape of a comatose female patient by a male nurse, in disturbingly ambiguous terms. Benigno (Javier Cámara) impregnates ballet dancer Alicia (Leonor Watling) whom he has cared for as a specialist nurse since the accident that left her in a coma; previously a full-time caregiver for his sick and aged mother, Benigno is an innocent, tender, self-sacrificing, and loving character, who puts his faith in talking to the inert beauty as the best hope of a therapeutic recovery. Punished for his crime with a prison sentence, he commits suicide, but his lesson in communicative care is not lost on the journalist he befriended, Marco (Darío Grandinetti), whose love for a female bullfighter (Rosario Flores) was blighted by his inability to talk to her on equal terms.

Here it is Alicia's miscarriage, as a result of conception through a rape, which redeems her from the coma and returns her to life. In simplistic terms, a stalker and rapist has engendered a kind of miracle through his obsessive love for a woman who for the better part of the film is merely a passive body; his violation of her is in some ways "benign," like his name. That Almodóvar creates a film of immense sensitivity and understanding from such a controversial situation testifies to his ability not to shock, but to take his audience to new and challenging territories of human love and vulnerability. For Benigno is not a macho aggressor; indeed he has been assigned to nurse Alicia because her psychiatrist father believes him to be homosexual. Under cover of an assumed gay innocuousness, he is free to live in a special kind of intimacy with Alicia's body, acting in some ways as a paradigmatic mother figure, rather than as predatory male.

Returning to *All About My Mother*, Manuela's all-embracing capacity for caring really becomes apparent when she takes the pregnant Rosa under her wing, at first reluctantly, as her maternal role has just been cruelly terminated by the death of Esteban. As nurse, cook, secretary, and shoulder to lean on she gradually recovers the strength and resolve to overcome the pain of bereavement and to reconcile herself to life's betrayals. Losing Rosa, her reward is to be blessed with a new baby boy, whose lethal inheritance as son of Lola who passed on the AIDS virus to Rosa she assumes with a new resignation and courage. Having tried to protect her own son, Esteban, from knowledge of his degenerate progenitor and having seen how that repression caused such suffering, she is now determined to face realities, rather than trying to hide unpleasant truths as Rosa's mother would wish to. In the last resort the film promotes tolerance and understanding, and even the deadly Lola forms an image of maternal tenderness as he cradles the newborn Esteban in his arms, inviting our sympathy, in contrast to the bigoted outrage of Rosa's mother.

All about Whose Mother?

Whose mother is *All About My Mother* really about? Ostensibly it is Manuela, mother of Lola's first son Esteban, who had written the title in his notebook with the intention of writing about her, and foster-mother of Rosa's baby. The dedication by Almodóvar quoted earlier suggests that the film is also about his own mother, Francisca Caballero. In his acceptance speech on receiving an honorary doctorate at the University of Castilla, La Mancha, Almodóvar referred to his mother as "the territory where everything used to happen," one of many unusual tributes he has paid to her. His frequent expressions of esteem for her could be interpreted within the most reactionary traditions of Spanish male chauvinism, in which reverence for one's own mother somehow could be turned into a lack of respect for all other women. As no other woman could possibly live up to the maternal ideal, the undervaluing, mistrust, and abuse of wives, lovers, or partners can be explained if not excused. Yet Almodóvar's tributes to his mother are not couched in such reverential and ultimately misogynistic terms. Rather she is acknowledged as the one person whose wisdom, tolerance, understanding, and encouragement toward her unconventional son were a source of great strength to the filmmaker, who set about breaking taboos and scandalizing the old intolerant Spain that still lingered on after the death of Franco. Finally, in referring to "all men who want to be mothers," Almodóvar may be revealing his own deepest desire, not to redeem the world, but perhaps to be a mother who gives birth to films of hope, survival, and redemption for all those who find themselves bereft and alone in this vale of tears.

While his unconventional and nearly always provocative examinations of human behavior reveal little or nothing in the way of spiritual or religious transcendence, Almodóvar's moral universe is strongly informed by the values he identifies with motherhood. The caring, nurturing, but never again stifling or denying mother figure, which Manuela becomes in *All About My Mother*, is somehow closely identified with those sorrowing but consoling images of the Mother of the Redeemer that so fascinate his cinematic imagination and that are such a vibrant and characteristic feature of traditional Spanish popular Catholicism.

Reviewing the Chapter

1.   How universal is Almodóvar's picture of the Spanish Catholic Church? How different is it from the church of other European countries? Beyond Europe?

2.   What are the main features of the church, its history, its imagery, its doctrines, and its relationship with the arts that Almodóvar portrays—approvingly or critically?

3.   The films of Almodóvar always explore experiences of sexuality and the moral implications. *All About My Mother* ranges widely through family, mother-son relationships, transvestitism, HIV, AIDS, nuns, and pregnancy. The Ecumenical Jury in Cannes gave it its award. Why?

Notes

1.   Pedro Almodóvar, "Todos tenemos más miedo,"*El País*, September 3, 2002, 6 [translated by the author, as are all subsequent translations from Spanish]. The filming was for *Hable con ella* (*Talk to Her*, 2002).

2.   Pedro Almodóvar, *Todo sobre mi madre* (guión original) (Madrid: El Deseo S.A., 1999), 4.

3.   Frances Lannon notes that in Spanish brothels there were often pictures of the Virgin Mary over the beds.

4.   Isabel Piquer, "Almodóvar anuncia en el festival de Nueva York que rodará '*Mala educación,*'" *El País*, October 10, 2002, 39, and Paloma Leyra, "El cine ha sido mi auténtica educación," *Cambio 16*, October 13, 1997, 64.

5.   David Leavitt, "Almodóvar on the Verge," *Weekend Guardian*, June 23, 1990, 12–16.

6.   Pedro Almodóvar, "Industria e hipocresía," *El País*, April 22, 1990, 11–12.

7

Solidarity, Sharing, and Compassion: Walter Salles's *Central Do Brasil* (*Central Station*)

Jose Tavares de Barros

Central Do Brasil in Context

> *"Weep for the young boy, weep for Dora, weep for the father, weep for the mother, for the brother of the young boy, weep for the people, weep for Brazil. In short, weep for all of us."*
> —*Inácio Luiz Rhoden*

Directed by Walter Salles, *Central do Brasil* gained the attention of film distributors and of the public worldwide from the moment that it received awards at the Berlin Film Festival in 1998. *Central do Brasil* won the Golden Bear for Best Film and Fernanda Montenegro won a Silver Bear for Best Actress. The film was also awarded the prize of the Ecumenical Jury. Immediately after the Berlinale, it won an award for best script at the American Sundance Festival. A year later it won the Best Foreign Language film at the British Academy of Film and Television Arts (BAFTA) awards in London and was one of the five nominations for the Oscar for Best Foreign Language film in the United States, but the Academy chose the Italian tragicomedy, *La Vita è Bella* (*A Beautiful Life*), by Roberto Benigni.

It had been a long time since such hearty applause had been heard at the end of a film. This was not only the case at a privileged film festival like Berlin, but in many other countries as well where the film was screened. One of the reasons for this success was that in a world marked by an escalation of violence that touches individuals and society—which the cinema often sadly reflects—Walter Salles's film brought into action other values like solidarity, sharing, and compassion. Further, the emotional response elicited by the film from viewers shows that the director understood that his point of view coincided with a desire to change society, to expose the current conflict between the aspirations of civil society, and the incapacity of the state to respond to these aspirations.[1]

As a student of theology, Inácio Luiz Rhoden represents the viewer moved by the film:

> In its joyful weeping, *Central Station* discovers a country that, by its own troubles, finds in itself, in the heart of its people, the forces to overcome the difficulties of life. Perhaps there is an explanation for this. The dramatic tension of the film shows an impoverished Brazil, in which faith and fanaticism live together, solidarity and egoism, hope and despair, and more such contradictions. The utopia of the narrative is projected in a perspective of searching and dreaming, from a perspective that humanizes people and, consequently contributes to a real encounter with others and with ourselves. There is a [re]discovery of the other and the recovery of self-esteem, a return to sensitivity which brings back the possibility of a life in which there is place for liberty and dignity.[2]

Central do Brasil has as its background the faces of the Brazilian people— poor and forgotten by the authorities. Those who are looking for someone to write their letters, whether it be in the central station or in the rural Juazeiro do Norte, show that, in fact, they are no illiterates, even if they have to learn to read and to write something. In front of the little table of Dora, a retired teacher, situated in the hall of Rio's biggest railway station, Central do Brasil, we find the old and the young, blacks and whites, men and women. They come because they all wish to communicate, to show who they are and to show their struggle for survival. It is the skill of the director that, from the series of scenes opening the film, captures the emotion that is hidden in those faces, close-ups, as if they were three-by-four portraits, to be brought together later in the course of the narrative.

It is the same with the expressions of faith from the pilgrims in Northeastern Brazil in front of the Altar of Padre Cícero, who is venerated as holy man. Particularly significant is the contrast between the urban faces, insecure and tense, and the faces of the people from the interior, tranquil and happy, pious, reconciled with God and with life, despite the simple and poor conditions they live in. The central axis of the film is the unfolding of the story, tumultuous but transforming, between Dora and the little boy, Josué. The constant exchange of emotions and experiences is built on a succession of encounters and incidents, marked by the geographical and cultural landscape that progressively moves into a trajectory from the urban chaos to the tranquility of the interior. This is a special way of storytelling, in which the external action of the protagonists always reflects their interiority. In a certain sense it harks back to the Italian neo-realistic school and especially to the film, *Viaggio in Italia*, despite the cultural, historical, and stylistic differences between the world of Roberto Rosselini and the way Salles looks on the world. Some critics refer with a stronger emphasis to the films *Ladri di Biciclette* (*Bicycle Thieves*), *Umberto D*, and *Miracolo a Milano* (*Miracle in Milan*). Others point out the appreciation the director has declared for filmmakers like John Cassavetes (*Gloria*) and for Martin Scorsese (*Alice Doesn't Live Here Anymore*). The Italian critic, Fabrizio Bozzetti, acknowledges that *Central do Brasil* is an example of a cinema that is cultivated and conscious, essential and refined, which "looks to put together the simplicity of neo-realism and the fascination for landscapes in the desolate images of the new German Cinema and, yet, reflects the work of the actors of North American Film, but more intelligently."[3]

The Narrative of the Film

To increase her pension Dora (Fernanda Montenegro) writes letters for modest people in the entrance of the railroad station. One of her customers is Ana (Sóia Lira) from the northeastern area of Brazil, who with her son, Josué (Vinicius de Oliveira), expresses her desire, until then unspoken, to meet her husband again. That same day, as Ana leaves the station, she is run over by a bus. Josué is now an orphan in a double sense: His mother is dead and his father has disappeared. Dora takes care of the boy. At first she intends to sell him to a trader in human organs, but then she changes her mind and helps him to escape from this fate. She becomes more and more involved with Josué and finally decides to accompany him on a long trip into the interior of the country to look for his father.

Already in the railway station, Dora has used sentimental tricks to attract Josué to her house. The viewer, who identifies himself with the loneliness of the boy, does not suspect the perverse intentions of the woman to work together with the killer (Otávio Augusto). The temptation becomes clear through the contrast between the old television set and her new one that she drags through the alleys alongside of railway tracks, with all its noise, elements that characterize the first part of the film. But the story goes further. Her neighbor and friend, Irene (Marília Pera), a happy and communicative woman, reacts against the cynicism of Dora and forces her to confront herself with the absurdity of her criminal attitude. This is reinforced by the way Dora has abused the good faith of the weak and humble people. For weeks, Dora has accumulated the letters. She has not sent them. She has destroyed them or put them into the "purgatory" of a drawer. Dora's decision to travel with Josué indicates, at first feebly, the awakening of her sensitivity. The boy is an obstacle in the city. It is worth her while to help him at least to start his obsessive search for his unknown father. It is normal when she wants to protect the boy at times during the bus trip against the hatred of the criminals she has tricked. She becomes more involved in Josué's life, which is especially revealed at the moment in which she sends Josué out to play, because she wants to stay alone with the evangelical driver (Othon Bastos) to whom she is attracted. It is important to observe that the illusion of the woman and the pragmatism of the man are shown with both tenderness and fine irony. Salles and his scriptwriter do not use the stereotypes of the melodrama, but they give the characters an outlet of free expression of their sentiments. In one of the most expressive scenes of the film, Dora weeps softly, with her face pushed against the window of the bar, because the driver of the truck takes her self-deceiving dream far away.

The second part of *Central do Brasil* corresponds to a progressive plunging into the interior of the country characterized by the popular religiosity. During the uncomfortable journey of the pilgrims, the value of solidarity becomes immediately clear when a greasy meal is distributed, something that vexes Dora. This, by the way, does not have anything to do with her former cynicism. She starts to break with her corrupt and petty life at the moment she suggests to Josué the idea of placing on the rural altar the handkerchief that his mother had forgotten, leaving it on Dora's writing table. The real conversion happens when she becomes involved with the multitude of devotees, inspired by their singing in unison and by the light of the candles, and in her anguished run as she searches for the boy. The scene is characterized by the ascending movement of the camera, which suggests a horizon without any ending of suffering and of the prayers. Afterward there is a long lateral tracking shot that accompanies Dora's discomfort. The climax of Dora's despair—she passes out and collapses—takes place in a mystical atmosphere of the room of miracles in Juazeiro do Norte, the city of the saint Padre Cícero. In the marketplace, fireworks explode at the spectacular height of the feast. Silence follows. When the sun rises the following day, Dora's transformation is revealed. Now it is the boy who welcomes the women in his arms: It is like an inverse Pietà.

The episode of Dora's fainting in the House of Miracles strongly illustrates the need for the emotional dimension in a person's life. It is striking how the scene continues to show how the power of the unknown can change lives. In the moment in which Dora is confronted with a reality over which she does not have control, she feels herself obliged to act in ways different from what she was used to do. She has lived in a small, controlled, and predictable world. Now that she sees herself in front of something new, she feels her own sensibilities and discovers the change.

In the procession and in the Room of Miracles, faith comes to many people. Dora looks into herself and understands the importance of the feelings that were expressed in the letters she wrote. This scene illustrates with a particular force the opening and the change that a religious dimension can provoke in the life of a human being.[4]

Meanwhile the codependence between Dora and Josué is transformed by happiness and by some complicity, when the boy has the idea to promote the letter writing abilities of the teacher among the pilgrims. The illiterates continue to be the majority of the devotees of the "saint" Padre Cícero just like the people in the city who came to see Dora in the train station. The difference is that now the faces of the old and young people, like that of the grateful bride, infect the audience with an exuberant happiness that they experience through the images of the grace that has been obtained. This is without doubt one of the most significant scenes of the film: It reveals Salles's humanitarian vision and optimism. It is also one of the arguments used by critics to denounce this scene as complacent and sentimental. Now, in an ethical context, as opposed to the opening sequences, the work of writing letters will be again the source of survival. With the money (*reais*) that Josué receives from the contented pilgrims, he can buy the photo of saint Padre Cícero that he so wants. He buys Dora a dress and invites her to spend the night in a modest hotel. It is the beginning of a profound friendship.

The third part of *Central do Brasil* contains the search to find Josué's father and his consequent frustrations. The scene of the first approach is treated by Salles in a solemn tone. As Josué sees the house and the door of the place where his supposed father lives, he runs the small distance—which is for him long and dramatic—with great anxiety. As he enters the place where clothes are hanging to dry, he feels that another boy, who is his brother, is looking at him. From a corner of the room, he observes with curiosity objects and people, as if he is experiencing a completely new territory in his life. The supposed father turns before he enters the house. Josué's hope turns into deception.

> *Central Station* is a strange film, apparently simple and direct but, in reality, it is constructed with subtlety. (The director) wants to keep the focus on the protagonists and he lets the faces and the bodies of others who are in front or behind them, stay out of the focus. The result is a frenetic impression of movement, which is realised by simple tracking, some figures and an open screen frame. The young protagonist approaches the house which he thinks is his father's: [I]t is enough to show a shot of him, then the wind blowing the cloths which are hanging on a rope to dry, to give at this situation a huge emotional impact.[5]

Jessé, father of Josué, had in fact lived in that house, but because of his debts, he sold it and went off to live in another place. The search continues. Dora understands that the father is an alcoholic and she tries to protect the boy from him. She goes as far as revealing to the boy an intimate secret from her own past. She tells Josué the encounter with her father who left the family years before. She saw him by chance in a crowded street. He did not recognize his daughter. He glanced at her as if he were a cheap seducer, interested in attractive girls of that age. Dora confesses to Josué that she never again searched for her father. She puts into words the disappointment that she had kept to herself for years. She tells him even though she knows that the young listener is not capable of understanding her frustrations.

His father's brothers suddenly and by chance come into Josué's life. Isaías (Mateus Nachtergeale) is open for the news and is good-natured. He gives Josué a toy. Moisés (Caio Junqueira), the other brother, prefers to forget the past and the disgraceful condition of Josué's alcoholic father. It is true that they have built a house, where Josué can sleep in a bed between the two of them, undisturbed. But this conclusion is only partial and does not end the story. The final message, in reality, is linked to the long process of education, which the film proposes, as much for the characters as for the audience. Dora leaves, because she feels her mission is finished. Josué runs to her. Dora became important to him. What unites them from that moment on is the memory of the mutual discovery, with the photograph of the saint as testimony: "I have nostalgia about everything we did together," Dora confesses in the first letter, which she really signs when the bus drives away from Josué's new home. According to Sérgio Avila, *Central do Brasil* reminds us of the frustrating search for the father in *Paysage dans la brume*, directed by Theo Angelopoulos. But Angelopoulos's film has a certain coldness. The critic also observes that the film has affinities with *Cinema Paradiso*, but it avoids making a tribute to cinema, although there is the final scene with the monocle and the photograph, which shows the clear intention of the director to evoke tears from his audience. He criticizes, further, the disappearance, without any explanations, of the criminal, who has the trade in children's organs and the gratuity of the murder committed in cold blood at the railway station. According to this critic, this scene has as its aim only to provoke to shock the audience.[6]

The Construction of the Script

The idea for the story came from Salles himself, who had already made a short film on the theme a few years before. Initially it was a documentary about the life and the work of the polish sculptor, Frans Krajcberg, who came to live in Brazil at the end of the war. In one of the interviews, the artist made reference to a correspondence with a criminal, Socorro Nobre. She refers with tenderness to the sculptor from her cell in the women's prison. He was also a prisoner of his past, because he had lost his parents in a concentration camp. Salles visited Socorro, interviewed her extensively, and talked to her colleagues in the prison. This was a vivid experience for Salles, offering him the personality of the letter writer that became the narrative axis of *Central do Brasil*. Socorro, after she came out of prison, was the first performer in the film, dictating a letter to Dora at the opening.

From this idea, Marcos Bernstein and João Emanuel Carneiro, who was at that time twenty-five and a son of an anthropologist, wrote the script. Carneiro declared that the history of the film had a lot to do with himself. When he heard the story, he remembered a boy, called Jeová, who traveled with him to Salvador in a bus. He was nine years old and had never seen his father. He became excited sitting alongside Carneiro and explained to him how he imagined his father. When they arrived at the station, they found out that he was a drunk. Carneiro also said that when he was researching the film in the hall of the railway station, he did not find a writer, but he met some of the former customers and learned about them and their stories. During the filming, a lot of people came to ask the film crew if they could write real letters. They did and a lot of these letters were written and mailed. The young scriptwriter also expressed a view that is worth mentioning: "I believe that *Central Station* brings to the Brazilian cinema a new neo-realism. In Brazil, we like to tell stories in such away that performance always excels. *Central Station* changes this emphasis." Beyond the reference to the historical phase in Italian film history immediately after the Second World War, Carneiro explained the popularity of the film in that many people are tired of always seeing violence on the screen. They want to see human characters on television, human stories. Another argument for the positive impact of the film he offers is the structure of the script itself, closer to American cinema, a kind of mixture of European and North American cinema traditions.[7]

The Protagonists: Dora and Josué

Montenegro, a great actress of Brazilian cinema, also known for her memorable roles in theater and in television soap operas, comments about her acting in *Central do Brasil*: "The first challenge was not to be a face in the crowd. The challenge was not to act but to go beyond acting in making sure my face would not be in discord with the others or that it would not attract attention when I appeared in the middle of the crowd. When you are acting, your presence cannot be out of proportion. What is striking here are the faces of everyday people, people who are not stereotyped. It is the same for the young boy. He is a well-educated, very sensitive boy, but he is a street kid. You cannot say that the boy plays a typical role. I believe he succeeds, unbelievably as it may seem, to remain incognito. People rush out of the trains like a herd of buffalos, running off to their jobs and they come back to the trains running hastily again like buffalos to go to their homes, far away in the suburbs, stressed and tired, without even giving a glance to the boy."[8]

Vinícius de Oliveira, who plays Josué, was born in the slums of Manguinhos, a suburb of Rio de Janeiro. For a long time, Vinícius's mother took on a number of unstable jobs to support the boy and his three brothers. When Vinícius was just over eight years old, he started to visit the airport, Santos Dumont, in the center of the city, to earn some money as a shoeshine boy. His teacher at that time explained that the boy was never a criminal or a street kid. He had a good education, and he never went out in bad company. At the airport, Vinícius crossed Salles's path by chance. Salles was already involved with the preproduction of the film. He was not wearing ordinary shoes. So the boy decided to ask Salles some money for a meal, because he thought that the man had an honest face. The filmmaker felt that he had found the leading child character for his film. When he did the first screen test, it became clear that he not only had the intuition and the necessary talent for the role but also a great determination and an unusual capacity to memorize texts.

Montenegra shared Salles's same opinion of Vinícius. "To work with Vinícius was good because he was sensitive, proud and a fighter. He didn't have the habitual indulgence of a typical educated boy who is appearing in telenovelas. In these soaps, the child is always a wise guy, always eager to come to the world to teach the adults. Vinícius was not and is not like that. He experienced himself as an actor when he thanked the audience after the long applause at the Berlin Film Festival. Salles did a perfect job in directing this boy, but this was only possible because Vinícius was gifted enough to perform."[9]

Salles's Roots

In an interview at Soraia Vilela, Salles established a link between *Central do Brasil* and the Cinema Novo, the film movement that had international repercussions in the sixties and which provoked a short but real revolution for the Brazilian cinema. It was not just about the themes of the films, which put forward class struggles as a reaction against the power of the capitalist ideology but also about the aesthetics, expressed by Glauber Rocha in his manifesto *A estética da Fome* (*The Aesthetics of Hunger*). With a reference to the photo of Walter Carvalho, who preferred the use of natural light in most of the sequences of the film, Salles reaffirmed that the Cinema Novo nourished not only the European imagination but also that of young Brazilian directors. So if the links refer the Cinema Novo to the Italian neo-realism, it is possible to defend the existence of the vinculum of the film of Salles with the Italian postwar school, which represents a fundamental homage in the film history. This is shown through the use of film language as much as through the Brazilians' own film industry. These affinities can be seen in the following statements by Salles:

> [*Central do Brasil*] develops itself in the boy's road trip, searching for his father. What is of interest in the film for me is that the characters are obliged to leave their familiar urban neighborhood and let go of their perceptions of the world. They are confronted with the unknown and they change exactly for that reason; [*Central do Brasil*] tries to dialogue with Brazilian society. There is a fatigue in relation to what the seventies and the eighties have shown about Brazil. There is a fatigue in the eternal promises that we will be the country of the future or a country of the first world. This makes people forget the things which do really matter: relationships with others, with those who are different from ourselves. Possible relations of affection and friendship have been put in the bottom drawer. A lot of people, like Dora, come to the point that they don't care. She doesn't mail the letters she writes for the poor illiterates. Nobody bothered to question this. What is important is that moment when she actually mailed the letters and let go of her cynical world vision.[10]

Debate

On December 4, 1998, the French newspaper, *Le Monde*, the day of the premiere of the film in France, published on its first page *"A volta do Brasil"* ("The Return of Brazil"). Critic Jean Michel Frodon indicated three successive issues of suspense in the plot: Will Dora escape the criminals who are chasing her? Will Dora accompany Josué in his search for his father? Will Josué find his father? But he notes that these questions are surpassed and canceled by another that manifests itself during the trip through the backblocks of Brazil: How long did Salles resist the sentimentality and the clichés inherent in his script? The response of the journalist is positive. Salles has resisted this, because the film is also a reflection of the confrontation between an experienced actress and a young shoeshine boy. He finishes his article with a positive evaluation: From Rio to the Sertão, the film celebrates the re-encounter of a cinema that has its space and a history.

The praise of the critics for *Central do Brasil*, although in a significant majority, was not unanimous. To illustrate this and to summarize the disagreement of three or four Brazilian critics, I mention the article *"Da estética à cosmética da fome"* (*"Aesthetics to the Cosmetics of Hunger"*) by Ivana Bentes, a researcher and professor of cinema at the Federal University of Rio de Janeiro.[11] The starting point of this article is the famous manifesto of director Rocha, *A estética da Fome*, which he presented at the IV Rassegna del Cinema Latino Americano held in 1965 in Genoa. According to Bentes, the function of a socially oriented cinema should be to create in the viewer an unbearable, insupportable feeling for the realities represented in the film, producing a kind of "aesthetical apocalypse" that draws the audience out of their "immobility." This kind of cinema is opposed to that of the language of tears and silent, humanitarian suffering, which she considers a political discourse and an aesthetic incapable of expressing the brutality of the poverty. It transforms hunger into folklore and into tears.

They correspond to the ideal of the social, political films of the Cinema Novo, especially the classical first film of Rocha: *Deus e o Diabo na Terra do Sol* (*God and the Devil in the Land of the Sun*) made in 1964. The film gives a vision of how the workers and the revolutionaries see those who have the power and see the misery and manipulated faith that mark for the Brazilian *sertão* (desert). In this context, according to Bentes, *Central do Brasil* is falsifying the reality of the country, forming, as she calls it, a "cosmetic of hunger" and a "Romanticising of the desert (sertão)." Salles's film crosses the sertão of Glauber with the tradition of the Latin American melodrama. He cites other recent Brazilian films that carry on the mythical and fabulous line of the sertão, as in *Sertão das Memórias* (*Landscapes of Memory*), by José Araújo. People return to the slums or to the suburbs without prejudices or to a redeemed goodness as in *Um céu de estrelas* (*A Starry Sky*), directed by Tata Amaral.

It is not something new that the most radical critics resist any acceptance of emotions and tears as a mechanism for reading the reality of life. For them, indignation always results from a rational process, never from the spontaneity of the eye or the heart. In this line of thinking, any manifestation of kindness by humble people is probably because of the structure of domination and of exploitation by the privileged classes. Thus they are alienated from every way of overcoming their condition and of any optimistic openness. This is how Bentes sees *Central do Brasil*.

Mariza Leão does not agree with the opinion of Bentes. She has produced numerous Brazilian films like *Guerra de Canudos* (*Battle of Canudos*) directed by Sérgio Rezende. This film, inspired by the well-known book *Os Sertões* by Euclides da Cunha, focuses on the figure of Antonio Conselheiro, a mystical revolutionary who, in the nineteenth century, gathered in the sertão an independent community to defend the monarchy. But the republicans, who had only recently established themselves in the country, massacre this community. For the producer, the popularity of the films of Rezende and Salles reaffirms the competence and the courage of both projects. In the case of *Central do Brasil*, Leão declares, "To pretend to deny the possibility that in the universe there are stories of personal relations, intimate dramas, family conflicts or tenderness, the journalist pretends that she can take possession of this landscape changing it into a kind of environmental reserve for those who thinks their destiny is unique."

Leão argues that the country revealed by Salles is a real Brazil with a real sertão, real people, not characters constructed in a laboratory or as an idealization of the people and the sertão. This positive view coincides with the Christian perception in a speech of Rhoden, where he considers *Central do Brasil* as a mirror in which the everyday battle of life and death is reflected. For the theologian, the silences and the images of the film create for us a journey that ends with the feeling that the mission is complete and offers a perspective for entering into the promised land in which the characters can live a life with dignity.

The most recent film of Salles, *Abril Despedaçado* (*Behind the Sun*, 2002) is set in 1910 in the northeastern region. It is based on a novel of the same name by Ismail Kadré. Its subject is crimes of honor, which are taken for granted in rural cultures. The analyst, Jurandir Freire Costa, has observed, with reason, that this film has that unmistakable touch of the director, which can be described as excellent artistic quality combined with human tenderness. Freire Costa points out, in the last work of Salles, two questions that are his perennial questions: "Why the blindness in relation to our own suffering and to the suffering of others? Why do we accept violence if we can live in solidarity?" can also be asked of *Central do Brasil*.[12]

Reviewing the Chapter

1. How well does Salles portray the ordinary people of Brazil, in their daily lives, in their poverty, and in the difficulties to sustain family life?

2. How do audiences respond to the kind of religion and piety portrayed in *Central do Brasil*? How much is part of the Brazilian psyche? How much is simply the way of life of Brazil? What did the pilgrimage and the devotions at the shrine reveal about this religion?

3. Salles is a director with social concern. His movie shows an impoverished Brazil, in which faith and fanaticism live together, solidarity and egoism, hope and despair. Does he offer any leads for resolving some of these contradictions?

Notes

1. Interview: Jurandir Costa Freire, Folha de Sao Paulo, *Caderno Mais*, February 2, 1998.

2. Essay by Inácio Luiz Rhoden, theology student presented for the course, "A Igreja e os Meios de Comunicaçao Social no Brasil," directed by José Tavares de Barros at the Jesuit Instituto Santo Inácio, Belo Horizonte.

3. Article by Fabrizio Bozzetti, 1999, www.revisioncinema.com/ci_cdobr.htm (accessed February 7, 2007).

4. Rhoden, "A Igreja."

5. Bozzetti.

6. Sérgio Avila, "Folha de São Paulo," *Caderno Ilustrada,* April 2, 1998.

7. Gisela Campos, "Jornal do Brasil," *Caderno B*, March 29, 1998.

8. Deposition by Pedro Alexandre Sanches, "Folha de Sao Paulo," *Caderno Ilustrada,* April 2, 1998.

9. Carlos Helí de Andrade, "A estrela cresce," *O Globo*, Segundo Caderno, March 3, 1998.

10. Soraia Vilela in *Estado de Minas*, February 24, 1998.

11. Interview: Ivana Bentes in *Jornal do Brasil*, Caderno B, July 8, 2001.

12. "Condenados em nome de Glauber?" in *Jornal do Brasil*, Caderno B, July 10, 2001.

8

Observer of Everyday Life:
Carlos Carrera and
El Crimen del Padre Amaro
(*The Crime of Father Amaro*)

Luis Garcia Orso

Tiny, thin, serious, shy, quiet Carlos Carrera seems to feel like always going unnoticed, away from laughs and the hustle and bustle of social relations. But if you approach him, he is kind, respectful, and unaffected. He regards himself as an observer of everyday life, particularly of people we usually are unaware of. After observing, Carrera seems to meditate on such observed and experienced reality. From that, there will be material to tell in his film stories.

Luis Carlos Carrera González was born in Mexico City on August 18, 1962, but his mother was born in San Miguel el Alto, in the state of Jalisco. The highlands of Jalisco are famous in Mexico because of their conservative, strict, quite devotional Catholicism and without any native influence as in other areas of Mexico. This region is the cradle of the so-called war of "Cristeros," from 1926 to 1929, in which a great number of Catholics took up arms against the Mexican government to defend their religious beliefs. San Miguel el Alto was founded in the sixteenth century, and it is meaningful that its coat of arms shows a Franciscan friar and the column (twenty-one meters high) of the parish atrium. During his holidays as a child, Carlos Carrera spent days with relatives in San Miguel. He is familiar with the atmosphere of a traditional Catholic city, and he confesses that since he was a kid he felt attracted to the sorrowful and baroque effigies of Christ and the Virgin (Our Lady of Remedies and the Blessed Virgin are the most important representations in this city), conveying sorrow and sacrifice, ascetic attraction and sensitive displeasure, and sensuality and tragedy.

Carrera made his first Holy Communion when he was six years old, and he studied in the Catholic schools run by the Marist Brothers. Later on, he studied Communication Sciences in the Universidad Iberoamericana of Mexico City run by Jesuits. After that, he studied for a degree in filmmaking in the Centro de Capacitación Cinematográfica de México [Center for film training of Mexico]. Despite his religious background, Carrera considers himself quite an agnostic. He has been disappointed with stances and attitudes of leaders of the Catholic Church and of other believers, which he considers to be narrow-minded, intolerant, ignorant, and fanatic.

Carrera is demanding of himself when writing for and directing his films. He reveals that for each character of a story he produces a whole biography: birth place, social class and family, childhood, upbringing, growth environment and relationships, people and events in their lives, decisions taken in life and so on. Carrera considers that every actor or actress needs this biography to really interpret the character. On the other hand, he as a director and screenwriter is interested in following and respecting each character's life logic or way and that the film story entirely shows him or her to appreciate that character's behavior, decisions taken, truth, and life process. When the story and the film end, each character is not exactly the same.

Another work demand he imposes on himself as a producer in every movie is to create comprehensive story boards. Since he was a child, Carrera has been skilled in drawing, an ability further developed and used in his work. Some of his short films are animations based on drawing and plasticine modeling. Carrera also works and makes a living from commercials, provided that they are in accordance with his own convictions and ways of placing in society, and not only for profit and notoriety. In recent years, he has been an enthusiastic promoter of the up-and-coming stars in Mexican film industry with the movie company Malayerba, especially in the Festival of Guanajuato, which features short movies.

Carrera filmed his first animation work using a Super 8 camera when he was twelve. In 1984, when he was twenty-two, he made his first short film: *El hijo pródigo* (*The Prodigal Son*). His four-minute animated short film, *El héroe* (*The Hero*) won the Golden Palm in the Cannes Film Festival in 1994.

He has made five full-length films, which all tell unconventional love stories uncovering the mystery and contradiction of the human condition: *La mujer de Benjamín* (*Benjamin's Woman*, 1991) deals with the love obsession of an old bachelor village shopkeeper who kidnaps a girl and she eventually robs and humiliates him; *La vida conyugal* (*Married Life*, 1992) using black humor, portrays a married couple's long road of jealousy and infidelity, until the wife remembers that promise of "till death us do part"; *Sin remitente* (*Without Sender*, 1994) gives a close view of an old and lonely post office clerk who suddenly receives letters from an unknown romantic young lady who only plays with his feelings; *Un embrujo* (*A Bewitching*, 1998), is about a teenager's strong attraction and love for his schoolmistress, a solitary, liberal, and rejected woman, whom he meets again ten years later in the circumstances caused by the union and agrarian struggles of the 1930s in Puerto Progreso, state of Yucatán; *El Crimen del Padre Amaro* (*The Crime of Father Amaro*, 2002) follows the affair of a young newly ordained priest with a catechist girl in a small village in which power and hypocrisy strands of plot are developed.

In 2004, Carrera participated, along with three other Mexican directors, Antonio Serrano, Fernando Sariñana, and Alejandro Gamboa, in the production of the full-length film *Cero y van cuatro* (*Zero and Counting Four*). In this compendium movie, Carrera directs the story called *Barbacoa de chivo* (*Barbecued Billy Goat*), which is about the robbery of a religious statue by a poor man in need of money to buy medicine for his sick daughter. This unleashes the rage of the villagers. All his full-length films have received recognition by the Academia de Artes Cinematográficas de México (Film Arts Academy of Mexico), which indicates how outstanding his work is.

Carrera has won several prizes for each of his films in Mexico and in festivals in other countries (Cannes, Nantes, Montreal, Havana, San Sebastián, and so on). He admires directors like John Ford, Akira Kurosawa, and Luis Buñuel.

El Crimen del Padre Amaro

Carrera's movie version of a Portuguese novel published in 1875 (with a screenplay by Vicente Leñero, a well-known Mexican playwright who also received a Catholic education) was a controversial major box office hit in Mexico. With the discrediting statements by the leaders of the Catholic Church along with the recommendation of (also Catholic) moviegoers, the film went beyond itself and became a social phenomenon deserving attention. It invited its audiences to think about the human condition, about the structures of society, and about ecclesiastical practice and Christian life.

Leñero had already written a screenplay for this movie that the producer, Alfredo Ripstein, wanted to film several years earlier. When Carrera was invited to direct it, Leñero, along with Carrera, made five additional treatments to the screenplay. Production began in 2001, before sexual scandals of some priests were publicly revealed by the media—Pope John Paul II wanted to apologize for them and also wanted an investigation—and before the Pope made his fifth visit to Mexico in July 2002. By an agreement of the Mexican government with the movie producers, so that it would not seem rather impolite to the Pope, the film was commercially shown only after fifteen days had elapsed since John Paul II left Mexico.

However, groups of conservative Catholics and some bishops, who had not seen the film but only heard about it, launched a campaign of strong attacks, criticism, and demands against the film considering it as "offensive, blasphemous and sacrilegious" months before the film's premiere. Encouraged by so much gratuitous publicity for scandal and provocation, the Mexican public (most of them Catholic) crowded movie theaters and turned it into a box office success, the greatest in the history of Mexican cinema. On the other hand, Carrera's film was nominated for an Oscar, a Golden Globe, and a Goya. It also received nominations in the Festivals of San Sebastián, Havana, and Istanbul.

From the point of view of cinema, Carrera's movie has the defect of dealing with the stories of so many characters that he cannot go into any of them in detail about their journeys and problems. The characteristics of each of them, in their essential features, are merely stereotypes. Oddly enough, this does work with the general public, because it is easier for them to follow the story and to understand the characters. We need to remember that the Mexican general public has been formed by watching television soap operas.

Consistent with his movie themes of looking with benevolence and understanding at the contradictions in the human condition, the film offers a close look at priests as human beings, not divine beings. It also shows us something of our own human journey. Men struggling between what they desire in their vocation and what they really do, between what they want and what they are able to do, between what they want according to God and what they want according to flesh; men with hopes and temptations, with the happiness of their ministry and sadness for their mistakes, who are sensitive to others' sorrows, to sickness, solitude, sexual attraction, confusion, power blindness, and ambition. . . . Human beings, needy, sinners, and yet called to be willing to serve and to experience grace.

Priests are men placed in a social reality, which is also contradictory and sinful, tempting them, confusing them, defying them, and prompting their own decisions. The film discreetly sets, without great depth, the reality of the village that is also torn between sincerity and hypocrisy, between goodness and perversity, between innocence and corruption, and between love and confusion. Carrera does not idealize any character, but it seems that he does show the good side of Amelia, her mother, her boyfriend Rubén, and Father Natalio. They all live in a real world, in which sin and grace fight each other and in which selfishness is stronger than love.

El Crimen del Padre Amaro may be a good vehicle for portraying those three temptations revealed by Gospel (Matthew 4:1–11) into film: covetousness and attachment to material things, appearance and conceit, and power. When God through Jesus reveals that nobody is free of them, not even His Church, because they are always sinful and graceful and need conversion.

But temptation is overcome not by fleeing from it but by going through it to a greater reality where God only—and the Holy Spirit in everyone's conscience—invites again to conversion, generosity, humility, and to a love different from that one we selfishly call love.

As human beings and God's creatures, priests are invited to admit they are also needy and to open up to something greater to be released and redeemed. So it happens with Natalio before the sorrow and oppression of the poor people; with Benito before the recognition of his own loneliness and needs that have led him to sin; with Amaro to relive his first wish to unselfishly serve and to renounce power, which tempts him and which leads him to become conceited; with the bishop to leave his place of privilege and power to heartily understand what is happening to others. They are invited, but they must give their own reply.

The film shows with embarrassment the arduous and uneasy road to conversion, because Amaro prefers to be still trapped in his own desires, in his deceit to keep up appearances, in his ambitions of clerical power, in his inability to think of others—of Amelia, of village people, of God—in his inability to relinquish for love. The bishop prefers to overlook humility and continues in the power and haughtiness of controlling and making authoritarian decisions over others. Meanwhile, Natalio is still convinced that God's way goes through the suffering of the weak; and Benito returns to God by means of the sorrowful confession of his faults and by accepting his own weakness.

The end of the film shows Amaro's face full of confusion, grief, shame, which some viewers may find cynical, unemotional, or skeptical. It is not a clear ending to the film just as the acceptance of our own human contradictions and our own responsibility in sin is unclear and uneasy. However, why should we not think that it is an end that invites to awareness, remorse, and responsibility? The chorus in the village church prays for Amelia's salvation, for God's mercy, and in the final credits, the chorus praying in Latin confess: "Lamb of God who takes away the sin of the world, have mercy on us."

El Crimen del Padre Amaro is a film about many crimes, a filmed fiction showing contradictions and mistakes occurring in the life of a Mexican village and of its clergymen: deceit, lies, double moral standards, hypocrisy, breaking of priestly celibacy, political and ecclesiastical corruption, tyranny, arrogance, unlawful abortions, power of drug trafficking, and so on. It is not a sole crime but many crimes. "It is a film about hypocrisy," says Carlos Carrera. But truth is stranger than fiction both in afflictions and in benefits of the village people. Getting rid of afflictions and fostering the benefits of the general people shall be always a day-to-day task. The movie is valuable in helping us to see ourselves, to be aware, to accept our mistakes and their aftermath, to become responsible, and to invite us to be loyal to our hopes.

In summary, Carlos Carrera is a serious and consistent movie director, an acute observer and narrator of everyday life, of customs, and of common and ordinary people; of people who are overlooked and who are given no importance. In such people, the viewer finds characters producing mixed feelings, because in the films of Carrera, human contradiction is close, common, tangible; that is why it surprises us, disarms us, and at times, makes us upset. For Carrera's films, the human beings are the core of his stories—which are ours—and they are simply human.

Reviewing the Chapter

1. How does Carrera bridge the differences between the observation of daily life and filmmaking?

2.   How important is it for Carrera to create a complete biography of each character in his film story?

3.   How does *El Crimen del Padre Amaro* show audiences an authentic Christian life or its opposite? What profile of a priest does *El Crimen del Padre Amaro* offer?

9

The Son of Man (Facing Southeast): Jesus Christ in Eliseo Subiela's Films

Ricardo Yáñez

At the outset of Eliseo Subiela's third film, *Last Images of the Shipwreck*, the protagonist Roberto looks at the camera and says "I am a survivor and this is my story." These words can be the calling card of one of the most novel in style and prolific in films among all directors of Argentine movies in the last twenty years.

Subiela was born on December 27, 1944, and raised in the *porteño* quarter of Las Cañitas. He and his peers were a hard hit generation during the troubled years of Argentine history; these twenty-year-old youngsters had a strong political commitment and suffered harassment, persecution, torture, and death as many disappeared in the hands of the Argentine government from 1976 to 1983.

Subiela is married and has three children. In February 1995, when he had just finished his fifth film, *Don't Die without Telling Me Where Are You Going*, he had a heart attack and went through a triple bypass surgery. "Life is an everlasting miracle," he says. "Those who are not aware of this miracle are missing a lot and are not enjoying life. I am in constant awe and in harmony with these things."[1] Son of Spanish immigrants, he considers himself a *gallego* like his father who arrived in the port of Buenos Aires in 1934, just before the outbreak of the Spanish Civil War. Subiela had an agnostic and anticlerical upbringing but with a special sensitivity for the spiritual.[2] His father died when the filmmaker-to-be was twenty-one and before he could tell him his whole story. Subiela deeply felt this loss, so much so that the theme of the missing father repeats itself in the films of his initial trilogy.[3]

In his teens he was an eager reader and moviegoer. His favorite directors were Robert Bresson, Andrzej Wajda, Jerzy Kawalerowicz, Pierre Paolo Pasolini, Krzysztof Zanussi, and Ermanno Olmi—all of whom have strong Catholic backgrounds. Subiela does not know how he got hold of a New Testament book. "From that very moment on a very special relationship with Christ started to grow."[4] That adolescent of the late 1950s was deeply moved by a Jesus who is for the society outcasts and who is always in rebelion against the status quo. His readings took him to the San Benito Abbey, close to his home, to discuss with the priests different problems of faith that occurred to him. "As I read about Jesus Christ I became more and more interested in his figure and therefore I suspect that I am a [C]hristian, although not a Catholic."[5] He tried to study philosophy but finally he attended Universidad Nacional de La Plata to begin a major in film-making. There he met Roland Fustiñiana, one of the most outstanding critics and researchers of the country.

In 1963 Subiela quit the university to work passionately on his first short movie, *A Long Silence*. He started production with a photographic survey of the painful living conditions and forlornness of the inmates at the Borda Neuropsychiatry Hospital. He completed this documentary in nine months by using the professional equipment lent to him by Juan José Stagnaro, an outstand-ing commercial filmmaker. In this black-and-white movie we get a glimpse of Subiela's universe: the fear of madness, his criticism of the materialistic evalua-tion that society makes of people, the tension between reality and the world of dreams, love overcoming all evil, and Christian spirituality.

The camera moves through the inmates' rooms showing their hard life. It scrutinizes their faces and their lost expressions. Suddenly the image of an inmate praying, kneeling down, clutching a rosary in his hands, lingers on screen. "But love is a long way off," says one of the voice-overs, spoken by María Vaner. "No, it is in him," replies the leading voice, that of actor and director Lautaro Murúa. While this counterpoint is heard a close-up of the crucifix is shown; the inmate kisses the Christ image and squeezes it between his prayerful hands. The young filmmaker switches his attention to the hospital inmates strolling through the gar-dens and patios. A bell rings and the men slowly walk in files toward the chapel. At the door an image of the Pietà welcomes them. In the chapel the men sing and pray. The camera captures in detail four Via Crucis stations, intercutting them in parallels, mirroring scenes of daily life at the hospital. "Veronica wipes the face of Jesus" can be read on the image, and the next shot is of a nurse tenderly comb-ing an inmate's hair. The priest gives the blessing to the gathering and everyone sings, praising God. Later everybody comes to receive communion and then goes out, wandering off. Various theme and aesthetic elements of this short film are a clear approach to *Man Facing Southeast*, his second feature film.[6] *A Long Silence* won the first award at Viña del Mar International Film Festival in Chile and gave to the young filmmaker a big boost in his career.

Vaner introduced Subiela to her husband, Leonardo Favio, an actor who was working on his first film, *Crónica de un niño sólo* (*Story of a Lone Child*). Subiela acted as a publicity assistant and appeared in a short cameo. Next he worked for Ralph Pappier in *Esquiú, una luz en el sendero* (*Esquiú, A Light in the Path*) as assistant to the director and in the costume department. This was a biographical film shot in Argentina at a time when there was a lot of talk about Fray Mamerto Esquiú possibly being canonized as the first Argentine saint. Subiela did some other production work, and then in 1965, he shot his second short documentary,

About All These Stars, on the expectations of movie extras. It won a number of national and international prizes. This was the year that his father died, and he had to take charge of his family. During this time, he began shooting commercials.

In the mid-seventies he read Alejo Carpentier's novel *Los pasos perdidos* (*Stray Footsteps*) and tried to buy the movie rights but was not sucessful. He decided to write his own free version that in time turned out to be his first film, *The Conquest of Paradise*. It tells the story of a publicity agent who finds his dying father, whom he had thought dead for thirty years. He gets his father's will and decides to go with a group to look for a lost treasure. The real purpose of the expedition is to get to know his father through meeting the people in the group who were his father's friends.[7]

In 1983 democracy returned to Argentina, and with it, a great art boom took place, and movies were not an exception. In 1984 there was an all-time record of moviegoing, 62 millon people in one year. That year María Luisa Bemberg's film *Camila* was shown to more than 2 millon people in Argentina, success that has never been matched since for a movie produced in the country. It was the second Argentine movie ever nominated for an award in Hollywood. The following year Luis Puenzo's *La historia oficial* (*The Official Story*) won the Oscar, a great achievement for the outstanding quality of filmmaking in Argentina.

"A man arrives at an asylum for the insane, telling that he comes from another planet," is written on a note in an old scrapbook where Subiela used to jot down his ideas. In the democratic spring of 1983, he came across the old notebook. But the beginnings of *Man Facing Southeast* go back further. The filmmaker tells us that it all started when the title came to him in a surprising way. When he used to live in Vicente López (a quarter of Great Buenos Aires), there was a man who, every day, stood on a corner in his neighborhood staring for hours on end at a fixed point and then went away; the point happened to be the southeast.[8] Starting with the title and the storyline, he wrote the complete screenplay in a month. Following his past experiences and without paying attention to advice, Subiela decided to cast new people, actors who would fit the characters. Consequently Hugo Soto got the part of Rantes, the assumed E.T., a prominent artist who at the time was working in a play at the General San Martín Theater, the most important artistic haven during the years of the military dictatorship. Inés Vernengo, who would play the Saint, was a dancer in the same theater. For both of them this movie was their cinematic debut.

Soto became a close friend of Subiela, taking a role in his next film, *Last Images of the Shipwreck* and providing several sculptures for the film *The Dark Side of the Heart*. In 1995 Subiela released a new film, *Don't Die without Telling Me Where Are You Going*, dedicated to Hugo Soto's memory. He had recently died and had been considered at one time for a role in this movie.[9] It was he who had proposed Lorenzo Quinteros, a distinguished actor, for the part of Doctor Denis in *Man Facing Southeast*. In December 1985, with this cast, Subiela again filmed in the Borda Hospital: As he recalls, everything was like it was in 1963.[10]

Man Facing Southeast is a journey, a way that ends up on a cross (via cru-cis) and with a resurrection; but unlike the clear comparison between the images of the stations and those of the inmates as new Christs that young Subiela pro-posed in *A Long Silence*, in *Man Facing Southeast* the whole film is a stylized and subtle way of the cross. It starts with empty hallways and ends with the image of Denis studying the picture of Rantes, the Saint, and the absent father. The title sequences pass along corridors, which had already appeared in *A Long Silence*, an invitation to a walk, which is a search, to go out to meet, to try to get into this labyrinth of the souls of people in a neuropsychiatric hospital.

This is Denis's responsibility. He is a thirty-year-old psychiatric doctor who starts his morning by visiting the patients under his charge in the hospital rooms. In an interview with an insane man, the doctor is full of reasoning but without any human compassion. He has lost his professional zeal. Denis is a bereft human being without knowing it or even intending it, and he takes no risks wherever he goes through these well-known passages searching for someone. He meets Rantes, a young patient, who has mysteriously arrived at the hospital and has been assigned to his charge. This character is a Christlike figure who leads Denis to his conversion.[11] Subiela likes to play with two levels of interpretation, the direct one and the analogy;[12] the former corresponding to the dialogue between Rantes and Denis at several moments, which refers in a literal way to phrases or situations of the Gospels, and the latter corresponding to the images of the story. In a clear Christlike allusion, when Rantes arrives, he is registered as patient number 33 (the Gospel age of Christ during his Passion) under Denis's responsibility. When the doctor approaches Rantes's bed, another inmate in the room assures him—he will do it in several times in the film—that he is a good man coming from a faraway place, much like the testimony that John gave of Jesus as the Lamb of God in John 1:29. It is interesting to see how Rantes chooses to go out of his way to meet Denis—in a subtle way, almost imperceptible—as Jesus did with many people in the Gospels (John 4:6–7; Luke 17:11–13; Luke 19:1–3).

In the documentary that Subiela shot when he was seventeen, the hospital chapel scenes conclude the film. In *Man Facing Southeast* this setting is chosen to introduce Rantes. Denis enters the chapel and the music played by the new-comer on the organ sounds fascinating for those attending. The doctor waits for Rantes to finish his performance before interrogating him. An extreme close-up of Rantes's luminous glance and his line "Doctor, I come from far away, from another world" are enough to reflect his Christic identity. The Subielan Christlike figure shares with the Jesus of the Gospels the expression of the look (Mark 10:21a; John 11:33) and the hands (Mark 1:41a; John 9:6b; Mark 7:33–34). "He stares to a place that seems to be far away—Doctor Denis says trying to describe his particular gaze—Not far outside, but inside." When a man tells Rantes he is cold, Rantes caresses his head and offers his coat. In the circus arena, Denis's children cling to Rantes and he hugs them tenderly. In one of his strolls out of the asylum, he enters a restaurant and with a heavy heart, sees a mother with three starving children next to people enjoying a lot of food. With his telekinetic power, he offers the plentiful dishes to the indigent family, and with a glance, he invites the mother to accept them. Finally the needy woman picks up the food and he smiles, satisfied. The scene is backed by some Gregorian chant that clarifies in its audio impact, the Christologic sense that the director wants to communicate.

Rantes shares the telekinetic powers with Rosalía, the protagonist of *Small Miracles*, released by Subiela in 1997. Rosalía is a teenager who searches for maturity by helping others and looking for love. She also can move things, using her mental powers, but always—as she says—"to fulfill the desires of other people." She knows that it would be useless for her own benefit. She works as a cashier in a supermarket, and in her spare time, she reads for a blind woman. She also volunteers to read Fernando Pessoa's poems to a blind elderly man. Rosalía is a Christlike figure who always performs these "small miracles" in people's lives without ever losing the hope of finding the great miracle, her true love. Both characters have a human and mystic viewpoint of existence that makes them "crazy" in the eyes of others. Even Rosalía's mother, during a dinner at her daughter's place, considers her mad for looking for a man who truly loves her instead of taking men for the pleasure they can offer and later abandoning them. Although Rantes is in a neuropsychiatric hospital, he dares to express an ironic statement to Denis in one of the cross-examination sessions: "Everyone knows that I am insane." But there is a big difference between Rosalía and Rantes. She always has the word God on her lips: "Why God is so good to me?"; "This love was experienced only by Christ"; "I have to be grateful to God for his gift" or the countless times she says "My God" throughout the movie. Rantes on the other hand is quite moderate in his expressions about God, only to question the doctor as a member of the human race: "If God is in each of you, you are killing him every day."

If the human expression of Rantes resembles that of the Jesus that we know through the Gospels, his comings and goings are no less interesting. Rantes is an itinerant: He wanders through the hospital facilities, the gardens, and the research lab. He even sneaks out the asylum and later he goes out with Denis, to get to know the people and learn what is going on. This permanent attitude of wandering brings him in a broad sense close to the Jesus of the synoptic Gospels and in a special way to that of Luke's. Jesus is always moving around "going up to Jerusalem"[13] where he will have his passion, death, and resurrection. In his Gospel, Luke gradually announces the mission of Christ in Jerusalem; so does Subiela, through subtle lines of the dialogues along the film, on the tragic destiny of Rantes. He, the Christlike figure designed by Subiela, announces the final redemption to Denis. "We are preparing the rescue for the victims, for those that couldn't bear the fright, for those overwhelmed by horror. For those that have no hope at all."

Subiela deals again with redemption in *Last Images of the Shipwreck*, when he metaphorically shows searchers of salvation, shipwrecked people, out of a

shipwreck, which is the worn-out Argentine society as a result of the 1989 infla-
tionary economic crisis, and where the Christ figure will be replaced by a rebel
Jesus figure. The wanderer, Rantes, is contrasted with the one who, motionless,
stares at the southeast. The action of the character is balanced by those moments
of serenity, of contemplation in which, according to what he says, he is "transmit-
ing information" of what he sees in this world. But who is receiving that information? Who is he talking to? It is possible to think that his contacts are with the
Great Scriptwriter—an image that Subiela likes to use when he refers to God—
because, for the director, "life is a perfect script, full of mistery."[14] Rantes standing up in the middle of the deserted hospital gardens recalls for us an astonishing
scene from Pier Paolo Pasolini's *The Gospel According to Saint Matthew*. The
Italian director, one of the most influential on Subiela, "shows us Jesus kneeling
silent in early morning prayer, in communion with God."[15] In *Man Facing
Southeast*, Rantes prays.

That some of Rantes's companions become his close followers through their
everyday living together, and because of his communicative, helpful, and kind
nature, suggest that these people are like Christ's disciples.[16] When he walks in
the park they follow him. At night they line up to talk to him. When he passes by,
they try to touch him. They always stay close together like a small throng where
you cannot tell a face apart; except for Beatriz Dick, the Saint, the mysterious
young lady who visits the protagonist and who will be introduced as an extraterrestrial deserter because she has begun to feel emotions. She says she is a volunteer at a Salvation Army Home. From the first visit to the hospital, she catches
Denis's attention. She develops a prompt and fluid rapport, and she becomes his
lover. This encounter is sought for and celebrated by Rantes who, in the concert
scenes at the park, will symbolically join their hands. It is also the Saint who continues Rantes's mission, because she is the one who awakes in Denis the hope of
the second coming.

The Saint character, as described by Rantes, has a clear connection with the
rebel replicants of Philip K. Dick's novel *Do Androids Dream of Electric Sheep?*
that Ridley Scott adapted for *Blade Runner*. Rantes tells Denis "we are perfect
copies of human beings, except for one thing: We can't feel." The Saint had broken that rule; she had learned to feel. She had made the same mistake as the
Nexus 6, but she was not looking for immortality. Subiela paid his respects to the
writer by giving his surname to his character. There are literary references in the
film, the most remarkable of which is that of Adolfo Bioy Casares's novel *La
Invención de Morel* (*Morel's Invention*). The description that Rantes gives of himself corresponds to "a tridimensional corporate projection that makes possible the
communication between the extraterrestrial dimension and the human dimension."[17] It is precisely Bioy Casares's description of the trial that torments his
protagonist. There are also references to works of Julio Cortázar and other Ibero
and Latin American writers. As a matter of fact there are always some literary
allusions in all his movies.[18] In *Last Images of the Shipwreck*, the inventive genius

of Roberto Arlt is honored; in *The Dark Side of the Heart* poems of Oliverio Girondo and those of Mario Benedetti are evoked; and in *Small Miracles* the poetical works of Fernando Pessoa are mentioned.

Man Facing Southeast shows the beginning of the passion in a fine lyrical way in the concert scene at the park. Rantes and the Saint ask Denis to go out with them. It is evening and the orchestra is playing Ludwig van Beethoven's Ninth Symphony for a large crowd. Suddenly Rantes starts dancing; other couples, Denis, and the Saint join in. The crowd in the park is in a festive mood, while the inmates at the asylum sing and dance. Rantes quits dancing to become the orchestra's conductor and the leader of the joyful crowd. The musicians are now performing the beginning of the symphony's last movement. Where Beethoven wanted to include a vocal section, certain verses of Friedrich von Schiller's "Ode to Joy," verses which proclaim the joy of mankind when universal brotherhood shall be established under divine guidance,[19] Subiela decides to skip the chorus in this sequence, but the moving and powerful melody captures the crowd's emotions on screen and behind it. When an exultant Rantes hands over the baton to the conductor, he is acclaimed by the crowd. Through these images, the music and the lyrics, Rantes gives his message to the world and they receive him as a king. "And they said: 'Blessed is he who comes, the King in the name of the Lord! Peace in Heaven! Glory in Heaven!'" (Luke 19:38) as Luke relates of Jesus entering Jerusalem.[20]

The asylum authorities become worried about the inmates' sudden bustle so that they are already close to the outside gates. The enthused patients say that Rantes is leading the feast. Thus Subiela emphasizes the possible bilocation of his protagonist. The evening events get massive media coverage and speed up actions against Rantes whom, they state, is out of control. The authorities confront the insane messiah,[21] and as in Milos Forman's *One Flew over the Cuckoo's Nest*, he is condemned to an odd death, medication with tranquilizers and then lobotomy.

"Even if I were the Pilate of the galaxies, I wanted him out of my life," says Denis almost at the end of the movie. This is one of the roles that, from the beginning of the film, Subiela wants this character to play. The three meetings that Denis and Rantes have at the doctor's clinic rooms refer all the time to the Gospel confrontation between Jesus and Pilate, especially John's version (John 18:28–38). In those occasions Rantes talks of his identity and mission: "To tell the truth" in an ailing society. The director combines Rantes's image with the crucifix on the wall and the wind blowing through the window is as if it were the Holy Spirit assisting the Christlike figure brought before the doctor. "If I had powerful armies, I would understand your worries," Rantes tells Denis (Pilate), thus acknowledging his extrahuman nature, being from another world, and finally, his weakness. Denis, as the Roman governor did, will have to choose under pressure a conviction that he does not share.

One of the compelling ideas for Subiela to make this film was the fear of insanity. The whole story, but especially the sessions in the clinic, allows us to come closer to madness. A patient confronts his physician. A person quite open to contemplation and enjoyment of life confronts a man who lacks affection and who is the prisoner of his stereotypic reasoning. Rantes wants to persuade the doctor: "Why don't you look at insanity from this side? Why don't you stop pursuing the sad ones and those lacking spiritual fortitude?" Who is ailing? Who is insane? Subiela offers a great paradox, the word of truth in the mouth of the madman.[22] And then Rantes confirms this: "Everybody knows that I am crazy." But what kind of madness is this? The insanity of faith? Saint Paul will say "Jesus' death and resurrection is scandal for the Jews and madness for gentiles."[23] Rantes cannot grasp what is happening to the mind of the man that he supposes is impaired by "human stupidity." He would like to investigate the human brain. When he realizes that his time is up, he is seen tearing apart the encephalitic mass under a running tap while the water carries away the pieces. It is one of the most moving and poetic moments of the film when Rantes is confronted with his own destruction.

The medication prescribed by Denis starts to have an effect on Rantes. He turns more aggressive. He takes confrontative attitudes that recall Jack Nickolson as R. P. McMurphy in *One Flew over the Cuckoo's Nest*. Three times during the film Denis tells his patient: "I am not letting you down," reminding us of the triple negation of Peter the apostle. In the middle of the night Rantes is tormented by a nightmare. We see him tied to the bed across his forehead, chest, and waist. An extreme close-up shows his restless face as he cries: "Doctor, doctor why are you forsaking me?" Finally Rantes collapses, portrayed in a shot that refers to Jesus praying at Gethsemane. In the garden Rantes tries to stand up, still staring to the southeast, while other inmates are sitting on the grass in groups around Rantes. He tries to stand up again to no avail. The following shot has one of his companions carry him on his back. Rantes is being borne with his arms in the form of a cross.[24] The Saint takes him on her lap and, crying, tries to feed him, but his glance is lost, and the light that used to kindle his eyes is gone. This Pietà is the last image of Rantes in the film. Denis utters, with great disbelief, "the inmates did not believe that he was gone and said that he will come in his ship to fetch them." He finally admits that he expects the Saint to come back. Maybe his previously closed heart is being opened in some way as a kind of resurrection.[25]

Redemption is more clear and explicit in Subiela's movie, *Last Images of the Shipwreck*, considered in various ways as continuation of *Man Facing Southeast*. Roberto, the protagonist—also played by Lorenzo Quinteros—has his story told in a flashback that encompasses the whole film so that it ends with the beginning, and one realizes that the movie's addressee is the young son born of the love of Roberto and Estela. The father picks him up in his arms and carries him on his back. The landscape is a bright green meadow by a river under a deep blue sky. Roberto talks to the child: "If I did not have you and your mother, I would be very frightened to go through the night that waits before us." The young newcomer turns out to be a proof and a reason to be alive.

In 2001 Subiela was surprised by the release of the Universal production, *K-Pax,* directed by Iain Softley and based on Gene Brewer's novel. The film starred Kevin Spacey in the part of the inmate and Jeff Bridges as the doctor. It has suspicious coincidental similarities with the screenplay that the Argentine director wrote more than fifteen years before. According to Subiela, who is suing the American producers, "it's a clear case of plagiarism with the critics' consent."[26] In Softley's film, the character of the insane man (Prot) keeps a Christic profile but without the religious imagery or Gospel references. The only symbol that refers to divinity is the light that appears when Prot arrives at Grand Central Station in New York City. Images of church towers are seen in the movie, and there are some references to the Bible, but without the significant relevance given by Subiela in his film. The Argentine movie never reveals the true origin of Rantes, establishing an aura of mystery that enriches the story with many levels of interpretation. On the contrary, the British director of the American film is so interested in clarifying the real source of Prot's madness and his existential trauma that the movie becomes poorer.

Man Facing Southeast was released in the theaters of Buenos Aires almost a year after it had been shot. It had been previously screened in many festivals around the world. It won five international awards, in the festivals of San Sebastian, Toronto, La Habana, Cartagena, and San Paulo. This film was awarded its prize by the International Catholic Organization for Cinema and Audiovisuals, OCIC, at San Sebastian and also received a Commendation at La Habana. It was the national box office success of 1987, reaching the unheard-of figure of one millon viewers. The film also received nine awards from the critics of the country in the following categories: picture, direction, screenplay, actor (Lorenzo Quinteros), new male performance (Hugo Soto), new female performance (Inés Vernengo), music (Pedro Aznar), editing (César D'Angiolillo), and photography (R. de Angelis Jr.). The film was picked out by the reviewers of the country as among the top ten films of Argentine cinema between 1933 and 1999.[27]

For his movie, *Last Images of the Shipwreck,* Subiela won a Sundance Institute scholarship for a stage workshop of the screenplay. This film also received many national and international awards. The Canadian producer Roger Frappier (*The Decline of the American Empire* and *Jésus de Montréal*) produced his next film, *The Dark Side of the Heart.* The film starred Darío Grandinetti (Pedro Almodóvar's *Talk to Her*), André Melançon, and Jean-Pierre Reguerraz, and with eight hundred thousand dollars earned during its run, it was the box office success of the year and was also honored in many festivals around the world. In the following years, Subiela made many coproductions with Spain. Retrospectives of his career were shown in Portland (Oregon), Atlanta (Georgia), New York City (New York), and Sonoma (California) in the United States and in the rest of the world in Zurich (Switzerland), Bogota (Colombia), and Calcutta (India). In the second half of 2002, he had a scholarship at Stanford University (California). He taught some courses there and also took advantage of this time to think over and quietly put together his next project, *Lifting de Corazon (Heart Lifting)*. An Argentine–Spanish coproduction, the romantic comedy, casting Moro Anghileri (*Buena vida delivery*) and the Catalan actor Pep Munné, was released in 2005.

In *Last Images of the Shipwreck* Subiela adds in his story a Jesus figure. Estela (Noemí Frenkel), the prostitute who fell in love with Roberto, is fond of going to church to talk with Jesus (Alfredo Stuart), who comes down from the cross and enjoys the Milanese sandwiches that the young woman has brought for him. But one day, Jesus asks Estela something quite unusual. He wants ordinary clothes and a pair of shoes to get to learn how the common people live. This is quite close to the wandering ways of Rantes. Jesus is tired of being merciful with those who provoke suffering for their brothers and sisters.

In 2000, the filmmaker produced *The Adventures of God*, his artistically riskiest film, totally recorded in digital video, and the screenplay was developed as the surrealists used to. The Jesus figure makes an interesting intervention in the story where dream and reality live together—a Jesus that questions the identity of people that meet him, that laughs at his own images, and that pawns his crown of thorns to taste a coffee with a slice of bread and butter. In the oneiric world where Subiela emulates Luis Buñuel's *Un Chien Andalou* (*El perro andaluz* [*An Andalusian Dog*]), a lottery reminds Jesus over and over that he has to save the world. At the end of the movie the protagonist emerges from the sea—where Subiela's shipwrecks recur—alienated from his grey existence, and he decides to escape in his dreams with his love. In the middle of a road, Jesus is hitchhiking and gets a ride in a car that disappears at great speed.

This is the best image that describes Subiela, a survivor who never gives up his dreams, to question and to search. "The mission—he always repeats in each of his interviews—is to address to and stimulate the best in the human person and to struggle against death and violence."[28] Perhaps that is why in his journey the Nazarene always finds his place.

Reviewing the Chapter

1. What is *Man Facing Southeast*: a poetic stylization of madness, a sci-fi film, or a spiritual movie?

2. How do the Christlike and the Jesus figures rank in Subiela's universe having been educated in an agnostic atmosphere in Argentina during the 1950s and 1960s?

3. How could you trace influences of Pier Paolo Pasolini, Milos Forman, Ridley Scott, and several Ibero American writers in the work of one of the most personal Latin American filmmakers?

Notes

1. Eliseo Subiela interview by Ricardo Yáñez, Buenos Aires, January 2003, not published.

2. Yáñez, Subiela interview.

3. Paraná Sendros, *Eliseo Subiela* (Buenos Aires: Centro Editor de América Latina 1993), 7.

4. Yáñez, Subiela interview.

5. Yáñez, Subiela interview.

6. Sendrós, *Eliseo Subiela*, 8.

7. Sendrós, *Eliseo Subiela*, 17.

8. Yáñez, Subiela interview.

9. Diego Batlle, Pablo Marchetti, and Sergio Ranieri, "Interview with Eliseo Subiela," *La Maga* (Buenos Aires), June 14, 1995, 13.

10. Sendrós, *Eliseo Subiela*, 27.

11. Claudio España, *Cine Argentino en Democracia 1983–1993* (Buenos Aires: Fondo Nacional de las Artes 1994), 40.

12 Lloyd Baugh, *Imaging the Divine: Jesus and Christ Figures in Film* (Kansas City, MO: Sheed & Ward, 1997), 109.

13. Jean-Noel Aletti, *El Arte de Contar a Jesucristo* (Salamanca: Ediciones Sigueme 1992), 106.

14. Yáñez, Subiela interview.

15. Baugh, *Imaging the Divine,* 207.

16. Baugh *Imaging the Divine*, 206.

17. Sendrós, *Eliseo Subiela*, 30.

18. España, *Cine Argentino*, 120.

19. Homer Ulrich, *Music: A Design for Listening* (New York: Harcourt, Brace and Company, 1957), 267.

20. Aletti, *El Arte de Contar a Jesucristo*, 108.

21. Baugh, *Imaging the Divine*, 207.

22. Baugh, *Imaging the Divine*, 220.

23. Carlos Ferraro and Santiago Peluso, *Guia Orientadora de Peliculas Para Uso Educativo y Cultural* (Buenos Aires: COEDUC, 1990), 48.

24. Baugh, *Imaging the Divine*, 209.

25. Baugh, *Imaging the Divine*, 210.

26. Yáñez, Subiela interview.

27. María del Carmen Vieites, "Encuesta 100x100: las mejores películas del cine argentino 1933–1999," *La Mirada Cautiva*, number 4, September 2000, p. 11.

28. Yáñez, Subiela interview.

Part 4

Catholicism beyond Europe: Africa and Asia

Catholicism flourished during the early Christian centuries in the Roman provinces of Asia Minor and in Northern Africa (and St. Thomas was supposed to have visited India). The earliest of the church councils took place in Asian cities, especially Constantinople.

However, the clashes between the eastern and western centers of power in the empire, both political and religious, led to a schism between what came to be called the Catholic Church and the Orthodox Church that has lasted a thousand years. Catholicism came to be identified with the Roman, the Western church.

During the fifteenth and sixteenth centuries, Spanish and Portuguese explorers found the islands of the Caribbean and the lands which were eventually called Latin America. Besides crossing the Atlantic, they sailed into the Pacific and Indian oceans; the Spaniards, especially, making a new home in the Philippines and imposing their Catholicism. The Portuguese sailed further south, establishing a small Catholic colony in what was to become East Timor.

The Portuguese were more enterprising in establishing colonies in Africa, principally Angola and Mozambique. They also established a colony in Goa on the Indian subcontinent.

While missionaries went to India, China, and Japan in the sixteenth and seventeenth centuries, their success with conversions was limited. The missionary activity of the Catholic Church was a particular phenomenon of the nineteenth century, with many newly established religious congregations eager to establish foreign missions. The Irish and the French were the leaders in these endeavors, establishing churches, especially in territories colonized by the British and the French. Italian, Dutch, German, Belgian, and other missionaries soon moved into whatever area of the world had not heard the Christian message. While some regions, like the islands of the Pacific, embraced different forms of Christianity, Asia, with its strong Buddhist and Hindu traditions, was slow to respond. By the time of independence of many African nations in the mid-twentieth century, it was clear that Catholicism had been firmly established in many countries.

However, there are few directors with Catholic backgrounds from these two continents. The Philippines is the obvious place to look in Asia. Nicasio Cruz, who knew him well, writes on the first of the significant Filipino directors, Lino Brocka. Guido Convents, a friend of Gaston Kaboré and an expert on the different cinemas of Africa, situates Kaboré within the cinema culture of sub-Saharan Africa.

10

Finding his Place in Society, Local Stories with a Universal and Spiritual Dimension: Filmmaking by Gaston Kaboré

Guido Convents

> *"If African Cinema has a role to play, it should in my opinion, help the African people, African societies to dialogue with their own image. This was often forbidden to them. I don't want to make films with a message. You make a film, you produce images, so you provoke reflections. In fact, you produce a way of looking at the world, with which you confront the spectator. I believe in the force of the image and in its capacity to touch the mind of people."*
>
> *—Gaston Kaboré speaking at the Film Festival of Nantes, France, 1997*

Catholic Background

Gaston Kaboré was born in 1951 in the city of Bobodioulasso in Burkina Faso. He studied from the age of six until he was eighteen at a Catholic school conducted by the *Frères des Ecoles Chrétiennes* (De La Salle Brothers). His family belonged to the first Catholics of Ouagadougou. His parents' house stood in the shadow of the cathedral.

He then studied cinema and history and obtained his doctorate at the Sorbonne University in Paris. This is not without importance, because some of his films have a special way of looking into history. What makes the story of Kaboré special is that he belongs to a religious minority in his country; Catholicism arrived only one hundred years ago in this country, a former French colony. About 13 percent of the twelve million inhabitants of this Sahel country, one of the poorest of Africa, is Catholic; more than 50 percent is Muslim. The rest belong to Protestant fundamentalist groups (5 percent) or are followers of indigenous beliefs. In the reality of day-to-day life, it is easy to know if somebody is Catholic or Muslim, through their customs of giving a child a name. Catholics have typical western names like Jean, Gaston, Dieudonné, or Maurice.

In 1900 the White Fathers established mission stations in this part of Africa, which is on the edge of the desert and the savannah. Only in 1956 was the first local Catholic priest ordained as a bishop. After independence in 1960, it was believed that the people of this country could not live together. There are more than sixty different ethnic groups. In the last forty years Burkina Faso has experienced a great deal of political turmoil. As a poor country there is little money for education, health, and culture. Most of the Burkinabese are illiterate, which means, according to Kaboré, that the influence of the audiovisual media is important. He found it an appalling fact that his compatriots were seeing the world through the eyes of foreign filmmakers and television productions. It was one of the realities that brought him to cinema. He wanted to put into images stories that were relevant for the inhabitants of his country, which used the local languages and which respected history but also promoted tolerance between the religions.

For a man living in one of the poorest countries in the world and among a diversity of cultures as well as belonging to a minority, it was not easy to find his way into cinema. One of the explanations is that he became known as a man who lived according to human (catholic) values, for which he became respected not only by Catholics but also by the non-Catholics in his country and abroad. He became known for making films in which honesty, respect, solidarity, spirituality, and peaceful revolt against injustice are significant. At a certain point in his career, he was elected as the representative of all African filmmakers. He held this position for more than a decade. This means that the community of African filmmakers considered him as a man of dialogue, not a man of the extremist attitudes toward the former colonialists or simply a member of the filmmakers' world, who held different religious beliefs and political ideologies.

Filmmaking in Black Africa

To understand the significance of the films of Kaboré, they have to be put in the context of filmmaking in black Africa. There is not a huge amount of production. Each country in French-speaking Africa produces an average of only a handful of feature films a year. And there is the French tradition of the auteur theory, which means in the African context that every film mostly expresses the ideas of the director (who is often also the scriptwriter and the producer). Understanding the principal steps in the evolution of production in French-speaking Africa also gives an insight into the films of Kaboré. He is often considered to be part of the first generation of African filmmakers, from the period of 1960 to 1980, and a director of *soft* films, because he is not a man who calls for violence when confronted with injustice. He looks to traditional values and so is not considered as modern.

In 1977 Kaboré started teaching film in his home country, and with his students, he made his first film that year, *Je reviens de Bokin*. From this moment he defined himself as a maker of African cinema. For this first film, he worked with young people to tell a story in the local language, about a local situation, which also had universal interest. *Je reviens de Bokin* shows the adventures of a young tailor who leaves his small village to live in the big city. His somewhat naive dream turns into a nightmare. With this film, Kaboré touches an important socioeconomic aspect of development in African society, the flight from the countryside to the city. It is also a warning that going to the city or having strong beliefs in modernity or even in Western culture can end in disillusionment.

The way Kaboré looks at film expresses the view of most African filmmakers. His small number of feature films is not an example of political militancy as are those of the first African filmmakers who dominated the sixties and seventies, Sembene Ousmane (Senegal) or Med Hondo (Mauritania). They were, and still are, struggling with the effects of European colonization and neocolonization of Africa. They have tried and continue to try to explain the negative effects of colonial occupation on African society. They refer to historical facts, which do not appear in the official histories published by the former colonial powers. These pioneers blame colonialism for all the misfortunes of Africa of today. Kaboré looks at matters differently. His films show that he practices another kind of activism rather than that of the so-called political leftist pioneers.

In the first place, although he is aware of the colonial area, he is not obsessed by this period any longer. He focuses on contemporary society and tries to explain the changes that occur. He asks himself what went wrong when independence came to Africa more than forty years ago.

He tries to explain it in a story. In *Zan Boko* he tackles anew the important issue of contemporary human conditions in Africa. He situates his story in the contrast between city and country life, how the city swallows the countryside, and how values are lost because individualism no longer serves the community. It is not so strange to see in his films the fundamental human and spiritual values that an individual, as a member of society, has to appreciate as a responsibility to assure that society's well-being. From this point of view, the moment an individual forgets this, things go wrong for him and for society. Kaboré has said in discussion that he does not need to go back to the wrongdoings of colonialists in Africa. In this way his films touch not only typical African situations but also universal situations.

In two of his well-known films, *Wend Kuuni* (*The Gift of God*, 1987) and *Buud Yam* (1997), he does use precolonial African society to put forward positive and negative elements inherent in that society. The films can be considered as part I and part II of the same story. When asked if his long stay in a Catholic school influenced him in his way of making films, he said that in the first place the education he got from his family determined his worldview. He said that he learned from his father and mother what ethics are. His presence in a Catholic school only reinforced this education. In his films, family life is crucial, and he frequently stresses the importance of that family life. He puts his own life experience into these films. This explains the sensitivity for morality, respect for life, pledges made in words, and the consideration for the others in his films. They are filled with hope for the future and in the human race. This is one of the reasons why most of his films are directed toward younger audiences, and they are almost without violence.

Precolonical Times in the African Films of Souleymane Cisse and Mweze Ngangura

Kaboré is not the only director who analyses malfunctions in society without pointing at nineteenth- and twentieth-century colonialism and capitalism. A number of film directors use precolonial times to say something about the fundamentals of African society. It is as if they do not want their stories infected by colonial ideas or influences. In a sense, they do not blame the contemporary degradation of society on the results of the conflict between tradition and modernity. For them it is simple. In going back to precolonial times, they are reacting against Western historical writing about Africa. Prior to the independence of many countries, the official history of Africa stated that before the coming of the Europeans there was only barbarism, no civilization, and even no history. So situating stories in a precolonial period is done for different reasons. In the first place it is to tell Africans that they do have a history, a civilization, and that they were not barbarians before their continent was colonized.

In Mali, Souleymane Cissé belongs to the same generation as Kaboré. Cissé also uses the precolonial era to go to the fundamentals of African society, his way to answer Western ethnographical filmmakers. *Yeelen* (1987) is a story that has meaning not only for Africans but for non-Africans. It is about human beings, a lesson for life. There are no superficial images but rather an emotional and dramatic story that every member of an audience can identify with. It was made in Mali with the Bambara people and is based on their myths. It is a confrontation between a father and a son. In *Yeelen* the father has a kind of wisdom that gives him power over others. He can help the others with it or abuse this power. Traditionally, this knowledge is passed from one generation to the next. Through a series of initiation rites the son gets access to this power. The father cannot accept that his son will become his equal, or even, that one day he could become more powerful than himself.

The mother, who knows her husband and his ambition to conserve the monopoly of dominance, is afraid for the life of her son. She runs away from her husband with her son. Traveling in uncertain conditions and not being protected by his father brings to completion the boy's life experience. It is in fact a final initiation rite. The father pursues him and uses terror to find him. He abuses his special powers. He has such a huge desire for knowledge and dominating others that it will kill him. His son does the contrary. He uses his magical powers and life experience to help others. His uncle tells him the story of the Bambara people and why his father wants to kill him. The son then understands what is expected from him, and he will look for his father and ask for reconciliation. This is not what the father wants. Then the son understands that he has to sacrifice himself and take with him his father for the well-being of the people. It is the only way of assuring the future; they melt together into one bright light. His wife is pregnant. For his unborn child he leaves his story. It is symbolized by a piece of his clothing, which his wife has to give to his son and in that way his story and wisdom will pass to the next generation. He will find that bright light. In that way the unborn son will have the possibility to understand his father's love for him. The film shows that everybody can make choices in life, and that there is always hope. One day the (grand)son will understand that he is important for society. He has to transmit experiences and knowledge for the cohesion of future generations. It is a universal story of good and evil, of the old and the new, and of what is decent and not decent. It dramatizes the option of choosing for individualism or for society.

With *Yeelen*, Cissé brings to the screen the richness of the Bambara culture and tells it as a real gift to his own people. He showed it to Africa and the world in 1987 and won the Jury award at the international film festival in Cannes. Cissé is a socially and politically active director who finds in his own culture all the stories and elements to illustrate his vision of society. He is convinced that the Africans can find only real independence when they know and respect their own history, stories, and culture. In that sense the role of a filmmaker is important today in the world of media. They can give a sense of the world in which Africans lived and still live.

In the 1980s, African films like *Wend Kuuni*, *Yeelen*, and *Yaaba* (*Grandmother*, 1989) were considered by Western critics as "Calabas" films, which means that they were located in the rural areas, in small villages, and in farmer families. On the screen they saw not the real contemporary Africa but the rural countryside without cities. They had difficulty in understanding why African filmmakers made such films. For them it was a surrealist Africa that confirmed existing stereotypes. Africa was poor and full of small farmers without any technology and modernity. But, at the end of the decade African filmmakers started to put aside their complexes vis-à-vis city life.

The first was Mweze Ngangura (Zaire, Democratic Republic of Congo) with *La Vie est belle* (*Life Is Beautiful*, 1986), a musical comedy. He brought a complete other image to Africa on the screen. A man who migrates to the city in the

1980s works his way up in the leisure world of the capital, Kinshasa, which at that time had a population of more than four million. In the main role was one of the most famous African entertainers, Papa Wemba, who had succeeded in having an international career. The film was also the first African production sold worldwide. In *La vie est belle* the city makes all dreams come true.

In the following decade the new generation of filmmakers gave more attention to contemporary African life, the city with its everyday material problems of survival. As previously mentioned, Kaboré was not indifferent to this new trend, and he made *Zan Boko*. In this film and in others, such as Idrissa Ouedraogos's *Samba Traore* (1992), the modern city is seen as a place which corrupts and where decent living is almost impossible. Ouedraogo shows that respect, friendship, and a place in society have to be earned; they cannot be bought by money. Almost against the trend in contemporary African cinema of the mid-1990s, Kaboré returned with *Buud Yam* set at the same time as *Wend Kuuni*.

Children: The Future for Africa

Wend Kuuni is a story about children. After the first decades of independence, when film productions were highly political, film was an instrument of political conscience for adults. The second generation of African filmmakers, Kaboré, Cissé, and Ouedraogo, had another vision for political action and film. They were aware that a new future for Africa was possible only if children again found the essential aspects of life and society. They started to make films with children but also for children. It was if they wanted to bring those Africans, who did not know colonialism, back to the essence of Africa. This means looking for their identity. These filmmakers wanted to give to young people the strength to look at themselves through their traditions, their social and cultural context, and their history. After independence, Africans saw themselves in the mirror the West was putting in front of them. Western audiovisual productions dominated and still largely dominate the media in Africa.

Kaboré has fought his whole life against this appalling situation. He did this as a social and politically committed director who looks at his own culture to illustrate or to express his stories and ideas but also as president of the pan-African Federation of Filmmakers, which he served from 1995 to 1997. In fact, he makes the same points as some highly political filmmakers, Haïlé Gerima, Ousmane, and Hondo. For them African identity and real independence can exist only if Africans accept and know their own culture and history. These filmmakers are well aware that they have an important responsibility to their society that depends on their creativity. They are considered in their society as the contemporary griots. Some of them, like Danny Kounyaté (Burkina Faso), are actually traditional griots who use Western techniques (film, video, DVD, radio, and Internet) to tell the stories of their people. With films they have easy access to young Africans. African directors translate traditional values, such as tolerance and solidarity, as important for society, but less tolerance and too much solidarity (like gifts from other countries) can endanger society.

For Kaboré this has an enormous social impact. In 1992, with *Guelwaar*, Ousmane explained that a society that accepts gifts to survive cannot be independent. They will be at the mercy of their donors. Ousmane denounces the official and unofficial Western aid given to African countries or their politicians. Kaboré had already explained the problem with this ten years earlier. There was no need to point to the West (neocolonialism) to explain that it is a fundamental law for all human beings to find their own identity and respect by being responsible for their own future. *Wend Kuuni* is the title of his film. It refers to the name of a young boy, a name given to him by the family that has adopted him. It refers to the boy's past, which is unknown to the people. Name-giving in Africa is important, because it situates the individual in society. As the boy is not able to tell his story, he receives this name. But it makes his future problematic. He has to win respect and find his place among the others.

Wend Kuuni discovers in the village a man who has hanged himself, because his younger wife had decided to leave him. This event is such a shock for the mute boy that he rediscovers his speech. He tells his story to his adoptive family, in the way of a griot (voice-over). His father left the family one morning for hunting. He did not return in the evening. His wife waited for him for years. People in the village declared him dead, and a suitor wanted to marry the wife. The village accused her of witchcraft, because she refused this new marriage. She ran away with her son. During their attempt to escape she dies. Her son tries to find help but in vain. He is exhausted and nearly dead when a traveler finds him by chance. As the young boy awakes, he can no longer speak because of the traumatic events. The traveler leaves the boy with a family in a nearby village where he becomes Wend Kuuni.

With this film Kaboré treats other aspects of African life. In the past not everybody was equal. There were traditions (which often still exist in many parts of Africa) that discriminated against women. Women could not make their own decisions. They were bound in structures that kept them in a state of dependence. They were considered inferior to men. If conservative politicians in contemporary Africa were to enforce traditional laws and ways of life, it would not be an alternative for a democratic political regime. The film stressed the importance of solidarity for African society. The family adopted, unconditionally, a child in need.

Burkina Faso: Ouedraogo and Kaboré

With *Yaaba* Ouedraogo tells a similar story to *Wend Kuuni*. *Yaaba* won national and international success, Best Film at the Festival of Ouagadougou and Critics' Week prize in Cannes in 1989. It is a story of an old woman who settles herself not far from a village. She is alone, and the people of the village cannot understand an old woman without a family. For them it is not normal. It is suspicious. It is the same attitude toward Wend Kuuni by the boys of the village. In *Yaaba* the villagers consider the grandmother as a bad omen. The teenagers of the village tease her constantly. A young boy, Bila, befriends the old women. Knowing her better, he understands that the villagers are spreading hostile rumors about her, because they are ignorant and fear the unknown. Nopoko, a friend of Bila, tells the people that the old woman is dying. The villagers prefer to listen to a fraudulent healer rather than trust the experience and knowledge of the old woman. Against all odds, the old woman searches for a competent healer. She wants to rescue Nopoko. The old woman feels she can die in peace, because saving Nopoko has given a meaning to her life. She has found a place and found people who respect her and will do so after her death. Bila and Nopoko have accepted her, and she will stay in their memories forever.

Ouedraogo situates his film in his country without any reference to contemporary or colonial times. He tells the story of a normal village—without idealizing it. There is an unfaithful woman, a drunk, people who make wrong decisions, friendship, conflict between people of the same village, ignorance, and intolerance. He points out that not all healers are trustworthy. The director wanted to focus on a crucial moment in the lives of two children, the moment they start to think for themselves. They could see beyond the conflict between the village and the old woman. It is an appeal to have respect for older people in general and more specifically, for grandparents; values that are being eroded in Africa, which is rapidly transforming culturally, economically, and socially due to influence of media.

More than a decade later Kaboré made *Buud Yam*. It is a story about a crucial phase in a man's life: the day he has to make decisions and take responsibility. Kaboré goes back to the story of Wend Kuuni and looks at him again and his adoptive family. Wend Kuuni is now a young man of twenty. He has now lived for twelve years with his new family. The daughter of the family, Pungheer, is seventeen. Wend Kuuni sees her as his sister. The whole family lives in harmony, and they are happy. One day everything changes. A snake bites Pungheer. Somebody has to go and find an antidote. Wend Kuuni decides to leave the village and to search for the witch doctor who can provide the serum. The story seems simple, but it is not. Wend Kuuni and Pungheer have grown up as brother and sister, but they are not. They fall in love. This is not tolerated by the village and considered as incest. Wend Kuuni is also a stranger. The boys of the village consider him as an intruder who came to steal a woman that belongs to one of them. Some of the boys are jealous, because they cannot stand it that the strange boy is so well treated by his adoptive parents. For his birthday Wend Kuuni is given a horse, and his adoptive father made the harness. The young people of the village curse Pungheer, and she is bitten by a snake. Wend Kuuni is accused as being responsible.

As Wend Kuuni decides to look for help, it is not only a way of thanking his family who adopted him or to show that he cares about Pungheer. The voyage is also an initiation rite, a search for his own identity and place in the community. He is an intruder and not the brother of Pungheer. With commitment and effort, he has to prove that he is worthwhile to be a member of that village. The village has to know that they can count on him. He has to earn respect from the community, from his adoptive parents, and also from Pungheer. To earn respect means to do something for the community. During his long trip through the country, looking for the witch doctor, he proves that he can live and survive outside the adoptive family and that he has reached adulthood. He can make decisions independently. He does not need his adoptive family anymore, and he can stand as his own man. It is a rupture with the past. His long absence will give him the opportunity to find his own personality and to recognize his loving feelings for Pungheer. At the end of his odyssey, in which he has confronted many dangers, he returns with the antidote to the village. Saving the life of Pungheer, almost at the cost of his own life, makes his marriage acceptable to the village.

The film is a clear reevaluation of the traditional healers who were vilified by the Western rational scientifically educated doctors. Wend Kuuni's journey to look for the witch doctor is more than looking for medicine. To avoid more stress and gossip in the village, he has to do something to be accepted by society. The bite of the snake was only a pretext. The idea that traditional healers and Western doctors can learn from each other and can function as complementary to each other had already been a theme in several African films. In Moustaphe Diop's *Le medecin de Gafiré* (1983) from Benin, a young African doctor, with a Western education, arrives in a region where traditional healers have long worked to the satisfaction of the people. One of them explains to the young doctor that the Western way of looking to illness is not enough. He discovers that he can help the sick only if he collaborates with the traditional medicine men. This was also a conclusion in South Africa at the end of the Apartheid regime. The positive aspects of African healers, or Sangomas, were accepted. The government accepts their abilities, and they are integrated in the public health system.

Buud Yam is a kind of African western. The hero, Wend Kuuni, takes his horse and rides out for a noble goal: to save the live of his beloved. He experiences adventures in unknown territories. But there is an important difference between this film and most American westerns. The hero is not going to fight against other people. The people he meets are not hostile to him, but they help him to reach his goal. Wend Kuuni does not fight with them. He talks with them. His story began with an absence of words. In *Buud Yam* he becomes a person in speaking with others. He then goes to confront nature and the supernatural in the spirits of the woods, which is his struggle and perseverance to find his identity.

Kaboré wants to draw the attention of African children and youngsters to the images and stories of their own continent through his films. He wants them to discover their own environment and stories as seen through the eyes of an African.

It is his way of making them conscious of their identity. The world he brings to the screen is as interesting as are the images from other continents made by non-African filmmakers. The moment the new generations discover this view, they will find it easier to deal with their future. At that moment they will accept that their creativity and stories are as good as those of the rest of the world.

Kaboré and African Culture

It is clear that film and television production in twenty-first-century Africa by an African requires courage. He or she will be confronted by international, Western media production companies. For Kaboré it is the same struggle as in the sixties and seventies when UNESCO launched its literacy campaigns. Any person with common sense knows that an independent country without its own literature, its own press, is unthinkable. Kaboré and other African filmmakers consider film and audiovisual production in the same way. More than ever, their own audiovisual productions are, just as the campaigns for literacy, important and necessary for the own cultural, social, economical, and political development. Investment in culture is as necessary as the investment in other infrastructures, like hospitals, roads, or housing.

Kaboré explained at a conference of the International Catholic Organization for Cinema (OCIC) in Namur, Belgium, in 2000 that it demands an enormous courage for an African film director to make films, which is a titanic task, that will be seen by young Africans. He stressed the point that every time they see Western productions, instead of African productions, they are confronted with a society that is not based on solidarity, respect for others, or an intellectual and cultural enrichment and the struggle to obtain a better world for all. Most of these Western films are purely commercial products that reflect a society that stresses the right for individuals to express and enrich themselves with the cultivation of competition instead of solidarity. Kaboré sees how traditional and universal human values are lost in these audiovisual productions, which are the reflection of a model of neoliberal Western society. These films do not show the result of what happens when the balance between the interest of the individual and society is out of order.

Kaboré is not the only one who has discovered that these Western images on African screens provoke a schizophrenic world for many Africans. They see on television and in the cinema Western society, with its materialism and its consumerism on the one hand, and on the other, they see their daily life, their family, and their culture, which does not correspond to the world seen in the media and which cannot respond to fulfill the needs created by these media. The result is that the new generation of Africans, who see reality through the eyes of the foreign images, do not appreciate their own African productions.

"Is there then no hope for a change?" was one of the questions put to Kaboré at the Namur meeting. He replied that in the 1980s he was pessimistic, but then *Buud Yam* was released in cinemas in Burkina Faso. Children of his middle-class friends who were more concerned with the latest fashions from Paris and who were listening exclusively to Western pop music discovered *Buud Yam*. They looked at it as a Western and a road movie. Through the film they saw an unknown fascinating African world. They did not even know that they lived in such a splendid natural environment. For thousands of young people in Burkina Faso, the film became something of a cult movie. They went several times to the cinema to see it and even to make the same journey as Wend Kuuni. Instead of going on holiday in France, these youngsters began to appreciate and discover their country.

Conclusion

For Kaboré film and culture in general is an important vehicle for spreading values and a specific view on life and society. As the global audiovisual future becomes more and more dominant worldwide, it will have a more determined influence on the life of the inhabitants of the African continent. Through these images and perspectives, the danger of losing respect for their own society, culture, and values will be imminent. Along with losing ground with the own stories, this will undermine their own creativity and the development of the continent. The responsibility for an African filmmaker is immense. He or she should be faithful to his or her cultural roots. This is not important only for his or her own continent, but it contributes to the world's cultural variety. Films from the African continent should help audiences from other continents and cultures to discover Africa as seen by Africans. This leads to people respecting each other's way of life, thought, and cultural expressions. Kaboré shares Frantz Fanon's opinion that the struggle for every people in this world is the control and the knowledge of its own past, image, and identity. Images can alienate people, but they can also help them find their place in society. Kaboré said in the Namur meeting that his education as a Catholic in Burkina Faso helped him to recognize the importance of dialogue and also the importance of having faith in bringing significant stories for the people in his country. As belonging to a minority he never had the intention to bring up explicit Catholic themes—he felt he had to portray those values and spiritual meanings, which his religion has in common with others and which can be recognized as worthwhile.

Reviewing the Chapter

1.   Kaboré does not only look to the African society in which he lives, but he tries to give a comment on it. What does this reveal about him?

2. Is there a contradiction in Kaboré's Catholic education and worldview and the way he portrays precolonial society (before Catholicism arrived in his country)?

3. Is it important that people, like Kaboré, living in the poorest country of the world, use money to make films or would that money be better used in financing hospitals or schools?

11

The Legacy of Lino Brocka

Nicasio Cruz

Lino Brocka saw the world through the eye of the camera. At various times, movies provided him an escape from everyday reality and later became the medium to express his vision and dream for a better Philippines. Nothing in Brocka's parentage or early childhood was typical or straightforward. Lino's father, Regino Brocka, was a skilled carpenter, a boat builder, and a traveling salesman from the Bicol Peninsula in Southern Luzon. Regino was legally a married man when he met Pilar Ortiz, a beautiful woman from Nueva Ecija in Central Luzon, during one his business trips. This union begot Lino on April 3, 1939. Five years later, Regino's legal first wife filed a charge of bigamy against him, which eventually led to his conviction and incarceration in the Muntinglupa Penitentiary in the outskirts of Manila. Pilar decided to be near her husband, so she and the young five-year-old Lino lived in Manila. After Regino's release from prison, the family returned to the island where they lived a normal life.

Regino taught Lino the alphabet, arithmetic, and natural science as well as singing and dancing. Lino himself said, "I had vivid memories of my father because I had a very wonderful relationship with him. This island reminded me of *Blue Lagoon*, the film which starred Jean Simmons." But this idyllic existence was cut short when his father, in one of his business trips, never came back. For one week, Pilar would put a lamp on top of a cliff overlooking the sea, hoping that her husband would see it and find his way home. Until one day, the body of an unidentified man surfaced on the shore. The decomposed body was identified by Pilar as Regino. Thus, Lino's paradise vanished forever.

Lino's transition from adolescence to adulthood was marred by many tragic events that left indelible marks on his soul. To support the family, Pilar worked as a taxi dancer and later married a local fisherman. This marriage split the family; Lino was sent to live with his aunt, while Danilo, his younger brother, with his grandmother. Maltreated by their relatives, the two boys ran away and joined their mother. Lino was only ten, Danilo seven. They began working at odd jobs, like selling flowers at market places, where Lino would dance and sing heartrending songs about being an orphan. The only relief Lino found from this day-to-day struggle was at the movies; he saw a beautiful world in the movies, a world of fantasy, where everything was colorful, everyone danced like Fred Astaire, swam like Esther Williams, and sang like Deanna Durbin. Lino even tried breathing underwater like Esther Williams, and his failure convinced him that Americans could breathe underwater, but Filipino boys could not. Nevertheless, Lino loved the movies and lived that world in his dreams.

In school, Lino excelled in his academic subjects as well as in oratory, debate, and in anything theatrical and artistic. He graduated from Nueva Ecija High School in 1956 with six medals and a scholarship to the University of the Philippines (UP). Brocka's first year at UP was cataclysmic in many ways. His peers, who were Manila born and rich, did not accept him. This so affected his academic performance that he lost his scholarship because of poor grades. Consequently, to support himself in school he took odd jobs, like working at a music shop and washing dishes at the canteen. While studying at UP, Brocka joined the dramatic club. Trying out for a minor part with dialogue was a complete disaster because of his hackneyed English accent. "Madder, madder," as he skidded onto the stage, "look at the gurls in der baiting shoots (bathing suits)." The second take was no improvement. Frustrated, Lino argued, "That's the way we say it at home!" That was the end of his acting career. The would-be actor next tried prompting, but he delivered the lines so loud with the wrong expression that he was kicked out the dramatic club.

But this sad experience did not dampen his desire to become an artist. So, slowly, perseveringly, he edged his way back into the dramatic club as a stagehand, sweeping, pulling curtains, moving props and scenery, hanging around, desperate to be accepted. He even remembered standing in the heavy rain to get a taxi for the director. But the boy from the province went beyond sweeping and standing in the rain. He sat through rehearsal after rehearsal, mesmerized, watching, observing with keen eyes the directors, and listening to the actors deliver their lines. He learned about set design, how to position lights, how to improvise, and make do on a meager budget. So, when Lino left UP and the dramatic club, he had a solid knowledge of basic stagecraft from directing to acting to lighting the set.

The struggles and hardships of a young man from the province in search of the impossible dream were embodied in the story of Julio Madiaga in Brocka's masterpiece, *Maynila: sa mga Kuko ng Liwanag* (*Manila: At the Claws of Light*, 1975), which chronicled the travails of a poor country boy in search of the elusive dream in the dark city of light. *Maynila* may well be Lino's autobiography, a rarity among local movies in that he has succeeded in translating a fine social novel into a film that captures with remarkable impact the plight of an innocent young man who left his hometown in search of his sweetheart (the symbol of his dream of a good life). The search led Julio through construction sites, slums, crowded apartments, and sinister streets where the urban poor live, clawing their way to survive, suffering exploitation and deprivation. Julio is the prototype of all young people from poverty-stricken barrios lured to the enticing neon lights of the city, expecting a better life and destroyed by social forces for which their simple country background had not armed them. Theirs is a tragedy that is commonplace in developing countries where the city always seems to offer liberation from the abject poverty that is the lot of the poor in rural areas.

In *Maynila*, Brocka exposed the exploitation of the innocent and the weak in the big metropolis, by creating graphic images that cut through the heart and brought tears of compassion to the eyes. *Maynila* without being shrill in its socially relevant message, eloquently tells us about the economic conditions that grind down people who have naiveté and goodwill as their weapon. Brocka has given us a film that set high standards for motion pictures in the Philippine film industry, and for that alone Brocka deserves to be honored and revered. In the words of Brocka himself, "I am for socially relevant films. Since we are an underdeveloped country, we should use film as a vehicle of communication, for education to make people aware of the social realities in the Philippines. I only hope that it will not be all content. It is important to consider form in the art of making it; otherwise, it will make people shortsighted and myopic and thus lead them to another kind of exploitation. Form and content must go together."

Maynila was chosen as one of the 150 masterpieces of world cinema in Geoff Andrew's book *Film: The Critics' Choice*. Even before Andrew's book included Brocka in the list of all-time greats of world cinema, the Manunuri ng Pelikulang Filipino (Filipino Film Critics) had already given *Maynila* near unanimous approbation. It is the movies against which other Filipino films will be gauged and graded. It represents an artistic watershed for Filipino cinema. Those who saw the film in 1975 were amazed at its technical bravura—the exacting production design, art direction that tried to make sense out of the chaos of the city of Manila, with its false allurements and sinister enchantment, the editing that was well paced and lyrical (the final lynching of Julio intercut with the ravishing beauty of Hilda Koronel as Ligaya, his sweetheart, basking in the sun—a poignant and unforgettable montage), and the groundbreaking music that combined ethnic and semielectronic instrumentation. And there are the performances: the moving realism of Bembol Roco as Julio, the soft beauty of Hilda, and the ensemble acting that contributes to one of the most wrenching dramas in Philippine cinema. Clodualdo del Mundo wrote a screenplay that contained the stock characters of Philippine contemporary drama based on the novel written by Edgardo Reyes.

Brocka and the Mormon Missionaries

In 1961, Behn Cervantes, a stage and film director whom Brocka befriended in the UP dramatic club, was the one who introduced Brocka to a team of Mormon missionaries, largely to rid himself of them. Brocka listened, first out of politeness, recognizing that whatever the missionaries were preaching, their beliefs were deeply sincere. Slowly, Lino seemed to hear echoes of his father teaching him about honesty, commitment, and living what you believe. He responded to the Mormon concept that God has created the world for us and that we should feel good about ourselves, in contrast to the teachings of the Catholic Church about guilt. His parents were not practicing Catholics, so Lino never had any basic Christian upbringing. He never went to confession, because of fear; he also despised the sham religiosity of some Catholics he knew, who went to Mass, communion, and confession but communed with the devil in their daily lives; he looked down on some Catholic government officials who were corrupt, philandering husbands, unfaithful wives, and worldly men of the cloth; and he deplored the church's alliance with the rich and powerful, the pomp and elaborate ceremony associated with the church in contrast to the simplicity and frugality in Mormonism.

All this religious hypocrisy he found among many members of the Catholic Church was the theme of his much-acclaimed film, *Tinimbang Ka, Ngunit Kulang (Weight, but Found Wanting*, 1974). Brocka became one of the first Filipino converts to the Mormon Church, and he agreed to go to Hawaii on the two-year mission required of all male Mormons, in part to get away from the Philippines and the meaningless life he felt himself to be living. He was not a perfect missionary, but he learned a lot about himself. But the idealism with which he joined the church soon became tempered by the realization that the Mormons were no different from the Catholics: Some believed and lived the credo, while some did not; some did their work honestly and humbly, while others curried favors from their superiors; some supervisors gave their teams leeway while others insisted on obedience. If he had any religious experience during his two-year stint as a Mormon missionary, it was during his year at the Kalaupapa leper colony in Molokai Island that he experienced a religious renewal. His involvement with lepers and the multinational staff, working together in projects, putting on performances, and going fishing revived the idyllic times he had with his family in his hometown. Although the lepers led miserable lives, they faced life with cheerful good humor. Even their funerals were happy occasions, because they believed that after death they would be whole and clean again. Brocka had a lot of time to think and he began to put his own life into some kind of perspective. He formed his own credo for living: to be grateful for what he had, not to clutter his life with non-essentials; to reject the excuse that something is futile and therefore not worth doing; finally resolving that "life will never put me down, I shall prove stronger than life."

After completing his missionary commitment, Brocka attended the Mormon Church College of Hawaii to complete his college education and then left the island to go to the United States, still searching for the impossible dream. But his life in the States was a nightmare. He arrived in San Francisco with only $50 in his pocket. He lived among the hoboes in the "tenderloin district" until he found a job at Fisherman's Wharf. Here he had to scavenge for food in trashcans and after five months of choking and drowning in his own life, he felt overwhelming homesickness for the Philippines.

On his return to Manila, his old friend, Cervantes, introduced him to Cecile Guidote, founder of the Philippines Educational Theater Association (PETA). For the first time in his life, he really felt that he belonged somewhere, his first love, the theater art. Here is where he met the benevolent Jesuit priest, Father James B. Reuter, an American, who revived his dormant faith in the Catholic Church. The kind Jesuit gave him board and lodging in the Jesuit residence. Brocka fondly recalled this period of embarrassment and commented, "I'm sure Father Reuter knew I was stealing food from the fridge in the Fathers' kitchen, because he knew I was hungry and he made sure no one else knew about it. If Father Reuter asks me to do anything, go anywhere, even to Timbuktu, I will go." Although he was critical about the Catholic Church, he remained close to the Jesuits, especially to Father Reuter, his counselor and mentor, who encouraged and believed in Lino's crusade for social reform through his films. Through Father Reuter's recommendation, Brocka was invited as a guest speaker at the International Convention of Catholic Communicators held in Manila in 1977. Another Jesuit, Father Nicasio Cruz, was also instrumental in bringing to the public, through his film reviews, the films of Brocka. Father Cruz accompanied Lino in promoting his film *Tinimbang Ka* to different public and private schools and seminaries. His endorsement of the film made *Tinimbang Ka* a box office hit. Brocka remained a Catholic at heart, thanks to the Jesuits, until his death.

Brocka directed his first film, *Wanted: Perfect Mother* (1970), at a time when Philippine cinema was full of clichés. It did fairly well at the box office but his second film, *Cherry Blossoms* (1972), was a financial disaster. Discouraged, Lino abandoned directing movies and devoted himself to acting and directing plays for PETA, but the lure of cinema was so great that he founded his own movie outfit, called Cine Manila, by selling his car and mortgaging his house. His directorial debut as a producer was *Tinimbang Ka*, a tremendous success at the box office, thanks to the critical review of the film by Father Nicasio Cruz, S.J. *Tinimbang Ka* marked the first that a serious film was also a commercial success. Even the department of education made the film required viewing for all schools, public and private. The movie tackled as one of its themes the role of the Catholic Church in Philippine society. It subtly attacked the hypocrisy of the church for the poor where the rich and powerful were given special pews. He also criticized pious religious church organizations, like the members of the Catholic Women's League, who indulged in gossip while going about their religious duties.

Brocka and the Social Milieu

Unlike many Filipino producers and directors of his time, Brocka disagreed with the notion that the majority of the Filipino moviegoers could not possibly appreciate subtle and meaningful subject matter or fine, underplayed acting, that more violence, more sex, and more fantasy layered onto overused plots were necessary.

Brocka tried to bring to the consciousness of the Filipino people through his films the real political situation in the country, especially the exploitation of the poor, the corrupt officials of the government, the widening gap between the rich and poor, the profligacy of Imelda Marcos, and the dictatorial regime of Ferdinand Marcos.

Insiang (the heroine) was a social comment on the plight of the slum dwellers of Manila: mother and daughter sharing the same man as lover. The daughter, played by Lino's favorite leading lady, Koronel, takes revenge on her mother by plotting the murder of her live-in partner without feeling any compunction. It was a hit at the Cannes Festival but criticized locally for presenting an unflattering view of the Philippines; but Brocka defended his view to show the poor who fight to survive with dignity in the most abject conditions rather than show the merry-making of public relations agents. But one could interpret the film as a plea against the slums and advocating a return to the countryside.

Another movie, *Jaguar* (1979), tackled the plight of the poor amidst an urban setting. It is about a young man's fascination with the lifestyle of the rich and powerful (Lino's dream as a deprived youth). In the beginning, Poldo, played by Philip Salvador, has the mentality of a dog; when you pat him on the head, he wags his tail. So, Poldo follows orders from his boss blindly until he finds out that he is using him as a pawn. Just like Insiang who plotted killing her mother's lover and Julio in *Maynila* who murdered the Chinese who abducted his sweetheart, Poldo would have almost killed his boss had the police not intervened. From glimpses of individual gestures, practices, and weaknesses of the poor, small acts that color his cinematic mural, Brocka trained his sight critically on society and antilabor organizations, like the government, the church, police, military, hospitals, and institutions that caused oppression and suffering. He dramatized police brutality, the absence or lack of justice in the judicial system, and the apparent silence and indifference of the church and the clergy. *Jaguar* was entered in competition at the Cannes Film Festival in 1980, and another Brocka socially relevant film, *Bona* (1980), starring Nora Aunor, was included in the Cannes Festival Directors' Fortnight in 1981.

Brocka often did a string of unabashedly commercial projects to pay off his debts and those of others that he charitably assumed and saved enough money for his producers so he could make a truly good one. Lino knew he could not change the Filipino film industry overnight, but he also believed that there was always room to bring in a little more sense and sympathy into the most contrived and convoluted plot, so he worked with and within established formulas and conventions, taking melodrama as an artistic and political challenge rather than disdaining it. He dissected Filipino motherhood in *Inay* (*Mother*, 1977), tracked down a domestic drama in *Ina Ka ng Anak Mo* (*You're the Mother of Your Child*, 1979), made a lawyer out of the famous megastar Sharon Cuneta in the movie *Biktima* (1991). Brocka liberally drew on the story of his own youth in San Jose, Nueva Ecija, and his rebellious youth in *Miguelito: Batang Rebelde* (*Miguelito: the Rebel Youth*, 1985).

In the 1980s, nightclubs, disco houses, and beer gardens featuring skimpily-clad women gyrating sensuously before a pack of sex-starved males proliferated not only in the city of Manila but also in the cities all over the country. Macho dancing, on the other hand, catered to the gay crowd and live sex shows for the sex maniacs. These young men and women are forced by extreme poverty to engage in this dehumanizing kind of job to support their families or to send their siblings to school or earn money for their own schooling. Brocka made the movie, *Macho Dancer* (1988), to expose and explore this flesh trade, the exploitation of the human body, to the public's consciousness. Despite its relevant message, the brilliant performances of the lead actors, the stark realism of Joe Totanes's photography, *Macho Dancer* went beyond the boundaries of a tasteful expression of creativity and attacked the viewers' common sense of decency and moral values. *Macho Dancer* was a box office disaster locally, because the conservative Filipino moviegoer was not yet prepared psychologically and emotionally to accept such a sensational topic. The Toronto Film Festival gave it a standing ovation when it was shown out of competition. Emboldened by the critical success of *Macho Dancer* in film festivals abroad, Mel Chionglo made *Sibak* (*Midnight Dancers*, 1994) also about macho dancers. It also received favorable reviews in Toronto Film Festival and from several film festivals abroad. This was followed by a movie on live sex shows, *Live Show* (2000), directed by Jose Javier Reyes. It featured not only live sex but also male frontal nudity. The Board of Censors, pressured by the Catholic hierarchy and the government, banned the film from being shown in the Philippines.

In the final phase of the late 1980s, Brocka somehow established the box office formula that blended the best qualities of a popular movie drama, melodrama, and political statements, which characterized his films. Except for the French-produced *Orapronobis* (*Pray for Us* but translated as *Fight for Us* for commercial purposes, 1989), the films made during this period were by no means of equal stature to such Brocka classics as *Tinimbang Ka*, *Maynila*, *Insiang* (1976), *Bona*, and *Jaguar*. But social corruption and political evil and social inequalities were exposed even in films like *Miguelito*, *Gumapang Ka sa Lusak* (*Dirty Affair*, 1990), *Hahamakin Lahat* (*All Be Damned*, 1990), and *Sa Kabila ng Lahat* (1991).

No amount of publicity can prepare one for the frightening exposé by Brocka in *Orapronobis*. In terms of its artistic courage, the film has ten times the ferocity of a Costa-Gavras movie. Brocka and screenwriter, Pete Lacaba, succeeded where Costa-Gavras did not in films like *Z* (1969) and *Missing* (1982). They were not able to film their stories of right-wing brutality in their own country. Free from the repressive arm of the Marcos dictatorial regime, the movie took full advantage of the liberalism of the Aquino government in launching a critical attack on its policy of supporting the vigilantes organized by the military to combat the communists in the hinterlands, the criminal relic of the Marcos era. It also took potshots against the Catholic hierarchy, which remained silent and passive about bringing relief to the poor and justice to the oppressed. *Orapronobis* is a sterling tribute to the power of cinema at a point when cinema is fighting off the influx of video as the consumer's medium for motion picture art. *Orapronobis* shows that nothing can equal big screen spectacle when it comes to sheer impact. It is this edge that precisely accounts for the uproar this film caused. Ironically, *Orapronobis* was banned for public viewing in the Philippines until the present.

As a political statement, *Orapronobis* worked, but as a piece of artistic truth, it failed. While purporting to present a true picture of human rights violations under the Aquino administration, it played too cavalierly with facts, presenting a merry muddle of events that had dubious historical basis. Brocka and his team were only too inclined to smear the Aquino government, and they got funding from foreign sources to do so. It was a movie consumed by its own hate and weighed down by its ideological baggage. Ultimately, it was a cynical movie, but its images remain scorching and memorable, haunting, composed by a hurting and human artistic sensibility. Brocka's last masterpiece might have grated too politically, but again and again, he never faltered in his humanity. He was, after all, a man of many wild and immodest passions and drives. He had a strong will, stubborn flaws, honed by his miserable past. There was no way a man like Brocka would have left the world the same way he found it. It is time lesser mortals thanked him that he did not.

The films of Brocka have the typical scenario of the Third World, which is esteemed in Africa, India, and China. In terms of dramatic aspects, the best is Satyajit Ray's *Apo Trilogy*. It is Brocka's being faithful to the genre (film noir) that makes his films the true eyewitness cinema of his country. At the time of his death, Brocka had acquired a reputation as the conscience of Asia. He will be missed not simply as the spokesman for the Philippines and Southeast Asia but for his manner of igniting his films, far from the traditional ways, without an equivalent today.

Reviewing the Chapter

1.   Does Brocka deserve the reputation as the conscience of not simply the Philippines but for the rest of Southeast Asia?

2.   How do *Maynila: sa mga Kuko ng Liwanag*, *Orapronobis*, and other lesser films of Brocka reflect the sad memories of his childhood days and his later life, depicting an angry man, filled with hatred and discontent toward any kind of institution, like family, church, and society in general?

3.   Can a movie like the highly politicized *Orapronobis* be considered great or a work of art if it is weighed down by its ideological baggage?

Other Resources

Andrew, Geoff, ed., *Film, The Critics' Choice: 150 Masterpieces of World Cinema Selected and Defined by the Experts* (New York: Billboard Books, 2001).

Aquino, Michael, and Sara Guia, *Lino Brocka: His Art and His Message* (Manila: Masters thesis, Ateneo de Manila, 1998).

CCP Encyclopedia of Philippine Art: Vol VIII Philippine Film (1994).

Deocampo, Nick, "Edison vs. Brocka," in *Pelikula: A Journal of Philippine Cinema* (University of Philippines, College of Mass Communication Foundation, March-August 2000).

Hernando, Mario A., *Lino Brocka: The Artist and His Times* (Manila: Cultural Center of the Philippines, 1993).

Part 5

Catholic, Agnostic, Atheist

Some people describe themselves as lapsed Catholics. Some are believers but do not wish to have any affiliation with the institution of the church or its practices. Others do not believe any more. And that is that.

There are others who, sometimes for serious reasons, at other times out of anger, bewilderment, or different priorities in their lives, declare their disbelief in God, church, and church teachings. Sometimes this is done with great bitterness and subsequent antagonism. For others it is a parallel to Luis Buñuel's journey from Catholic upbringing through disillusionment and attack on religious hypocrisy to "Thank God, I'm an atheist." Whatever the attitudes or stances that Buñuel took in his life and films are traced by Tom Aitken, and he shows that Catholicism in great detail pervades his career.

Krzysztof Kieslowski, despite filming his own *Dekalog* and achieving fame and worldwide respect (and the admiration of the churches), chose to be seen as a Polish agnostic. Lloyd Baugh has written a thesis on Kieslowski and explores the nature of his agnosticism.

Marc Gervais, who taught Denys Arcand at University in Montreal, situates him in his French Canadian setting and examines the rapid, often extreme, responses of Catholics during the 1960s and 1970s, a kind of widespread antichurch rebellion. This is reflected in the major films of Arcand's career, *The Decline of the American Empire* (1986) and its Oscar-winning sequel of sixteen years later, *The Barbarian Invasions* (2003) and his masterpiece, *Jésus de Montréal* (1989). In a filmed interview for the documentary, *Jesus Christ Moviestar* (1990), Arcand asks how anyone could make a film about Jesus, "because we don't know anything about him."

These directors from Catholic cultures declare that they do not know and cannot know anything about God, but nevertheless, they make classic movies on that subject.

12

Sacrilege, Satire, or Statement of Faith? Ways of Reading Luis Buñuel's *Viridiana*

Tom Aitken

In 1960, when Luis Buñuel made *Viridiana*, he had been an exile from his native Spain since 1938, living in Los Angeles, New York, and Mexico. Before he left Spain he had made (in Paris) two surrealist films with Salvador Dali and *Land without Bread*, a documentary in which peasant poverty was contrasted with the church's wealth. Between 1932 and 1947, when he moved to Mexico, he directed no films, but from that time on, content to make whatever films came his way, with whatever actors he was offered (sometimes most unsuitable ones), he became known as a craftsman who consistently finished on time and under budget. One commentator disapproves, writing that "he compromised himself with outright commercialism."[1] It makes better sense to say that he was simply learning his trade.

He had been from his youth an iconoclast, a hater of the Catholic Church and of bourgeois morality and of the unholy mixture of the two which, in his view, constituted Franco's Spain. He later wrote in *My Last Breath*, "I have always been impressed by the famous photograph of . . . ecclesiastical dignitaries standing in front of the cathedral of Santiago de Compostela in full sacerdotal garb, their arms raised in the Fascist salute. . . . God and country make an unbeatable team; they break all records for oppression and bloodshed."[2]

It would be true to say, however, that while he delighted in being a hostile critic of the church, he was also an obsessively fascinated one.

His iconoclasm was essentially anticlerical, linked with his attachment to anarchism and surrealism and to what, in a less perversely complex man, we might call his social conscience—or his feeling that there was a great deal of social injustice in the world. In 1950 in *Los Olvidados* (*The Young and the Damned*), about juvenile delinquents in the slums of Mexico, he returned to something like the mood of *Land without Bread*. In 1958, in *Nazarin*, he portrayed a humble and unworldly priest who attempted to live according to the example given by Jesus but was despised for doing so by those for whom religion was merely formal public observance.

He rejected as misguided interpretations of the film that depended on his supposed feelings of sympathy for the priest. (One reason for this, however, was his irritation when some people chose to see *Nazarin* as an attempt at self-rehabilitation.[3]

But even if many people, including Catholics, misunderstood *Nazarin*, what happened two years later, when Buñuel set about making a feminine companion piece, became a bizarre comic saga, stage-managed by Buñuel himself. The rest of the world obligingly played its appointed roles. The role he allotted the Franco government was that of incompetent idiot.

In 1960, having been a Mexican citizen for ten years, Buñuel applied for a visa to return to Spain, which, to his surprise (he says), was granted. He revisited the scenes of his childhood. On the boat back to Mexico, he decided "to write my own screenplay about a woman I called *Viridiana*, in memory of a little-known saint I'd heard about when I was a schoolboy. As I worked, I remembered my old erotic fantasy about making love to the queen of Spain when she was drugged, and decided somehow to combine the two stories."[4]

His decision to film *Viridiana* in Spain partly reflected its quintessentially Spanish character, but an element of careerist calculation was involved. Much of his best work was virtually unknown in Europe and America. He wanted to establish an international reputation, which was unlikely while he continued working only in Mexico.

When the project was announced, his friends among the émigré Spanish Republicans in Mexico were outraged. He was accused of treason, of kowtowing to Franco. Republican anger, however, was rapidly assuaged once they saw the film. It was not so much a gift to Franco as a bomb that exploded in his face.

Viridiana, a novice about to take her final vows, visits her uncle, Don Jaime, a landowner who has allowed his estate to fall into decay. He proposes marriage, and when Viridiana rejects him, he tries to trick her into it by claiming that he ravished her while she was unconscious. He dies, leaving the estate to Viridiana and Jorge, his illegitimate son. They manage their shares of it in quite different ways, he attempting to restore the estate as a working farm, she (having explicitly abandoned convent life) throwing open the outbuildings (all she will accept of the property) to beggars and outcasts. In return she demands only a little routine work and attendance at daily religious observances.

One afternoon, when Viridiana, Jorge, and Ramona, the housekeeper, are absent in the nearby town, the beggars break into the main house and in its luxurious dining room, stage a riotous party that concludes with them assuming the postures of Jesus and the disciples in Leonardo da Vinci's painting, *The Last Supper*. Further sensational events and an unexpected ending follow.

The script had to be passed by the Spanish censors, who suggested three changes. One concerned phallic symbolism in connection with Don Jaime's death. It was thought that Viridiana should not be seen praying alongside a crown of thorns, a hammer, and a nail, which were derived from traditional representations of the saint whose name Buñuel had borrowed. As for the unexpected ending, Viridiana should not be shown knocking on her cousin's door, and entering, the door closing behind her. Buñuel suggested that, instead, she should be shown settling down to a three-handed card game with Jorge and Ramona. This was accepted. In Buñuel's mischievous view (which, of course, he kept to himself) this merely made the scene still more suggestive.[5]

Disguise, deceit, and practical jokes were second nature to Buñuel. He was undoubtedly delighted by the discomfiture, in due course, of the Fascist government of Spain. Although it is widely assumed that the plot of *Viridiana* reflects his hostility toward the church, it does so in a more complex manner than is usually recognized.

It amused him that a nun should become the mistress of a rowdy household, which turned on its head the pious orderliness of the convent. And so Buñuel's biographer, John Baxter tells us, warming gleefully to his fantasy with the schoolboy relish for sacrilege and scatology he never, for all his exterior sternness, lost; "I thought that I'd enjoy seeing the beggars dine in the manor dining-room, on a great table covered with an embroidered cloth and candles. Suddenly I realized that they were in the position of a picture, evoking Leonardo da Vinci's *The Last Supper*. Finally I linked the Hallelujah Chorus with the beggars' dance and orgy, which became more startling like this than if I underlined it with rock and roll."[6]

On the face of it this is exactly what one would expect him to have said if the usual interpretation of *Viridiana* is accepted. But there is a great deal more to the scene than is indicated by Buñuel's words and Baxter's rib-nudging stage directions ("gleefully," "schoolboy relish," "sacrilege," "scatology," and so forth). And, to be pedantic, there is no scatology in the scene.

Viridiana was entered late in the Cannes Film Festival, where it shared the Palme d'Or and won a special French critics' prize for black humor. The Palme d'Or was proudly accepted by the Spanish undersecretary of cinema, the functionary who had discussed with Buñuel the changes in the script required by the Spanish censors. He had not seen the finished film and realized too late that Buñuel had made only the last of the suggested alterations. Buñuel himself, who was not present at the festival, but in Paris, undergoing treatment for Ménière's Syndrome (which later destroyed his hearing), was incredulous. How could Fascists be so stupid?

A day later the Vatican newspaper, *L'Osservatore Romano*, ran a piece by a Spanish Dominican describing the film as "sacrilegious and blasphemous." Franco sacked his undersecretary for cinema and suppressed all of Buñuel's films. (Buñuel, anticipating this, had taken negatives of *Viridiana* to Paris.) When Franco, years later, saw the film, he reportedly wondered what the fuss was about.

Buñuel responded by wondering how you could shock a man who had committed so many atrocities.[7]

This chapter discusses the film in the terms listed in the title: sacrilege, satire, and statement of faith. The conventional idea would be that the first two are obviously correct, while the third is a clear nonstarter. Buñuel, after all, not long before he died, said "Thank God I'm still an atheist."[8]

Satire

Most critics have seen *Viridiana* as a satire, in more or less bad taste, on the Catholic Church. Many, while praising the film, even perhaps considering it Buñuel's masterpiece, have disliked it. Parker Tyler says it leaves a bad taste in the mouth. Isabel Quigly wrote in *The Spectator* that "Buñuel has all the hatred: what he lacks is the necessary antidote—love." Christopher Tookey, of London's *Daily Mail*, writes that it is "a nasty piece of work, concerned with emphasizing all that is most ungrateful, cruel and insensitive in human nature." The orgiastic parody of *The Last Supper* looks "like a juvenile attempt to shock."

If the film is a straightforward satire it must be a parable about the condition of Spain. Tyler tells us that "the film's leading allegorical figures represent the Church (Viridiana herself), old world aristocracy (Don Jaime), male youth as it inherits the modern tradition of forthright, cynical agnosticism (Jorge), and last but not least, the pariahs that form a universal underground in our harassed world (the sheer have-nots devoid of all scruple and possessing a potential of combustion parallel with that of the atom bomb itself)." On this reading, the decayed estate is Spain itself, presided over by an aging, weary dictator, emotionally stultified by events that happened decades earlier, who passes his time by playing and listening to masses and requiems. His attempt to seduce his niece Viridiana represents—well, what does it represent? Viridiana herself is well-meaning, naive, sentimental in a cold-hearted way, applying, arguably, the wrong solutions to problems she has failed to identify accurately. So what, in terms of political parable, can Don Jaime's attempt to ravish her mean? Had Franco's establishment ravished the church? That, surely, would be to credit the church with having resisted Franco, something Buñuel was not disposed to do. Whatever it means, it does not constitute an attack on the Church. Viridiana is sincere in her behavior throughout. Tactless, even cruel in her dealings with her uncle, she is honest and never underhanded.

Dilys Powell preferred the notion of parody to that of parable and thought the result superb:

> Buñuel goes far beyond attacking professional religion and the practices of celibacy and self-mortification. He assaults the basis of a creed which he sees as upholding a callous and decaying society. The Christian myths are savagely parodied. A band of the maimed, the halt, and the blind, recipients of Viridiana's

charity, drunkenly reenact the Last Supper and after it fall to coupling behind the sofa, while a repulsive outcast puts on the veil and crown of the Bride and scattering the feathers of the murdered Dove, joins in dancing to the Hallelujah Chorus. This is not the simple derisive reaction against the forms of religion that many inquiring minds go through in early life (and from which many permanently adolescent minds never emerge). It is the expression of a hatred, which has developed and which has matured. For Buñuel the Church is "antilife."[9]

Parts of this reading are flawed, because they require us to assume that Buñuel rejoices in the actions of the outcasts—that, as an anti-Fascist, anarchist, and reputed Communist, he must be their supporter. He denied, however, having joined the Communist Party and said that at the end of the 1950s he lost sympathy with its fanaticism. He felt that its dogmas left out at least half of what makes us human.[10] His enjoyment in contemplating the beggars as lords of misrule is tempered by critical presentation. Perhaps, as Viridiana supposes, they are lost souls who have been destroyed by society. But as a group, he makes clear, they are ungrateful, selfish, stupid, and incapable of cooperating with each other. They are liars and cheats, who hate each other at least as much as they hate wealth and privilege. In taking revenge, in a muddled drunken way, on society and the church for evils they have suffered, they are cutting their own throats. Our sympathy remains with Viridiana and is reinforced by the brutal attempted rape of her which follows. The would-be rapist, rather curiously, is a painter of religious pictures— but (although he clearly stands for religious and artistic hypocrisy) this chapter suggests that another reason for his presence is conceivable.

Viridiana cannot therefore represent the church as hated by Buñuel. She does little to deserve hatred. She could be kinder to her besotted uncle, but after all, she has her virginity to defend, and Buñuel does not try to make us think the worse of her for this. Organizing the beggars when they arrive at the estate she is a bit bossy but is hardly an oppressor.

But if she does not represent the church, who or what does?

The Mother Superior of Viridiana's convent appears twice. Initially one might, with effort, convince oneself that she is telling Viridiana to visit her uncle merely because Don Jaime gives the convent money. If, subsequently, she is coolly unemotional about Viridiana's decision to leave the convent, this is sensible to the point, almost, of neutrality. Short of bursting into "Climb Every Mountain," she could scarcely be more like her opposite number in "The Sound of Music." Similarly, Don Jaime's taste for doodling sacred songs on the harmonium, while not notably cheerful, hardly amounts to an intolerable weight of stifling dogma and intolerance.

Can we then deny that *Viridiana* is in any sense satirical? That might be difficult. Samuel Johnson tells us that in satire wickedness and folly are censured, and Buñuel clearly set out to do that in this film.[11] His brand of satire is that of an anarchic reactionary. It is not mere mudslinging indicative of contempt, although both mudslinging and contempt may seem to be involved, especially to someone who hopes that the claims of the satirist are untrue. It is, rather, an attempt to contrast what an institution or person claims to be, and should be, with what in fact it is.

Buñuel described himself as "a fanatical anti-fanatic," and what he satirizes most consistently in *Viridiana* is the folly, as he sees it, of trying to right the wrongs of the world.[12] *Viridiana* is an ironic tragicomedy about the ineffectuality of good intentions. When Jorge frees a dog he sees being mistreated he fails to notice another one being treated in exactly the same way. (The dog he has freed, incidentally, does not appear to want to be taken from its inconsiderate master.) According to Buñuel's sister, he loved animals and suffered grievously when shooting this scene because the reality was so common and to attempt to cure Spanish peasants of their ingrained habit of cruelty was to tilt at windmills.[13]

If Viridiana had succeeded in reforming her beggars, there would still be other beggars left in the world. But she was in any case doomed to failure. Like the dog, they are ungrateful for the kindness they are offered. In insisting that they recite the "Angelus" while Jorge's workmen are busily getting on with their work, she is naive and impractical. (As with all the religious music and texts in this film, Buñuel has chosen here something precisely and mischievously relevant to his theme, because this devotional prayer includes the words "Behold the handmaid of the Lord, be it done unto me according to your word" and "The Word was made flesh, and dwelt among us." In casting herself by implication as "the handmaid of the Lord" Viridiana is both presumptuous and ineffectual.)

Buñuel's satire, then, is directed at an aspiration, not an institution, an aspiration found as often among unbelievers as among Christians.

Sacrilege

L'Osservatore Romano's Spanish Dominican preferred "sacrilegious and blasphemous" but the word *blasphemous* is not included here. Why not? The word derives from Greek roots, which together suggest damage to reputation. Within Christian theology the basic meaning is speech, thought, or action that manifests contempt for God. Aquinas defines it as a sin against faith which attributes to God that which does not belong to him or denies him that which is his due.[14] Is *Viridiana* blasphemous?

Here we must take into account cultural differences between Spaniards (at least in Buñuel's day) and the rest of us. Blasphemy has, or had, a special role in Spanish life. Buñuel tells us that the Spanish language is capable of more scathing blasphemies than any other language he knew. Curses elsewhere are typically brief and punctuated by other comments, but the Spanish curse tends to take the form of a long speech in which extraordinary vulgarities—referring chiefly to the Virgin Mary, the Apostles, God, Christ, and the Holy Spirit, not to mention the pope—are strung end to end in a series of impressive scatological exclamations. In fact, blasphemy in Spain is truly an art: "In Mexico, for instance, I never heard a proper curse, whereas in my native land, a good one lasts for at least three good-sized sentences."[15]

We might wonder whether, in a world inhabited by grown-ups, blasphemy is a useful concept. It has often been invoked by religious authorities anxious to suppress mockery, but any severe criticism of religious beliefs, especially one that carries an emotional charge, may be deemed blasphemous. In any case, it is difficult to pinpoint blasphemy in *Viridiana*.

God himself is hardly mentioned. His name is sung in the Hallelujah Chorus during the beggars' riotous party, but we may want to distinguish between Buñuel showing us some beggars being blasphemous, and Buñuel making a blasphemous film.

At one point a white bird is killed. The allegorists suppose this must represent the Holy Spirit. Again, we may note, the man who kills the bird is a despicable character, not someone we are supposed to admire.

The charge of sacrilege is easier to sustain, but you do not have to have been educated by Jesuits—as Buñuel was—to question it. Sacrilege is the violation of any sacred person, place, or thing. Thus, the attempted rape of Viridiana when she is a novice is sacrilegious. Her subsequent misadventures take place after she has abandoned the cloister and perhaps do not count.

Three major works of Christian art, one pictorial, two musical, are treated disrespectfully. Leonardo's painting is imitated fairly exactly, but is it violated or profaned? More seriously, is the actual *The Last Supper* itself damaged by this parody? That depends. The moment when the drunken beggars suddenly pose for a photograph, and the photographer lifts her skirts at them, is usually thought of as a contemptuous gesture from the writer/director, and Baxter tells us that Buñuel conceived the scene in these terms.[16]

But as has been suggested, there is more to the sequence than a puerile attempt to shock. Surrealism was another of the complex factors in Buñuel's creative drive and, although I do not consider this a notably surrealist film, surrealism was for him a way of rebelling against those aspects of reality that he detested. It may be that beggars' riot is surrealist in mood. It is an inexplicable event in which reality is both present and, as it were, left behind. Its lack of logic may be presumed to reflect the workings of the subconscious mind. It also fits closely another of the complications of Buñuel's personality: He advocated revolution but was appalled when it occurred. He wrote of the outbreak of Civil War in Spain, that "I, who had been such an ardent subversive, who had so desired the overthrow of the established order, now found myself in the middle of a volcano, and I was afraid."[17]

Perhaps, if we want a rational explanation for the scene, we may assume that the beggar who is himself a painter of religious pictures has put the others up to the jape and coached them in what positions to adopt—although in that case we might expect him to sit where Judas sits, which he does not.

Why do the beggars burlesque Leonardo's *The Last Supper* as opposed to anybody else's? They have presumably never seen it, yet they produce a more or less accurate reproduction of the groupings. Perhaps it is frequently reproduced in Spain. For the film's likely audience, clearly, the fame of the painting will maximize the shock—and, if you will, so does the sacrilege or blasphemy. But there is another reason for Buñuel's choice, one much more relevant to the film as a work of art. Many earlier painters had represented the Last Supper as, in Kenneth Clark's words, "the moment of communion, a moment of calm in which each apostle might wish to sit alone with his thoughts." Leonardo, however, "chose the terrible moment in which Jesus says 'One of you will betray me.'"[18] The beggars' party is a betrayal of Viridiana—she who has fed, clothed, and sheltered them. And what is heard in the moment of silence as the pose is struck: the sound which reproached Peter after he denied knowing Jesus, a cock crowing. If this scene is a sacrilegious gesture on Buñuel's part, it is a carefully worked out and extremely ambiguous one.

The extracts from sacred choral classics that are used in the film are similarly there for other reasons than mere shock value. Early in the film Don Jaime plies Viridiana with wine and drugs and is only prevented from ravishing her by a last minute accession of conscience. This takes place to the musical accompaniment of that part of the Mozart "Requiem" in which the words "let eternal light shine upon them with Thy saints" are being sung. Could these words have aroused Don Jaime's conscience?

The Hallelujah Chorus, which accompanies the party scene, is used in a more obviously frivolous way. But it is surely significant that the choir is cut off in midphrase, at "And He shall reign . . . " omitting "for ever and ever." This is obviously a denial of the proposition that "the Lord God omnipotent reigneth," but although this, according to Aquinas's definition quoted previously, is at least technically blasphemy, because it denies God that which is his due, at the same time it makes the use of this music in this scene part of the film's serious argument.

We might also reflect that Leonardo's picture and Mozart's and Handel's music are not themselves objects of worship. They are objets d'art, and if we are tempted to say that they ought to be revered we might consider two other items in the dictionary of misdemeanours: idolatry and superstition.

Let us agree for the moment, then, that neither blasphemy nor sacrilege offer complete accounts of what Buñuel is doing in this film. Is it in any way a statement of faith?

Statement of Faith

It seems clear that Buñuel's attitude to God was to a significant degree bound up with his attitude to the church in Spain and the Catholic dictatorship of General Franco. This he hated and despised. But even about Franco he was more ambivalent than he was sometimes prepared to admit. In *My Last Breath* he wrote: "I've never been one of Franco's fanatical adversaries . . . I'm even prepared to believe that he kept our exhausted country from being invaded by the Nazis."[19] His collaborator Jean-Claude Carrière believed that this statement contributed to national reconciliation during the turbulent decade after Franco's death in 1975. Buñuel also gave the dictator credit for having helped save Spanish Jews.[20]

His attitude toward the church had similar touches of ambivalence. He wrote:

> To be frank, the only civilization I admire is the one in which I was raised, the Graeco-Roman Christian . . . I love the cathedrals of Segovia and Toledo, which for me are living worlds in themselves . . . that incomparable spectacle of the *retablo* [a series of carved panels behind an altar], with its baroque labyrinths, where your fantasies can wander endlessly in the minute detours. I love cloisters, too.[21]

The title of this notorious film embodies a curiously gentle side to his attitude toward the Church. He derived the name Viridiania from a little-known saint he had heard about when he was a schoolboy. An Italian, she lived in Castel Fiorentino in the thirteenth century, spending thirty-four years of prayer and penitence in seclusion there. She was visited by St. Francis in 1221. Her death, in 1242, was announced by a sudden miraculous ringing of bells in Castel Fiorentino. Her life of seclusion (she had earlier been married, probably under pressure from her parents) may have been inspired by a pilgrimage to Santiago de Compostela, in northern Spain—which may be the connection in which Buñuel heard of her. But why should he have remembered her? Perhaps because her name suggests greenness, in several senses appropriate to his character.

As *Nazarin* and *Viridiana* show, he thought Christianity impractical and naive. But, although he proclaimed Jesus an idiot, it is not difficult to detect, in both those films and in *La Voie lactée* (*The Milky Way*, 1969) an implication that there is, at least theoretically, a truer, more admirable version of Christianity than that being practiced by the church. But, of course, like Viridiana herself, that truer Christianity is necessarily so vulnerable to attack and betrayal as to be useless.

Buñuel had good reason to despise at least some aspects of the Catholicism of Franco's Spain. It may follow that his view of Christianity in general was necessarily a distorted one. This chapter is not trying to make him out to be a closet Christian, but his films are among the fruits of Catholic, Fascist Spain. If the uncompromisingly violent anger that is commonly attributed to him might seem to be the only possible response to the privileges and wealth enjoyed by the church during his youth—when so many Spaniards lived in abject poverty—ironic amusement seems more characteristic of many of his films, including *Viridiana*. He frequently denied that his films attacked anything. *La Voie lactée*, he said, is neither for nor against anything at all.[22]

Surprisingly often, it must be said, his characters utter quasi-religious sentiments, which seem entirely sincere and also seem not to be being mocked by the

director. One says, "My hatred of science and my horror of technology will finally bring me round to this absurd belief in God." In *La Voie lactée*, he uses an
image derived from one of his own vivid dreams. The Virgin, shining softly, holds
out her hands to the dreamer.

> It's a very strong presence, an absolutely indisputable reality. She speaks to
> me—to me, the unbeliever—with infinite tenderness; she's bathed in the music
> of Schubert. . . . My eyes full of tears, I kneel down, and suddenly I feel myself
> inundated with a vibrant and invincible faith. When I wake up, my heart is
> pounding, and I hear my voice saying: "Yes! Yes! Holy Virgin, yes, I believe!"
> It takes me several minutes to calm down. The erotic overtones are obvious, yet
> they always remain within the chaste limits of a platonic devotion.[23]

Buñuel even argued, when provoked, that *Viridiana* was essentially a devout
film, "because in every scene there is an underlying sense of sin. The old man
cannot violate his niece because of this." The Mexican cameraman Gabriel
Figueroa believed that Buñuel was "only irreverent; not against Catholicism. The
irony is that even though his films are labeled anti-religious and anti-Catholic,
Buñuel is actually preparing for his next life, trying to come nearer to God all the
time. He is one of the most religious of men." Orson Welles said that Buñuel was
"a deeply Christian man who hates God as only a Christian can. . . . I see him as
the most supremely religious director in the history of the movies."[24] Whatever
we may think of these judgments, however, Buñuel did not feel called on to practice the Christian virtues. In 1977, while making *Cet obscur objet du désir* (*That
Obscure Object of Desire*), he was approached by an elderly Dominican who confessed that he had written the article in *L'Osservatore Romano* denouncing
Viridiana. He had now changed his mind and asked Buñuel's forgiveness. Buñuel
threw him off the set.[25]

During the last months of his life Buñuel became dependent on the visits of
a Catholic priest. Every afternoon at five, Father Julian Pablo appeared (in non-
clerical garb, at Buñuel's request). Sometimes they sat in silence, sometimes they
debated points of Catholic dogma. Both denied that Father Julian was trying to
persuade Buñuel to be reconciled to the church. "He knows more about the
Church and its doctrines than I do," said the priest.[26]

It is neither over-ingenious nor merely provocative to say that for Buñuel,
atheism was indeed a faith and one that he devoted much of his life and work to
asserting. Atheism, he said, forced him to live "in shadowy confusion,"[27] thus
keeping his moral freedom intact.

Viridiana illustrates in a coolly detailed way the atheism that Buñuel
embraced with such fervor. He could not simply ignore "this absurd belief in
God" but was driven, as Orson Welles said, to hate the object of that belief. If *The
Last Supper* scene in *Viridiana* is a wild parody of Leonardo's painting, so also is
Buñuel's life and work a parody—sometimes wild, often anything but—of faith.

There is something much more than mere jokey paradox in his utterance quoted at the beginning of this chapter:

Thank God I'm still an atheist.

Reviewing the Chapter

1.　To what extent, if at all, did the circumstances of Buñuel's life affect the films he made and the way he made them?

2.　Describe and discuss the ways in which the characters in *Viridiana* can be regarded as satirical figures.

3.　Which characters in *Viridiana*, of any, do you find sympathetic? Why?

Notes

1.　Parker Tyler, *Classics of the Foreign Film* (London: Spring Books, 1966), 244.

2.　Luis Buñuel, *My Last Breath* (London: Jonathan Cape, 1984), 170.

3.　Buñuel, *Last Breath*, 215–16; John Baxter, *Luis Buñuel* (New York: Fourth Estate, 1994), 6–7.

4.　Baxter, *Luis Buñuel*, 2–3, 255–56; Buñuel, *Last Breath*, 234.

5.　Baxter, *Luis Buñuel,* 6.

6.　Baxter, *Luis Buñuel*, 3–4.

7.　Baxter, *Luis Buñuel*, 255.

8.　Buñuel, *Last Breath*, 171.

9.　For quotations from Isabel Quigly, Christopher Tookey, and Dilys Powell, see Christopher Tookey, *The Critics' Film Guide* (London: Boxtree, 1994), 905–06; for those from Parker Tyler, see *Classics*, 244–47.

10.　Buñuel, *Last Breath*, 166.

11.　Samuel Johnson, *A Dictionary of the English Language* (London, 1755).

12.　Buñuel, *Last Breath*, 228–38.

13.　Buñuel, *Last Breath*, 36.

14.　St. Thomas Aquinas, *Summa Theologiae*, First Part of the Second Part, Vice and Sin (Paris, 1270–1271).

15.　Buñuel, *Last Breath*, 159.

16.　Baxter, *Luis Buñuel*, 3–4.

17.　Buñuel, *Last Breath*, 153.

18.　Kenneth Clark, *Leonardo da Vinci* (London: Viking, 1998), 93.

19.　Buñuel, *Last Breath*, 170.

20.　Baxter, *Luis Buñuel*, 243.

21.　Buñuel, *Last Breath*, 220, 222–23.

22.　Buñuel, *Last Breath*, 245.

23.　Buñuel, *Last Breath*, 95.

24.　Baxter, *Luis Buñuel*, 2.

25. Baxter, *Luis Buñuel*, 256.
26. Baxter, *Luis Buñuel*, 312.
27. Buñuel, *Last Breath*, 174.

13

The Christian Moral Vision of a Believing Atheist: Krzysztof Kieslowski's *Decalogue* Films

Lloyd Baugh

"I don't believe in God, but I have a good relationship with him."[1] This offhand and typically ironic comment of the Polish filmmaker, Krzysztof Kieslowski, on the issue of his faith belies the utter seriousness with which he investigates the issues of God and of human existence before God, of faith and hope, and of Christian moral behavior in his ten-film *Decalogue* series. Like many filmmakers and artists, Kieslowski is reticent to speak of deeply personal issues; he speaks readily and eloquently of cultural and political themes, of the film scene in Poland and internationally, of the technical and aesthetic dimensions of his own films, of films and directors who have influenced him; but regarding his personal life—his relationship with his wife and daughter, for example, or his own religious beliefs—Kieslowski reveals little of substance. In most of the interviews he gives, the God and faith issue never comes up, and when it does, Kieslowski sometimes deflects the question with a humorous or enigmatic answer. In one somewhat unusual interview, he distinguishes between the God of the Old Testament—"a demanding, cruel God . . . who doesn't forgive, who ruthlessly demands obedience to the principles which He has laid down"—and the God of the New Testament—"a merciful kind-hearted old man with a white beard, who just forgives everything." Kieslowski then adds, referring to the God of both the Old and New Testaments, "I think that an authority like this does exist."[2]

Further complicating the issue of Kieslowski's belief or disbelief, most of the critical analytical material on the *Decalogue* films either avoids the God and faith issue or skirts it—for example, speaking only vaguely of Kieslowski's Polish cultural Catholicism—thus effectively undercutting any serious consideration of the question of his personal belief. Exceptionally, some French critics perceive and understand Kieslowski's "concern with the transcendent," characterizing his position with the paradoxical but expressive term, "secular theism,"[3] and one

Polish critic, with a clear sense of the Catholic tradition of his country, recognizes in the *Decalogue* films "evidence of profound meditation of revelation" with a "positive outlook on the question of the transcendent."[4]

Inspired by a painting in the National Museum of Warsaw that depicts in ten small frames specific violations of each of the Mosaic commandments, Kieslowski's *Decalogue* represents in ten short films (fifty to fifty-five minutes each), characters attempting to come to grips with specific moral crises brought about by the complexity of living in the postmodern world. Situated in the contemporary urban setting of Warsaw and more specifically in a grey and anonymous Marxist-socialist condominium complex, the films are in no way simple illustrations of the commandments but rather sophisticated investigations of what these ten chapters of the Mosaic law can mean for women and men today. In a sense the films, each hinging on one or more existential moral crises, dance around the commandments, sometimes coming close to their traditional meaning and other times apparently diverging far from that meaning, questioning it, or developing it in new and original directions.

Three Autobiographical References to God

However, as this chapter considers, elements of the Christian experience of God are common to the lived experience of many of the characters in the *Decalogue* films; in three of the films, Kieslowski embodies direct, thematic references to God and faith, so pointed and clear that they seem to reflect dimensions of Kieslowski's own experience. In the Catholic-born but agnostic university professor of *Decalogue One*, to whom Kieslowski pointedly gives his own first name, the director represents a journey from skepticism and indifference regarding issues of religious faith—the man answers his little son's anguished questions about the meaning of life, death, and the soul with technical scientific explanations that are clearly unsatisfactory to the boy—to the first evidence of a renewed faith in the God of his youth. In the conclusion of the film, Krzysztof, grieving from the accidental death of his son for which he accepts responsibility, enters a Catholic Church, expresses his anguish in the violent gesture of pushing down a temporary altar, perceives a sign of God's mercy, and submits to a kind of personal baptismal rite. About this rebellious act, Kieslowski, who like his film's protagonist denies the existence of God, comments paradoxically, "In an act of rebellion, we come to recognize that someone who did not seem to us to exist, in fact does exist. Rebellion is a manifestation of the faith that one denies . . . clearly he [the protagonist] is rebelling against God."[5]

In the same film, the sister of the protagonist—Kieslowski, too, has a sister—is a practicing Catholic and indeed arranges for her little nephew to attend religion classes at a nearby parish. When the boy inquires about God, she gives him a warm hug; the boy says that he feels loved and his aunt explains that "God is in that [love]." If Irena's vivid and concrete faith in God as love, in the God of Love, is in contrast to her brother's agnosticism—she explains to her nephew that both she and his father were raised Catholics but that early on, the father found another way of understanding the world around him, the way of reason—her reaction to the boy's tragic death is also in contrast to Krzysztof's. While he goes into a church and prays, Kieslowski has Irena wander through the deserted night streets, crying, in a response that clearly suggests a moment of agnosticism, normal in that terrible situation and evidently a dimension of the religious experience of Kieslowski and, in fact, of many true believers.

In *Decalogue Two*, one of the protagonists seems to propose further dimensions of Kieslowski's complex experience of faith. An old man, a medical doctor and surgeon, has for many years been something of a recluse, a reaction to the tragic death of his wife and two young children during the Second World War. When the wife of a patient that the doctor is treating presses him for information about her husband, he coldly keeps her at a distance. In frustration one day, she confronts him: "Do you believe in God?" In a quiet voice, full of pain, he responds "I have a private God. . . ." In the reticence of the old doctor, in his apparent rejection of formal religious practice, there is much of Kieslowski.

Then in *Decalogue Eight*, Kieslowski creates a character who in some ways is parallel to the doctor in *Two* and close to himself. Zofia—the reference to the Greek word for wisdom is transparent—is about the same age as the doctor and a university professor of moral philosophy. Kieslowski represents her in a crowded amphitheater directing a seminar on the "ethical inferno," that is on the great difficulty of making good moral decisions in the confusion of the postmodern world. Zofia's pedagogical method, she demonstrates and later explains, is to present her students with concrete cases of moral crises and moral decisions—a method clearly parallel to Kieslowski's "pedagogical" method in the *Decalogue* films—thus putting them in a position in which the "Good"[6] in each of them will express itself and direct them to make the right moral judgments and decisions. In response to an interlocutor's comment, "I've never read anything in your work about God," Zofia answers, "I don't go to church, I don't use the word 'God,' but that does not mean he does not exist." The woman's position, her approach to the issue of God here—her own belief and her method for raising the God issue with her students—is precisely that of Kieslowski in his ten films.

Moral Themes in a Christian Perspective

If *Decalogue One*, *Two*, and *Eight* underline in a more specific way than the other films in the series, the God and faith issue from a Christian perspective, they, as well as the other films, also approach this issue indirectly, by representing a wide range of moral themes that are clearly Christian in their substance or in their reach. Three of the films, *Two*, *Three*, and *Nine*, for example, investigate the crucial theme of faithfulness in marriage. In all three films, one or both partners have broken their marriage vows: in *Two*, the wife, Dorota, who is pregnant by her lover; in *Three*, the husband, Janusz, who, after attending Midnight Mass with his wife and children, deserts them on Christmas Eve to be with his former mistress; and both protagonists in *Nine*, a young surgeon who admits to have had many casual affairs in the past and his wife who in the present time is having a casual affair with a university student. These cases of infidelity are different among themselves and clearly all complex human situations, but in the course of each of the films, Kieslowski leads all six protagonists, out of love for their partners, to understand, appreciate, and regret the moral wrong of their choices and to choose freely to end their illicit liaisons and renew their marriage commitments.

A corollary theme to that of the sacredness of marriage in Kieslowski's films is that of the utter sacredness of the child—a theme often underlined by Jesus in the Gospel—and of the awesome responsibility of the parent toward the child. In *Two*, the example, the old doctor, still grieving forty years after the tragic death of his children, does all he can to save the life of an unborn child, and in the conclusion of the film, and reflecting a beautiful sense of the superabundance of grace, the husband of the mother of that child anticipates with joy the birth the child though clearly it is not his.

In *Four*, Kieslowski neatly shifts the meaning of the fourth commandment—"Honor your father and your mother"—to the responsibility of the parent for the child. A precocious nineteen-year-old girl announces dramatically to her fortyish and widowed father, that he is not her biological parent, supporting her contention with convincing evidence, and then she initiates an elaborate seduction attempt. The father/non-father struggles to resist the temptation and in the end, courageously proclaiming that the true meaning of parenthood is far more an existential, moral reality than a biological connection, he reaffirms his responsibility as father, saving his daughter and himself from a terrible moral tragedy.

Further regarding adult responsibility for children, in *Five*, Kieslowski has a young man condemned to death confess to his lawyer that he is responsible for the tragic death of his little sister, a sin/crime that has made him into a pariah and finally brought him to an ignoble end. In *Eight*, a terrible sin of irresponsibility committed forty years previously against a little Jewish girl seeking refuge from the Nazis, the source of much guilt and anguish in the protagonist professor ever since, becomes the motivation for her statement of moral principle that nothing is more important than the life of a child. And in the course of that film, Kieslowski represents the grace of forgiveness and reconciliation between the sinner and the victim, now an adult but still carrying the pain of the earlier rejection. Finally in *Nine*, Kieslowski points to the adoption of an orphan child as a sign of the reconciliation and new hope for the couple of protagonists, a sign that their marriage, previously childless by their irresponsible design, is now going to be lived responsibly and fruitfully.

In all the *Decalogue* films, Kieslowski insists that human life is sacred and to be protected and fostered, clearly a fundamental Christian principle. He represents the death of the little boy in *One* and the little girl in *Five* as particularly tragic events, terrible moral failures of those responsible, and he makes clear the joy with which the birth of a child must welcomed: the first-born child of the lawyer and his wife in *Five*, which serves as one of the few signs of hope in that otherwise bleak film, and the joy of the father/non-father of the child to be born in *Two*. Further in *Two*, Kieslowski adopts a clear antiabortion position, when, despite the protagonist Dorota's decision to abort her unborn child if her husband, who is not the father of the child, survives his cancer, Kieslowski shifts the narrative to bring miraculous healing to the dying husband and to give life to the unborn child. Again in favor of life, in *Nine*, Kieslowski saves the protagonist from the tragic absurdity of suicide, giving him hope and love, and in *Five*, he represents as unspeakable horrors both the cruel and unmotivated murder and the even more terrifying state-sanctioned execution of the killer.

The Fundamental Christian Pattern of Sin, Grace, Forgiveness, and Reconciliation

To be a Christian is to believe that one's personal sinfulness is met by saving grace in Jesus Christ; it is to experience that grace personally in the fundamental human dynamic of repentance, confession, forgiveness, and reconciliation. In the *Decalogue* films, Kieslowski refers to this most basic Christian moral pattern over and over again and not in peripheral actions but in the central moral dynamics at work in the protagonists. The possibility, "the prospect of redemption in the Christian pattern"[7] is a clearly a theme that pervades the entire *Decalogue*.

This redemptive pattern is easily recognized in the ultimately fruitful struggle of Dorota in *Two* to reconcile with her husband; in the final confessions and reconciliations between the unfaithful husband and his wife in *Three*; and in the healing confession and reconciliation between the daughter and her father in the conclusion of *Four*. Confession of sin, forgiveness, and reconciliation is the basic salvific pattern at work in the conversation between the condemned man Jacek and his lawyer in *Five*. In this remarkable scene, the young lawyer, a good and righteous man, is more a sacramental presence, more a priest/confessor than the actual priest who appears later in the execution scene. This same salvific theme is the fundamental pattern of the entire narrative of *Eight* from the beginning, with the woman sinned against taking the role of the accuser, and the woman who sinned, then confessing, seeking forgiveness and accepting reconciliation, in a remarkably beautiful, sacred, and fundamentally Christian moment.

In *Nine*, both partners in the marriage have sinned against each other in a variety of ways. Then in the course of the film, and not without much struggle and pain, they both recognize the destructive power of their sinful behavior, they confess to each other, and they begin a long process of healing reconciliation. If *Ten* seems at first to be about the dangers of coveting material goods, in fact, behind this evident theme, and despite the comic tone of the film, unique in the *Decalogue* series, there is another and more significant dynamic, that of the reunion and reconciliation of two estranged brothers, who, in fact, in the course of the film betray each other. Kieslowski's lingering close-ups on the faces of each of the betrayers make clear their awareness of the gravity of their sin, but then, in the final scene of the film, they confess to each other and in a burst of laughter—echoed inevitably in the satisfied laughter of the viewers of this exceptional film—effect a spectacular reconciliation that is an exceptional moment of pure grace.

In the Christian tradition, the saving grace of Jesus Christ expresses itself in the context of the Christian community, in favor of the building up of that community, which is the Mystical Body of Christ, in favor of the breaking down of the barriers of egoism, fear, and sinfulness, between people that destroy that Body. As we have suggested already, in most of the films of the *Decalogue*, Kieslowski investigates this theme of the creation of community and communion out of diversity and self-isolation. Some of the examples of this breaking down of barriers are dramatic: the passage from animosity to friendship between the desperate wife of the dying man and the reclusive old doctor in *Two*; the final salvific conversation between the wholly unsympathetic young punk killer and his lawyer in *Five*; and the reconciliation between the jealous and suicidal doctor and his wife in *Nine*, who in the breaking down of the barriers between themselves, also graciously open up their relationship to an unwanted child.

The Icon and the Cross: Essential Christian Symbols

In his exploration of these Christian themes, Kieslowski makes conscious use of concrete Christian religious objects and symbols, a technique of reinforcing these themes that is never heavy-handed, out of place, or kitsch, as is often the case with filmmakers who have moved away from the faith. In these ten films, the wealth of concrete religious references cannot be justified simply as Catholic cultural background. The care with which Kieslowski subtly embeds these references in the text of the films, so fully in synch with the development of the plot and the characters, and the unequivocal significance to the film texts of the transcendent God these Christian references point to clearly suggest Kieslowski's sincerity and seriousness.

Twice in the *Decalogue*, Kieslowski inserts visual references to sacred icons; both times they are of the Madonna and Child, and so images of the Incarnation of God into human experience and into all of its ambiguity. In the conclusion to *One*, the protagonist Krzysztof, having in anger toppled the altar in the church, finds himself face-to-face with the icon of Our Lady of Czestochowa. Tears of dripping wax form on the Madonna's face as she cries both for her son who is to die and for Krzysztof's son who has just now died. Because the nature of the icon is to point the viewer beyond himself or herself to the transcendent, this image clearly suggests that in that moment of Krzysztof's terrible suffering, God is in communion with him and shares his pain. In *Eight*, another icon of the Madonna and Child, again surrounded by lit candles, a sign of God's incarnation as light into the darkness of human existence—*"Lux in tenebris lucet"* (John 1:5)— watches benevolently over the protagonists as each enters a shadowy, menacing courtyard to face a moment of dark truth about herself. There is an uncanny sense that when, soon after their encounter with the sacred icon, the two women reconcile, the icon and the God it points to are somehow responsible.

Over and over again in the *Decalogue*, the perceptive viewer notes visual references to crosses, the Christian symbol par excellence of the redemptive death of Christ for the salvation of humanity. In the facade of the unfinished church in *One*, seen from the outside several times in the film and then from the inside in its conclusion, a huge cross associates the passion of Krzysztof to that of Christ and prepares for his baptismal act in the sign of the cross. The gold cross on the chain around the neck of the troubled Elzbieta in *Eight* and that worn by the suffering and suicidal surgeon Roman in *Nine* also point to the event of salvation that they are living through, despite the darkness of the present moment. Then, in the latter case, Kieslowski has Roman go to what he believes will be his death literally under a cross in the bell tower of a church, a cross which the director expertly holds twice over the man's head in the composition: The Christian mystery of death and resurrection are moving in Roman's life and he will be saved. Twice in *Six*, Kieslowski creates abstract crosses in the background of crucial actions of the protagonist Tomek: in a window as the young man "steals" the telescope that will permit him to get close to and save the woman he loves and in the door of the building toward which Tomek climbs after his rejection by the woman and as he is about to shed his blood for her salvation; the allusion to the saving event on Calvary is clear.

Repeatedly in Kieslowski's series, the words *God* and *Jesus* are used, beyond the previously noted discussions of God. The young killer in *Five*, for example, as he looks on the bloodied face of his agonized victim, exclaims "Jesus!" More a prayer, a Christian prayer—in the face of the horror he is committing—than a blasphemy, it also suggests Jacek's recognition of the suffering Jesus in his victim; clearly in the shocking close-up of the bruised face of the victim, blood flowing from his head as if from a crown of thorns, Kieslowski is making a visual allusion to the crucified Christ.[8] The wife of Roman in *Nine*, on hearing on the telephone the voice of the husband she thinks dead, says softly, "God, you're there," unequivocally a prayer of thanksgiving. And in *Ten*, in a beautiful moment representing the ongoing reconciliation of the two estranged brothers, one of them says, "God, I feel free." He too, perhaps without fully realizing the significance of what he is saying, seems to be thanking God for the grace received.

Hope in a Broken, Fragmented World:
The Providential Man of Mystery

There is little doubt that Kieslowski places his characters in a fragmented post-modern world vitiated by a breakdown of moral values, by lonely, anonymous living, by materialism and practical atheism. In this broken world he allows them to commit a wide variety of sins: the denial of God, the violation of the Sabbath, marital infidelity, lying, stealing, killing, to name only a few. But in the Christian pattern, Kieslowski also offers his characters hope. In the black-humor prologue and the closing credits of *Ten*, Kieslowski inserts on the soundtrack of the film the violent and outrageous hard rock lyrics of one the brother protagonists and his "City Death" band: "Kill, kill, kill/Screw who you will/Lust and crave/Pervert and deprave/Every day of the week. . . . On Sunday hit mother/Hit father, hit brother/Hit sister, the weakest/Steal from the meekest . . ." The words represent an ironic anti-decalogue, a comment on the behavior of the *Decalogue*'s characters and on the duplicity of human nature, something suggested by Kieslowski as one of his motives for making these films: "What fascinates me about the Commandments is that we all agree that they are just and appropriate, but at the same time, we violate them every day. They interest me because they allow me to examine the moral ambivalence of human beings."[9] But Artur's song inevitably is perceived by sensitive viewers as ironic precisely because in all but one of the films, Kieslowski represents characters who, though initially lost, ambivalent, or wandering dangerously in patterns of sinfulness, succeed in overcoming their immorality and in restoring moral/spiritual order in their lives.

In the complex challenges to moral behavior that face the characters in the *Decalogue* films, referred to by the professor of moral philosophy in *Eight* as an ethical inferno, these people need help if they are to survive and bring hope to the world. And Kieslowski gives them help, in each other, in fortuitous events of grace, and in the mysterious character who appears in nine of the ten films, in a different guise and with different behavior each time. Kieslowski responds to questions about the Man of Mystery with characteristically enigmatic comments: "There's this guy who wanders around in all the films. I don't know who he is; just a guy who comes and watches."[10] They are comments that do not do justice to the importance both structurally and morally/spiritually of this enigmatic figure, whose discrete appearances and timing are specifically coordinated in each film with a precise motive, a precise effect, and a specific significance. Generally speaking, the Man of Mystery has a spiritual identity and role: At times he represents the presence of God, at times the providential hand of God; at times he accompanies the protagonists anonymously and invisibly (to them, not to the viewer of the film) rather like a guardian angel.[11] Artur Barcis, the actor who plays the Man of Mystery, suggests significantly that at times his character "might be Christ who could meet a person at any time."[12] In some situations the Man of Mystery interferes directly in the actions of the protagonists and normally when he appears, his presence signals a positive shift in the narrative, the presence and action of grace.

In *One*, the Man of Mystery, framed repeatedly sitting in front of a blazing fire on the edge of an icy pond, is a beacon of light and warmth in the otherwise desolate winter landscape; in his contemplative stance and in the warm red and orange colors of his appearance, he is identified by Kieslowski with the icon of the Madonna and Child at the end of the film. Further, in the editing of the film, he is unequivocally identified with God and love. Directly, if silently, he challenges the protagonist Krzysztof before the tragedy, and in the film's conclusion, he receives in death little Pawel, the innocent victim of his father's idolatry.

In *Two*, the Man of Mystery clearly is a life-giving force, present as a doctor at Dorota's declaration of love to her dying husband, a declaration that becomes a healing experience for him; he is also present as the doctors make a decision that indirectly prevents an abortion. In *Three*, he is disguised as a tram driver at the most dangerous moment in the illicit couple's game of brinkmanship; his providential presence prevents a tragedy and sets them on the right path. The Man of Mystery appears as a canoeist in *Four*, manifests himself to the precocious daughter, clearly preventing her from opening a letter that might do her and her father much harm, and he reappears in the same guise when, in the conclusion, the right moral order is restored between daughter and father, as if he wishes to confirm that order, as if he is a visible expression of it.

In *Five*, the Man of Mystery is a road surveyor, who makes eye contact with the young murderer, evidently trying to dissuade him from his terrible decision. Later, in an allusion to the superabundance of unmerited grace, the Man reappears twice in the prison on the day of Jacek's execution, once with a ladder, as if preparing to meet Jacek in death, to take him "down from his cross," and once for the young lawyer, as if to strengthen him for his talk with Jacek, a meeting that becomes an opportunity of saving grace for the condemned man.

In *Six*, the Man of Mystery meets the protagonist/Christ figure twice, once when he succeeds for the first time in communicating his love to the woman and again when he is about to give up his life for her, acting here almost like the ministering angel from heaven who comes to Jesus in the Garden of Olives (Luke 22:43). He appears as a student in the seminar of Zofia in *Eight*, in which he clearly participates in the suffering of both women during a violent verbal confrontation, and no doubt this presence of grace is instrumental in the later reconciliation of the women. In *Nine*, the Man of Mystery is a bicyclist, whose guardian presence twice saves the life of the suicidal surgeon; here, as in *Two*, Kieslowski suggests that the Man's saving grace works parallel to the grace of the deep love of the victim's wife for her husband.[13]

Human Freedom: The Possibility of Refusing Grace

A fundamental, constitutional element of the Christian experience is the exercise of human freedom. The teaching and practice of Jesus, the entire New Testament, and two thousand years of Christian history make it abundantly clear how the person called by God in Jesus is free to accept the call of grace or to refuse it. Kieslowski respects this essential pattern of the possibility of the failure of grace, the refusal of salvation in his films. Though overwhelmingly, the Polish director represents the successful experience of salvation and hope and love, in *Seven*, he radically shifts register and creates a moral/spiritual wasteland. Easily the bleakest of the films, *Seven* does not manifest any opening to grace or hope, and its psychological violence is far more shocking than the physical violence of *Five*. Two women, mother and daughter, are aggressive and violent opponents, struggling for the affection of the daughter's little girl, legally adopted at birth by her grandmother. The women, both seriously unbalanced emotionally, insist repeatedly that they "love" little Anka, but neither woman is capable of love. They can only battle each other to possess her like an object, body and soul. The two scenes in which the birth mother insists hysterically that Anka call her "mother," a request obstinately rejected by the little girl, are truly horrific.

Given the moral principle proposed by Kieslowski and Zofia, the professor in *Eight*, that there is no higher value in this world than the life of a child, the violence against this child in *Seven* suggests that the sin of the two women is indeed grave. This is why Kieslowski limits the providential Man of Mystery to one brief and ambiguous appearance in *Seven*, at the train station in the concluding scene, kept far from the protagonists, hobbling across the background on crutches.[14] Where there is no love—for both Kieslowski and for the Jesus of Christian faith, the gravest sin—divine Providence, the power of grace, represented by this mysterious figure, has no power to function. The final shot of the film, a terrifying close-up of little Anka standing on the station platform, literally halfway between her grandmother-mother and her mother-sister, her mouth wide open as if to scream, but no sound comes out. The allusion to Edvard Munch's painting "The Scream" is undeniable. Like the dark, distorted, despairing world of that painting, the world Kieslowski represents in *Seven* is tragically closed to love and so, closed to grace and to God.

If *Seven* represents the possibility of utter moral failure, for lack of love, then *Six* represents a resounding moral/spiritual success in a strictly Christic pattern. In *Six*, Kieslowski adopts an entire narrative and moral pattern directly from the New Testament to examine the human dynamic of the experience of saving, redemptive love. *Six*, as already suggested, narrates the story of an innocent young man named Tomek who deeply and chastely loves an older woman, a woman given to promiscuous sexual activity; she brutally rejects him and in a conscious attempt to save her, Tomek sheds his blood. The young man's sacrificial act redeems the woman as she is converted to a new and chaste way of expressing love, in a remarkable

dynamic of salvation that includes the elements of repentance, confession, and reconciliation. When, late in the film, Kieslowski reveals the woman's name as
"Maria Magdalena," the minimally astute viewer recognizes that New Testament
reference[15] and uses it as a hermeneutic to reexamine the personality and behavior
of Tomek in the entire film, concluding that in him, Kieslowski has created a
metaphorical representation of Jesus Christ, a classical Christ figure.[16] Thus, the
director roots both the sacrificial saving love of Tomek and the conversion to love
of Maria Magdalena/Magda in the archetypal Christian pattern of confession of
sinfulness, contrition, amendment, and salvation.

The Fundamental Christian Law of Love

As this chapter has pointed out, in his *Decalogue* films, Kieslowski examines a
wide variety of human behavioral patterns, both sinful and graced, a thematic pattern consonant with the title and basic concept of the series and their reference to
the Old Testament Mosaic law. However, there is an abundance of evidence in the
films suggesting that behind and within Kieslowski's focus on the moral imperative of each of the Mosaic commandments and on the relevance of these moral
principles today, the Polish film director has a more essential and much richer
moral/spiritual focus, that is, on the New Testament commandment to love as the
most fundamental moral imperative for men and women today—a moral imperative that, as Jesus teaches, transcends the individual focus of each of the commandments. In Matthew 25 and Mark 12, Jesus proposes the love of God and the
love of neighbor as the greatest commandment, the fulfillment of the Old
Testament law. Then in a profound spiritual insight into the words of Jesus, St.
John develops the great commandment when he insists that love of neighbor is a
prerequisite for love of God and for contact with God: "No one has ever seen
God. If we love one another, God lives in us . . . those who do not love a brother
or sister whom they have seen, cannot love God whom they have not seen." (1
John 4:12, 20)

The evidence of Kieslowski's focus on the New Testament law of love is
overwhelming. Much of it has been at least alluded to in this chapter, but here, a
concluding synthesis. The experience of Christian love is present, somehow, in
all the films and not only as a theme but rather as a central dynamic. In the
Decalogue films, the sins committed are all sins against love: the infidelity of the
wife in *Two* and the rejection of a needful child in *Eight*; the cruel seduction in
Six and the morbid suspicions of the husband in *Nine*; the mutual betrayal of
brothers in *Ten* and the tragic narcissistic possessiveness of the grandmother and
mother in *Seven*. The graced moments of conversion, forgiveness, and reconciliation are all expressions of love: the presence of God in the love between the
father and son in *One*; the victory of responsible love in *Four*; the sacramental
power of the caring love of the lawyer for the condemned man in *Five*; Magda's

wonderful conversion by love and to love in *Six*; and the final affirmation of for-
giving and hopeful love in *Nine*.

Clearly the *Decalogue* films provide a magnificent catalogue of case studies
of how the Christian virtue and gift of love lead the women and men who love
and are loved in graced journeys from isolation to integration, from egoism to
altruism, from manipulation to caritas, from doubt to belief. In these films, the
women or men who love move forward, overcome barriers, and are integrated
into each other and into the fabric of society. Kieslowski leads them, often along
difficult paths, from sin, to forgiveness, to love, to grace, and thence, to God. It
is difficult to imagine a more deeply Christian journey.

Christian Love in the Later Films:
Veronica and *Three Colors: Blue, White, Red*

Kieslowski's vision of the law of love as the only hope for moral survival, for
touching God and for being touched by God, and so for human salvation, does
not end with the *Decalogue* films. The Polish director carries forward this essential Christian vision into the four films that follow the *Decalogue* series, his final
four films.[17] In *La double vie de Véronique* (*The Double Life of Veronica*, 1991),
perhaps the most mysterious of his films, Kieslowski examines in the experience
of the two young women called Veronica, the miraculous power of the transcendent experience of loving across the barriers of time and space and even death.
Then, in the providential puppet master/teacher Fabbri, he refines the character of
the Man of Mystery of the *Decalogue* films, and suggests in Fabbri's encounter
with the French Veronique, nothing less than the graced meeting of the human
being with the God of love.

In the *Trois couleurs* (*Three Colors*, 1993–1994) trilogy, the saving power of
love—in the New Testament sense—is a constant theme. In *Blanc* (*Three Colors:
White*) love transcends the betrayals and infidelities of the two protagonists to
bring hope into their broken marriage, and in *Rouge* (*Three Colors: Red*), a deli-
cate love relationship between a reclusive old man and a young woman brings
renewal, hope, and life to both of them.

But it is especially in *Bleu* (*Three Colors: Blue*) that Kieslowski's Christian
moral vision expresses itself with rare beauty and power. The film's protagonist, a
young woman, Julie, after the unspeakable morally and spiritually debilitating
tragedy of the sudden death of her husband and daughter and through the experience of being loved by gentle and patient people, learns again to love. At first, Julie
wants only to hide from people, to isolate herself, to refuse all connections and ties
that might lead to love, and as she sees it, to further pain. But gradually, as she
receives love and allows herself to respond spontaneously with gestures of love,
small at first and then awesome, Julie recognizes that love cannot die, that her good-

ness, her natural impulse to love, cannot be suppressed. She opens again to the experience of being loved and of loving, and in this experience she finds salvation.

The conclusion of *Bleu* (*Three Colors: Blue*), one of the most powerful spiritual moments in cinema, is the clearest statement of the Christian heritage that informs Kieslowski's films; a montage of visual images of the moral resurrection of love in Julie accompanied on the soundtrack by a piece of music she has created and by the words she has added to the music, the words of St. Paul's hymn to love in 1 Corinthians 13:1–13—"For if I speak in the tongues of mortals and of angels . . . and do not have love, I am nothing." The words, sung in the *koiné* Greek of the New Testament, translated into English in subtitles, confer a powerful Christian focus on *Film Blue*; they also serve most eloquently as a fitting Christian/moral coda to the ten films of the *Decalogue*.[18]

Reviewing the Chapter

1. *The Question of God*: This chapter proposes that the protagonists in the *Decalogue* films sooner or later face and deal with the "God question." Is your own experience of God always a direct reference point in your life or do you sometimes experience God in indirect ways, which are nonetheless authentically "of God"?

2. *The Decision to Love*: In the *Decalogue* films, the protagonists are called to make the decision to love, to give love, to receive love, or let love change their lives, clearly the fundamental vocation of the Christian. Does this ring true to your experience of love? With which of the films do you, and your experience of love, identify most closely?

3. *The Providential Man of Mystery*: In the *Decalogue*, Kieslowski has the Man of Mystery function as a providential figure. Have you had the experience in your own life where in critical moments you felt the presence of someone acting in your favor? Did you identify the person or persons with God's providential love?

Notes

1. Alberto Crespi, "La mia Bibbia senza certezze" ("My Bible with No Certainties"), *L'Unità*, September 19, 1989, 78.

2. Danusia Stok, ed., *Kieslowski on Kieslowski* (London: Faber and Faber, 1993), 149, 150. In contrast to these statements, in another interview, Kieslowski declares: "I am not a believer. For forty years I have not entered a church." Quoted by Tadeusz Sobolewski, "La solidarietà dei peccatori" ("Solidarity among Sinners"), in *Kieslowski*, ed. Malgorzata Furdal and Robert Turigliatto (Turin: Museo Nazionale del Cinema, 1989), 69.

3. Christopher Garbowski, *Krzysztof Kieslowski's Decalogue Series: The Problems*

of the Protagonists and Their Self-Transcendence (New York: Columbia University Press, 1996), 7. Beyond what Kieslowski might in fact believe, Garbowski speaks several times of his rejection of the Church, noting that "the director never felt himself attached with the institutional Church as such, or with Catholicism in particular," and that "Kieslowski himself had not much use for institutional Christianity." 6, 7.

4.   Garbowski, *Decalogue Series*, 7.

5.   Furdal and Turigliatto, *Kieslowski*, 27–28.

6.   The word is capitalized in the published text of the screenplays of the *Decalogue*: Krzysztof Kieslowski and Krzysztof Piesiewicz, *Decalogue: The Ten Commandments* (London: Faber and Faber, 1991), 228.

7.   Furdal and Turigliatto, *Kieslowski*, 68.

8.   Several critics note the allusion, and one of them sees it as reference to the horrific image of the crucifixion by Grunewald, adding that the image seems to be repeating the words of the dying Christ: "Father, forgive them. They do not know what they are doing." Garbowski, *Decalogue Series*, 18.

9.   Crespi,"La mia Bibbia senza certezze," 78.

10.   Stok, *Kieslowski on Kieslowski,* 158. Generally speaking, the critics do not know how to interpret this Man. Only three dare to suggest in him some level of spiritual significance. Gina Lagorio, *Il Decalogo di Kieslowski: Ricreazione narrativa* (Casale Monferrato: Piemme, 1992); Garbowski, *Decalogue Series*; and Emanuela Imparato, *Krzysztof Kieslowski: Il Decalogo: Per una lettura critica* (Rome: A.I.A.C.E., 1990).

11.   The allusion is to the poem, "Angel Surrounded by Paysans," by Wallace Stevens, in which the speaker says of himself, "I am the angel of reality. . . . Yes, I am the necessary angel of earth. . . ." Imparato, referring directly to Stevens's poem, refers to Kieslowski's Man of Mystery as the "Angel of the possible," *Il Decalogo*, 13–20. Several other lines the poem uncannily describe Kieslowski's Man of Mystery: "Am I not, / Myself, only half of a figure of a sort, / A figure half seen, or seen for a moment, a man / Of the mind, an apparition . . ." Wallace Stevens, *The Auroras of Autumn*, in *The Collected Poems* (New York: Knopf, 1989), 496.

12.   Garbowski, *Decalogue Series,* 18.

13.   In *Decalogue Ten*, the Man of Mystery is not present, effectively substituted by the transcendent, salvific reach of the grace of the exceptional humorous, playful tone and theme of the film and especially of its conclusion. The connection between the experience of joy and the experience of the Transcendent is made by the theologian Walter Kasper, who categorizes situations of great joy as being "disclosure situations," in which Holy Mystery breaks into human experience and reveals itself the subject. Kasper, *The God of Jesus Christ* (London: SCM Press, 1983), 85. Supporting the idea of Kasper though using different terminology, the sociologist Peter Berger qualifies the experience of joyful play, of laughter as "ec-static," and as one of the "signals of transcendence" in human experience. Berger, *The Sacred Canopy: Elements of a Sociological Theory of Religion* (Garden City, NY: Doubleday, 1969), 60.

14.   The Man's presence in *Seven* is so low-key that few of the critics notice him. My theology students, perhaps more sensitive than most to the spiritual meaning of this figure, almost always point him out and recognize immediately why Kieslowski represents him this way.

15.   In fact, in the Gospel, there is no conclusive evidence that Mary of Magdala (mentioned in Matthew 27:56, 61; 28:1; Mark 15:40, 47; 16:1; Luke 8:2; 24:10; and John 19:25;

20:1, 18) is a sinner. But from the sixth century onward, the tradition erroneously associates Mary of Magdala, Mary of Bethany, and the sinful woman in Luke 7:36–50. In the popular understanding, however, Mary Magdalene is the sinner saved by Jesus.

16. I have written a detailed analysis of the Christ metaphor operative in *Decalogue Six* and in its longer, original, version, *A Short Film about Love*. One is, "A Christ-Figure in Two Films of Kieslowski," a chapter in my *Imaging the Divine: Jesus and Christ Figures in Film* (Kansas City: Sheed and Ward, 1997), 172–84. A more detailed analysis of these films and their original script appear in *Gregorianum*. The articles are titled: "Cinematographic Variations on the Christ-Event: Three Film Texts by Krzysztof Kieslowski—Part One: *A Short Film about Love*" 84, no. 3 (2003), 551–83; and "Cinematographic Variations on the Christ-Event: Three Film Texts by Krzysztof Kieslowski—Part Two: *Decalogue Six* and the Script" 84, no. 4 (2004), 919–46.

17. Kieslowski died in Warsaw on March 13, 1996, of a heart attack following open-heart surgery. He was only fifty-four years old.

18. Since this chapter was written and submitted to the editor, Peter Malone, another major essay of mine has been published that, for the first time in Kieslowski scholarship, analyzes at length the nature and function of the Mystery Man—there I call him the "Silent Witness"—as a figure of Divine Providence. Lloyd Baugh, "The Grace of Divine Providence: The Identity and Function of the Silent Witness in the Decalogue Films of Kieslowski," *Gregorianum* 86, no. 3 (2005), 523–48.

14

Jésus de Montréal:
The Vision of Denys Arcand

Marc Gervais

May 1989: the Cannes Film Festival. I remember the feeling, call it elation, for we had just seen the international premiere of Denys Arcand's *Jésus de Montréal*. And as the festival continued, so did Canadian elation: The film folk from around the world—well, the serious ones anyway—were immensely impressed, sharing what seemed to be a general consensus that here indeed was the festival's best film, destined to win nothing less than the Palme d'Or in the official competition.

Cannes hosts the world's premier film festival, attracting thousands of film professionals. But the city really is not large: you keep bumping into people you know. Well, I had known Arcand for some decades. As part of my Jesuit training, I was his professor for what was supposed to be a university course on one William Shakespeare. And here we were, in Cannes, our roles having evolved, one of us the festival's darling, and the other (myself) a fledgling critic. Arcand had a bad cold, but that was not going to stop him as, racket in hand, he was rushing down a side street, on the way to a tennis court, and myself, naturally, admonishing him about his health. "I know, but I'm just fine. (long pause) It just doesn't get better than this." Denys was letting the moment happen, savoring it, and putting the experience into context.

But the fates love to work their own scenarios: *Jésus de Montréal*, to the fury of France's prestigious *Le Monde* and countless other critics (myself included), was beaten for best film by Steven Soderbergh's *Sex, Lies and Videotape*. Understandable, hindsight-wise: jury chairman that year was Wim Wenders, a dedicated devotee of American movies of the quirky variety, and much more attuned, methinks, to Soderbergh's world than to Arcand's.

But there was no doubt about it: Arcand was no longer just a promising prospect, he was in—especially if you happened to approach quality cinema the way I did and still do. As so many others, I had attained film maturity growing up in Hollywood's Golden Age and then coming into serious contact with neorealism and the ensuing richest period of film creativity ever, from the early fifties, say, to the late sixties. It is during that period that we became aggressively conscious of the immense artistic possibilities of film: Movies could, indeed, be great works of art; they could reflect culture, reality, our deepest doubts, fears, aspirations, the mystery of it all, or the human condition, just as literature and the arts have been doing, in their own right, for millennia. Cinema, we proclaimed, could play a privileged role in the advance of human consciousness.

So, during that period, giddy with these kinds of convictions, it became normal to await with impatience the next new discovery, and still more, of course, the next movie gem by a Roberto Rossellini, Federico Fellini, Michelangelo Antonioni, Ingmar Bergman, Alain Resnais, Francois Truffaut, Jean-Luc Godard, Kenzo Mizoguchi, Akira Kurosawa, Satyajit Ray, and so many others.

By the mid-seventies, alas, that incomparable creative outpouring was seriously diminishing. The truly great films were now much fewer and farther between. Other forces (the previous economic "realities") were reaffirming their overwhelming control, their understanding of popular entertainment, show business. Once again—to use a meaty metaphor—filet mignon was swamped by hamburger.

And so, by 1989, you can imagine our reaction when a film such as *Jésus de Montréal* appeared on the screen, with its obvious concerns, depth, intelligence, consciousness, technical skill, and artistry—its stamp of personal creativity, *elation* indeed.

Jésus de Montréal did garner some major awards at Cannes, including the Jury Prize. Many still rate the film as the finest Canadian feature ever made and maybe the best film ever on Jesus. It swept the Genies (Canada's Film Awards) for 1989, and it was a great box office hit in Canada. *Jésus de Montréal* also won the Ecumenical Award for artistic excellence combined with insight into the spiritual dimension of humanity. The citation read: "Because of its incisive contemporary re-reading of the Gospel in a rich and complex filmic form, playing on the relationship between spectacle and reality." Yes, and much more.

Quebec and Catholicism

All of which may lead neatly enough into this book's major concern: how, and to what extent, the Catholic background of certain film directors influences their filmmaking. A wee drop of historical contextualizing is peculiarly necessary at the level both of Arcand's personal background, and, given its rather unique nature, of the history of that part of Canada called Quebec. The context is what we might call (somewhat exaggeratedly) "Catholic culture going through an almost schizophrenic transformation."

It all goes back to a difference of colonizing approaches in the good old days of European triumphant. Britain and France started extending their tentacles into North America at about the same time, the 1600s. The British were talking real immigration into a new land, with fertile Protestant settlers creating a new agrarian society based on farms, with development to villages, towns, and cities. France, on the other hand, sent professionals, soldiers to protect the King's domains, explorers to discover yet new realms for His Majesty's enjoyment—and nuns for the schools and hospitals for the relatively few farmers and tradesmen. Add to that priests to minister to the spiritual needs of the new colony, and to convert the native *savages* to the Catholic Church. By 1763, when the French definitively ceded their New France territories (what corresponds in part nowadays to the Province of Quebec) to the British, the French colonists numbered barely sixty thousand, while the New England colonial population to the south numbered nearly three million.

New France had always been an extremely Catholic settlement, and the power of the clerics was huge, extending well beyond the religious sphere. This did not change when the British took over in 1763. Keenly aware of the constant threat of the ever-expanding, independent-minded, rambunctious Americans still officially subservient to the British Crown, in Canada the British (Anglicans and Protestants) wisely made an enormous, well-nigh unheard of concession to the conquered French settlers: in return for their cooperation and peace, the Catholics would enjoy freedom of religion. As a result, the power of the Catholic Church was now stronger than ever, overwhelmingly the main force in perpetuating some sort of French culture.

The situation became more obvious scarcely a dozen years later, when the American colonials actually rebelled against British rule (1776). When they wooed their northern neighbors to join them, they met total rejection: Catholic Quebec was not about to strike an alliance with the anti-Catholic Americans they did not trust. Quebec Catholic culture turned yet more in on itself; already feeling abandoned by France, cut off from recent centuries of European thought (rationalism, modernism, whatever) the French-Canadians learned with disgust about the excesses of the French Revolution, the guillotine and the enthroning of the Goddess of Reason on the high altar of Nôtre-Dame.

And so, the conquered descendants of New France were, to a surprising extent, on their own, the religious, cultural, political elite happy to develop their uniqueness, their adherence to an older, premodernist, Catholic culture. This, of course, proved a mixed blessing: a kind of religious, cultural freedom mitigated by intense clericalism coupled with severe control and a spirituality tinged by old-time French Jansenism—a recipe, surely, for creating serious problems, resentment included. And in any case you cannot stop new ideas (read European Enlightenment) from making their way, somehow or other, into the consciousness of educated people. Be that as it may, Quebec certainly became one of the most Catholic territories in the entire world—and this lasted over 150 years into World War II.

Arcand's Background

In 1941, in Deschambault, a tiny village on the Saint Lawrence River, about one hundred miles northeast of Montreal, Arcand was born into a family that was "middle ground between working class and bourgeoisie" (Arcand's words). His father was a river pilot and a "well paid technician." You might say that Arcand was born in quintessential old Quebec, the one I have been sketching in oversimplified terms. The only way the Arcands could afford to give their children a good education was to buy a house in Montreal and move there. This they did in 1953.

Little did they know—especially Arcand's mother, I would expect, who, as a young woman, had dreamed of becoming a Carmelite nun. Those were the closing years of Maurice Duplessis, the legendary Quebec Premier famous for his piety and his not totally holy compact with certain high-ranking church ecclesiastics and for repressive measures at just about every level of life: economic, political, social, and religious. But the time of unstoppable change was imminent, as Quebec literally caught up, in a few years, with hundreds of years of European modernist evolution. "The Quiet Revolution" is what Quebecers called it. One spectacular example of the changes that were to take place in the 1950s, 1960s, and 1970s: Proportionately speaking, almost nowhere else in the world, in terms of control, percentage of adherents, and vitality of practice, did the Catholic Church lose so much—and that even at a time when throughout the Western world the Church was suffering such heavy losses.

Arcand, from the beginning of his teens, spent his high school and college years at Collège Sainte Marie, a renowned Jesuit school in Montreal. No doubt Arcand would enrich his Catholic heritage with a strong philosophical and theological grounding, along with the riches from the rest of the classical humanities curriculum —spiced, no doubt, with whiffs of existentialist insight that were still the rage at the time. The winds, indeed, of contestation could be felt. For example, certain Jesuits were in serious trouble with Monsieur Duplessis and some of the Catholic hierarchy because of their severe critique of big business and its antilabor practices.

Of course, this was hardly the mainline orientation of Collège Sainte Marie, and the students and some of their professors may not have been aware of what really was going on. The college remained essentially orthodox. But a new kind of consciousness was fast developing. It was there, in 1957, that Arcand encountered Shakespeare, and so many other things. Besides, there was a famous theater at Sainte Marie, which still exists: the Gésu. Arcand loved it, worked there, learned, and made a little pocket money. Also, there was a film club (Quebec was way ahead of the rest of the world in this), a kind of extracurricular initiation into film culture. An immense discovery for him—and for the writer of this piece.

Indeed, these were important years—and Arcand's earlier cultural understanding was becoming immensely richer, more complex—and of course confused and disoriented. Bachelor in hand, he left the relatively unthreatening Sainte Marie and went on to the Université de Montréal, which was far more implicated in the cultural revolution that was changing Montreal. He obtained his Master of Arts in history and a strongly developed critical sense—and a devastating insight into the limitations and contradictions of all systems. Arcand was ready to take the plunge.

Early Career: Out of the Frying Pan and into the Fire

One of the things that attracted Arcand was film, and more or less fortuitously, he landed a job with the National Film Board of Canada. In the early sixties the Film Board (NFB) was already enjoying legendary status, richly earning its reputation as the true beginning of serious filmmaking in Canada. Not yet venturing into feature fiction movies—Canada obediently left that to Hollywood—the NFB was still dedicated totally to documentary, animation, and experimentation. Centered in Montreal, it was divided into an English Unit and a French Unit. And there's the rub. The NFB had been founded by John Grierson at the beginning of World War II to foster Canadian unity. But the times had changed, and here was the NFB's French Unit pushing French Canadian nationalism—seething with contestatory energy, flirting with Marxist economic and political analysis, and to an extent, even espousing separatist Quebec nationalism.

It is an extraordinary place to learn movie making, and Arcand plunged in. While he began mostly with rather innocuous and innocent documentaries, he learned the basics, and he worked with colleagues many of whom were steeped in an aesthetic of cinema shaped by a political-social conscience and consciousness. France and the film world were exploding with the Nouvelle Vague and such and you could be sure that the petits cousins in Quebec wanted to be part of the big movement.

Eventually, Arcand became a recognized name among this elite company, for among his documentaries were some of the most severe, most biting social/political/ideological film critiques yet seen in Canada. A few acquire real notoriety, suppressed for a time, then censored, and eventually released.

Arcand, then and now, could never be wholly pinned down to any specific ideology or militant movement. His "problem": Not only does he possess the tools of intelligence, passion, and education permitting him to expose capitalism's control of Quebec life, its exploitation of the workers, and the neutering of valid Quebec culture, but he is burdened with a terrible awareness and an anger at the victims as well, at their attitude of helplessness and their cultivation of submission to the system—for their own profit. And for him, it's not just the usual villains Quebec loves to blame (Ontario and "the English"). Already, for Arcand, it is specifically the presence of a certain American cultural and economic imperialism.

Arcand strikes even deeper; and here he is indebted to another current, the French existentialism of his earlier school years. He is burdened with a keen sense of the futility of all systems, a kind of existentialist recognition of generalized absurdity, with the concomitant anger and protestation. At least, let us say, that is part of the equation.

During the sixties and seventies, Arcand took leaves of absence from the NFB, to direct feature fiction films. These, if anything, are even darker, angrier exposés of the rich exploiting the poor, of the loathsome vulgarity and gross materialism that was then Quebec society. Call it a touch of Sartrian nausea? Indeed, the soul of Quebec was sick; and those struggling for something else seem doomed to futility. Ironically, perhaps, the virulence of the indignation also had echoes, one is tempted to suggest, of some of the old-time pulpit fulminations of the good old Catholic heyday of Arcand's childhood.

But this is no Savanarola, and there are no religious overtones. Arcand's cinema during this period cannot be typified as religious. There is indeed an innate moral thrust; and, yes, there is a caring, a concern for those aspiring to something else. But all seems overwhelmed by the nausea and anger—and that includes even the rich doses of humor that lighten the fundamental irony.

And the Catholic Church? Insofar as it appears at all, it is seen from a sociological vantage point—and found wanting.

The Decline of the American Empire

Had Arcand's career progressed no further, he certainly would have his place as a worthy contributor to the Quebecois film output of those days. However, in 1986, Arcand stunned the Canadian scene with *The Decline of the American Empire*, sweeping the Genie Awards (Canada's Oscars), and all manner of other awards in Canada and other parts of the world—including Cannes, where he won top prize in the prestigious Directors' Fortnight.

Here was an Arcand creating in another dimension, revealing a "true artist," a poetic sense, a brilliant command of sparkling high comedy dialogue, and the ability, nay, freedom to balance his devastating wit and awareness with tenderness, concern, dare I say even love for his characters. One senses a side to Arcand not totally removed from one of his French cinematic heroes, Jean Renoir, that unique mix of connivance and sympathy, of tragic awareness of human frailty, yet intuitive embracing of a life force.

The Decline of the American Empire focuses on a group of university professors, men and women he probably knows well, witty, articulate, self-aware—and in their self-knowledge and libidinous lifestyle progressively revealed to us as probably lost, as they share a weekend by beautiful Lake Memphremagog in Quebec's eastern townships. To attribute their reasonably comfortable, sexually muddled lifestyle to the effects of the American way of life in decline (as the film does) may seem a bit simplistic—but then think of it, the world's number one power and its overwhelming dominance in everything, from money and excessive consumerism including the world's richest and most evil businesses, such as pornography, the arms game, drugs. But I digress. . . . Three years later, Arcand would surpass this with his greatest achievement, *Jésus de Montréal*.

1989 and *Jésus de Montréal*

I shall attempt to focus in privileged fashion on this film, pleading anew that the rather long preamble was necessary if we are indeed to understand certain essential aspects of Arcand's creation. The roots of *Jésus de Montréal* are profoundly embedded in the feelings, knowledge, and judgments of that old-time Catholic Quebec culture that Arcand grew up in, in the North shore village of Deschambault. And by that I mean also things such as a personal, loving, living relationship difficult to explain rationally. And it is indeed well nigh impossible, on the broader scale, to conceive of the historical part of Quebec without this immense, central figure of Christ—or at least without reference to a certain Quebec experience of Catholicism as described so far.

But this childhood Jesus is definitely seen through the eyes of a film director who, by 1989, is fast approaching fifty. By 1989, it bears repeating, Quebec had made an enormous cultural leap. Even modernism's idols, such as Darwin, Marx, and Freud, scarcely had time to achieve icon status and by 1989 one had to add the post prefix before their names, for Postmodernism, that hybrid mix, was at its peak, challenging, mocking both modernism and the previous Catholic culture of the past. And so that left us human beings, with all our pretensions and ambitions and so-called knowledge, relegated to the role of mere pawns in a game of cultural substitutions, including "reality out there." Even while admitting that you are touched by longings, hopes of love, even the possibility of finding meaningfulness, what you have to cultivate in this cultural mode is achieving "cool": Enjoy the game, the irony, the "humor" knowing more or less that we're all drifting.

From the beginning of *Jésus de Montréal*, Arcand reveals that he is a master of the game. We sit in the darkness of the cinema theater, and all we see on the screen is a graininess—darkness. Then, voices, intensely, dramatically uttering desperate words, gradually we gather that there are two actors—and then we see them, performing on the stage, the camera moving, cutting back and forth. We are mesmerised by the power of the words, the intensity of the acting: serious stuff, this, a climatic confrontation between two characters from Dostoyevsky's monumental novel *The Brothers Karamazov*: The essential cry rings out as one character abandons the other in his prison cell, leaving him alone in a despairing monologue about modern man facing nothingness, because he has destroyed the presence of God within himself.

The anguish is theatrical, unbearable, as, finally, he hangs himself. Cut to the audience (within the film), their faces exalted, transformed, troubled, some of them weeping. Then a standing ovation, shouts of deep-felt "bravo." Arcand pushes the actors pretty far, though certainly not to the level of caricature. We know they are acting, yet we are moved, even troubled (like the audience). This movie, we may feel, is going to be tackling pretty serious aspects of the human condition.

The audience that we eventually see, however, is another matter—Quebecers would certainly recognize most of them: show biz types, stars, critics, talk show hosts, a typical opening night "paper" audience that hopefully will publicize the play. And their apparel, make-up, and such are a bit much. We cannot help smiling at Arcand's view of them, even although we share the emotional impact they have just experienced. But when Arcand cuts to backstage, caricature pretty well takes over. The visitors, too, are performing; the dialogue becomes silly, at times even nasty—though the actors we see in the play are the exception: Arcand always treats them with respect, even affection (except for the ones who actually have nasty key roles in the Arcand movie).

And then the handsome lead actor, somewhat extenuated, detached after the stage high of his performance, frees himself from a high-powered, predatory female television producer (played by a distinguished Montreal actress) who is trying to pin him down for her next major campaign ("*l'homme sauvage*"), as he recognizes in the background another actor saying "Now there's a real actor."

That other actor, dressed nondescriptively casual (not that different, perhaps, from the attire of the real Jesus of Nazareth of two thousand years ago, has been quietly watching. "Daniel, when did you get back? And what are you doing here?" "I'm trying to get inspired." "For?" "I'm doing Jesus."

Cut to the credits, the cinema overflows with glorious, well-known sacred music (Pergolese's Stabat Mater: "And there Jesus' mother Mary stood") played by an orchestral ensemble and sung by two young women backed by a choir. A huge circular stained-glass window illuminates all from the background: We are in the choir loft, the young women, faces softly illuminated and their voices, indeed beautiful. Classical music qua familiar beloved religious icon. No caricature here, no falseness, no irony: We are genuinely moved. The credits still roll as Arcand cuts down (wide, plunging high-angle shot) to the now familiar figure of Daniel, the actor who is "doing Jesus," standing small, below, looking up, Montreal's huge and most recognizable icon, St. Joseph's Oratory.

A series of reverse angle shots (from above and from below) alternate. By now, we, the real movie audience, have had plenty of time to interiorize—and to be moved by the sacred beauty and to become thoughtful. A tall fiftyish/sixtyish, rather handsome priest dressed in business suit and roman collar, appears, walks over to Daniel: "Ah, there you are—come, I want to show you something." Cut to Daniel watching a video of "the Jesus Passion Play" that has been staged by the "Sanctuary" (the movie's name for the real "Oratory" we have just seen). In fact, a passion play actually was staged in the summer for many years on Mount Royal, near St. Joseph's Oratory.

This time, Arcand pulls out the stops: the video is a series of almost unbelievably caricatured scenes of pseudo-religious piety surrounding Jesus's Passion.

We cannot help laughing—and we can almost hear Arcand's laughter as well. What in heaven's name is going on in this movie?

The priest explains that he has been staging this version of the passion play for years, that it is now seriously outmoded, that it needs updating, reviewing, whatever. Would Daniel do it? Daniel accepts. He recognizes one of the actresses in the video (Constance), with whom he studied in theater school. "Yes, she's talented," replies the priest. "If you wish, by all means use her," and then the plot of *Jésus de Montréal* is launched.

Arcand and His Audience

The viewer is off-balance, intrigued, amused, and confused. The obvious insistence that this is all a show, that this is controlled manipulation, a self-reflective exercise in art (read cultural fabrication) makes us wonder what Arcand is up to. How does he want us to react—and why? What is his attitude, what is his agenda: self-serving, show-off prestidigitation, mockery of the whole Christ Passion mystique long informing our culture? One need but think of the brittle superficiality of the show people, the control mechanisms already hinted at of the church presence and of the advertising business—and Arcand's distaste.

Daniel is an actor of mysterious recent background, who must engage in research and must form a team of actors, and rewrite (i.e., make contemporary) a passion play.

So we find him in a soup kitchen. Indeed, his attire would almost qualify him as one of the recipients. But Arcand has tricked us again, playfully: As Daniel extends his soup bowl, he is served by Constance, whom we recognize from the Passion video. Next they're sitting eating—and talking: oh yes, she likes to help out here—and it does save her a bit of money. "Where are you staying?" she asks. "Oh, here and there." "Good, come with me, I've got lots of room in my loft." So—it's still early in the game—we are beginning to catch subtle parallels with, or allusions to, the New Testament. "Jesus" (who will be played by Daniel himself) seeks Constance out, and she, very much like Martha, sister of Mary Magdalene, will be seen constantly helping people, preparing meals, constant indeed in her life of charitable service. And already I apologize for my rather literal heaviness, so foreign to the movie's relaxed, easy openness.

And then she brings Daniel to another actor played by Rémy Gerard. Yes, his name happens to be "Peter"—and broke, he happens to be dubbing a porno film—played by France's distinguished film star, Marie-Christine Barrault. We are astonished—and it is all hilariously crazy. Peter is only too happy to join Daniel.

And then he leads Daniel and Constance to another kind of recording studio, where another actor (played by Robert Lepage, in reality a Quebec actor/ writer/director well-known across the world for his progressive, free-form theatrical experimentations). He is doing voice-over for a (literally) awesomely

overwhelming documentary on the origins of the universe. We watch with the
stunned actors, sharing the moment—but alas, we also see him decline Daniel's
invitation, despite being mightily attracted to join.

Cut to a stunning young woman: We learn that she is from Paris, classically
trained—and doing modeling and commercials obviously anchored in sexual
exploitation. Fighting with her director boyfriend—we feel his bullying and his
contempt—she rebels, walking out on him. Lost, desperate, and afraid—we find
her knocking at Constance's door. No doubt about it, however she may have been
heard this intense "Magdalene" is "seeking Jesus." Back in Constance's loft the
three are joined by the voice-over experimental actor. "I've thought it over: would
you let me do 'to be or not to be' if I join you?" Rejoicing!—and how smoothly,
with what freshness has Arcand led us into the parallel with the Gospels' Jesus's
choosing of his apostles—only now, they will be only four, plus Daniel,
actors/stagehands, a tiny company of five in what will be a free-form, almost
street-theater style of presentation.

Arcand further makes the enterprise of organizing his material appear effort-
less and none too obvious, as he mixes these moments in with other kinds of plot
character. His first morning on waking up in the loft, we see Daniel playing with
single mother Constance's little girl, who walks out of Constance's bedroom, and
the Oratory Priest, putting on his tie. He is naturally somewhat embarrassed as he
says to Daniel: "As you see, not all priests are good priests." The priest's name,
by the way, is Père Leclerc (a common French name meaning, literally, the cleric). Ah yes, the clerics. There does seem something real in the relationship, but
essentially, as she confides to Daniel, this is another of her charitable deeds.

The Figure of Jesus

Daniel, meanwhile, is plunging into his research on Jesus. We see him perched
high up on a sort of balcony in a huge library, holding a huge tome: *Crucifixion
in Roman Times*. A strange lady comes by with a pushcart full of books: "Are you
searching for something?" Daniel answers, "Yes, I am searching." Wisely, profoundly: "Then you will find," as she wheels her articles away. And we are tempted to giggle: another incarnation of contemporary spirituality. Not for long.
Daniel is standing outside an imposing university building with another man, a
"real Quebec" cleric. This priest is a rather nervous professor of theology.
Furtively, he hands some documents to Daniel: "Please be careful. Don't tell anyone I gave you these photocopies." As Daniel objects, he insists: "Remember, the
Church still runs the Theology Faculty." The two, in imposing high angle shots,
are dwarfed by the building as the priest speaks about "the latest historical findings about the real Christ. If this ever gets out . . ." As the two part, Daniel walks
slowly, pondering, ultimately to be framed by the camera in a long-held composition with a cross in the background.

No doubt about it, Arcand is tightening the game. In the Gospel narrative, clearly the priests of that time and place were against Christ, opposing his views: They were his chief persecutors. In *Jésus de Montréal*, we do not see a single priest or church official who is sympathetic, brave, fundamentally honest, helpful to others, or "spiritual" to any degree. Far from being Jesus-like, they are impersonal, institutional figures, out of touch, caretakers holding on to jobs, without joy or vitality.

And an opposition is set up by Arcand: the church, on one hand, and Jesus/Daniel, whose own way of the cross has begun. The results of his research (presumably Arcand's research in writing the script for the movie) find their way into the new passion play, one which puts Daniel in serious opposition to the church authorities.

Those findings, many of which seek to "deconstruct" the "divine Jesus" of traditional faith and devotion, are highly contentious and far from being accepted by most of the world's leading biblical scholars, but seem more or less to be accepted by Arcand for the most part. All of which leads to the obvious question: Where is Arcand in all of this, what is he up to, and what is the audience to make of it all? Or perhaps one should face another uncomfortable possibility first, one that might well stand in the way of a serious analysis of the movie. To put it crudely: Is *Jésus de Montréal* a sort of cheap shot anticlerical diatribe?

I smile as I write these lines, for that seems far from the spirit that animates this film, even if, more than once in the past, Arcand may have earned his reputation of unrelenting satirist and critic about so many things in Quebec. The best character study in the film, for example, may well be that of Leclerc, the priest who is revealed in all his weakness, yet whose dilemma we understand: The young man who long ago joined the Church, because, in his poverty, it was the only way for him to receive advanced education and thereby by be able to pursue his great love of the theater. In a powerful scene in the great Oratory Church as Daniel confronts him painfully crying out against what he feels is the compromise, the power clinging, the lack of real understanding of the people, Arcand gives Leclerc wonderful lines, showing his concern for the poor, the sick, and the downtrodden—how this church affords comfort and solace. But once again, no statement of spiritual belief, a terrible lack in whatever that indeed may be, is the crucial factor that explains the critically reduced number of priests left in Quebec since the mass exodus in the sixties and subsequent years.

But one essential position is clearly reiterated: The "Jésus" of Montréal cannot be identified with the existing institutional Catholic Church of 1989 as described by Arcand. Jesus as presented in Daniel's passion play is never heard making claims of divinity, divine sonship, things that the young Arcand would have been taught, would have recited over and over again in childhood days— something he would have shared with the overwhelming majority of the Quebec culture since its earliest days.

Arcand in many ways is actually affirming Jesus. Progressively, Arcand presents Daniel as a Christ figure. It is there, suggested in his attire, his words, and his attitudes: the honesty, the caring for the poor, the intense sense of moral values, such as truth and justice, the caring, insightful concern, and the unrelenting castigating of those who exploit others, the profiteers from corruption, and the hypocrites. And as a result, the mounting opposition thereby created with these forces. And perhaps strongest of all: his ability to see deep into the minds and hearts of men and women and to elicit a profound response in those whom he touches; his power to make them acknowledge their own profound desire for goodness, truth, for living genuine lives, for becoming loving human beings, and for refusing to give in to the corruption of the world.

One might say that the experience of Jesus that Arcand still clings to is that of the little boy who grew up in Deschambault, who never lost his love and admiration for that aspect of Jesus. Arcand readily admits this.

Arcand's text goes one big step further: His filmic text, with its shifts of tone, is embracing of everything from farce to high seriousness, its multilevels and multidirections point to a deeper, perhaps more tragic doubt. *Jésus de Montréal* is not a C. B. DeMille super spectacle literal, pious *The Greatest Story Ever Told*, neurotic transposition of *The Last Temptation of Christ*, or something akin to Pier Paolo Pasolini's profound and radically politicized *The Gospel According to Matthew*.

Daniel's modernized text is indeed radically different, a mix of obviously familiar Gospel parallel moments, new research commentary, and the close direct addressing of the growing audiences, much as the Gospel Christ engaged in. The media folk we have grown accustomed to by and large love it, the play is an immense success, and its effects, at times charismatic.

"Jesus" confronts some of the Oratory priests who come to watch it with appropriate Gospel inspired texts. The play is courting trouble. There are jokes; a few sympathetic bungling security officers and their own unconscious (hilarious) contributions—they are not the enemy, they are "the lowly."

The tension mounts, the tone becoming more and more obviously paralleling the historical Jesus in events within the play and events surrounding it. We are being drawn into tragic overtones and dimensions. Daniel being Daniel (Jesus being Jesus?) means, inevitably, showdowns with dark forces of the world.

In one extraordinary sequence, for example, Daniel accompanies the beautiful, vulnerable Magdalene actress for her beer commercial audition (she is desperate for money). As the producer and the director try to demean her for their own gratification and for the benefit of the boys who are the sponsors, Daniel explodes, "turning over" the precious television equipment (as Jesus did to the money changers in the temple) and actually slapping the female producer in the face, literally chasing everybody out. Daniel comes before a judge (played with humor by Arcand himself). The trial is delayed, thanks to the judge's pro-Daniel connivance and that of a sympathetic psychological expert.

The Temptations

Daniel is, at least momentarily, free, standing with a slick media lawyer in a posh circular moving restaurant atop a Montreal skyscraper. Accompanied by the standard bimbo, whom he treats with contempt, the lawyer weaves his pattern on Daniel: "let me handle your career and I'll make this city yours," as they look at the great city below them. Just mentioning these scenes means little, except for the obvious Gospel references to Christ in the temple and Christ being tempted by the devil. But the mastery of Arcand's artistic control and the intensity and relevance he achieves are overwhelming, translating the experience into our world, enriching our insight, our revulsion or guilt feelings over our own semiaware connivance—our sheeplike acceptance.

Arcand's profound anger at the abuse of the media world, the world of spectacle making and commercials and sexual exploitation that he, willy-nilly, is professionally part of, seems far more intense and personal than his disappointment in the contemporary Catholic Church. The viewer is outraged at the sleaziness of these overwhelming contemporary enterprises. Arcand makes us reflect on their control of cultures—one is tempted to say the corruption of it all.

As the media lawyer attempts to seduce Daniel, high, overlooking the city, one is overwhelmed by the cynicism, the destruction of all values, the obscenely easy money and luxury—compared with the countless victims below—and the relentless quest of the Big Money predators to control all, to reduce all to monetary "values." This is Arcand's skill, his ability to suggest so much that is hidden, his intense loathing of the corruption of spirit.

As one watches Daniel and thinks of the Christ of the Gospels, one realizes (as they did) that there is no place for Jesus, for his vision, and his values in this world. The magic of Arcand's art is that he uses no spectacular, souped-up dramatic means to bring us to this insight, but simply a low-key scene of media money smarts at work in a Montreal skyscraper restaurant.

Passion and Resurrection

Inevitably is indeed the word: Daniel is drawn into Christ's Passion. The comedy moments, the witty asides, and cleverness disappears: The "world" must crucify Jesus/Daniel. The ultimate, literal turning point occurs as Daniel is "doing Jesus," being nailed to a cross. In the last burlesque moment of the film, a mini-riot breaks out as the security officers follow their orders and attempt to close the show. Things get out of control: The profoundly moved spectators try to save the play and "Jesus." Accidentally, a beam wielded by a pro-Jesus professional wrestler strikes the helpless Daniel on the head. He slumps, unconscious, on his cross and the final lamentations begin, a Good Friday ritual, Montreal 1989 style.

The two actresses watch over him as an ambulance arrives. Like the women who stood by Jesus to the end—while the men scattered—they accompany Daniel to a typical major hospital. Dreadfully overcrowded and bureaucratized, the place is a shambles of patients waiting in hallways, corridors, and in the emergency ward, the women trying to fill out the forms. It is painfully dehumanized.

Then they find Daniel risen, walking in the corridor. "I feel okay, just a bad headache," as they walk out of the hospital with him. Cut to a Montreal Metro Underground Station as they await the train. Daniel begins to wander deliriously. In the bowels of the earth, he moves from one group of silent waiters to another, reciting apocalyptic end-of-the-world prophecies on the destruction of the city— as did Jesus on his final walk to Calvary. The words are similar; Daniel's voice a kind of keening, of intense spiritual suffering, *Dies Irae*. Constance desperately seeks a phone as Daniel slumps to the ground, unconscious, with the Magdalene actress holding him, weeping.

Now Arcand completes his final adaptation tactics. The same ambulance has returned and carried Daniel and the two women from the station, the people standing like statues, quiet as the dead. A huge poster proclaiming L'homme Sauvage, a man's deodorant, looks down with the handsome young Dostoyevsky actor, from the opening of the movie as model.

The ironies abound: Jesus is brought to the Montreal Jewish Hospital, a human haven (as it is, relatively speaking) among Montreal's major hospitals. Familiar emergency procedures (we have seen them in so many television shows) are followed, with efficiency and kindness. But they lose Daniel. The sympathetic doctor hesitantly asks the two weeping women: "But his heart is still healthy— his eyes—would you give us permission to transplant them?" A bit lost, the women agree. Arcand cuts to other procedures, the organs finally being flown to another Quebec City, Sherbrooke, where they are successfully given to two grateful recipients.

These scenes are at once clinical and cold, yet overwhelmingly moving when the recipients respond. Arcand then cuts to the aftermath where the media lawyer is talking to the four actors: Given Daniel's recent fame, a new theater company should be formed. "With Peter as the head?" Yes, they agree—in the renovating, experimental spirit of Daniel. All smooth, polite; the lawyer has won, it would seem.

Except for one of the four, our Magdalene character, who walks off. . . . It is evening, tears in her eyes, a beautiful view of the city as she stands somewhere on one of the mountain lookouts. A spirit of love and hope, as she faces the limitless vistas, transformed, sad, yet, indeed, a new person. Arcand then cuts to the Metro beneath the city, a place familiar to us. The two young women who were singing the Stabat Mater in the Oratory near the beginning of the film are doing just that once again—but now in the subway station—with occasional passers-by dropping coins in a dish at their feet. Once again the beautiful music sounds fill the theater as the camera tilts and travels up, gradually capturing a high dark concrete wall, traveling up—closing credits.

And we are left with the thoughts and the music. There is great sadness, yet a profound peacefulness, even exaltation and holiness in the midst of the profane.

And so Arcand has been true to the end, true to *Jésus de Montréal*, that is, this exercise in capturing a fundamental Quebec culture. The double language continues to the end—even the beautiful and tender Pergolese music gradually ceding to a quiet recorded contemporary musak-sort-of rock.

Daniel has died, but his heart has given new life to another man, and his eyes sight to another woman who was blind. Are these symbols of Jesus's resurrection and new vision or "miracles of modern science?" There is no simple answer to this kind of question in Arcand's film, no univocal way of explaining things, of pinning him down.

And for all the jokes, ironies, and double meanings for the possibility of subverting official Christian interpretations, there is no way of destroying these beliefs. The culture of that pre-1950s Quebec is not wholly extinct: A profound religious feeling permeates the movie, the ever-present Great Questions (that underlie the religious experience). Arcand can go no further in expressing himself, his culture, in this postmodern grappling with the mystery of Jesus and contemporary humanity.

As I write these lines on May 23rd, 2003, fourteen years later again here in Cannes, as the world's greatest film festival comes to an end once again an amazingly fitting postscript is being worked out. Denys Arcand, now 62 years old, is once again in contention, in his most amazing achievement yet: *The Barbarian Invasions* (*Les Invasions Barbares*), a kind of return to the characters and world of *The Decline of the American Empire* which he brought to Cannes in 1986.

But far more importantly—and however the decision may go—Arcand is enjoying his greatest moments as a film artist. And in terms of the piece just written, let me just add that *The Barbarian Invasions* could easily be analyzed within the terms of reference used for *Jésus de Montréal*. It is a film dedicated to life on earth and the mystery of death, a hilarious comedy of intense emotional power, celebration, love, and human destiny. And the search? Right to its final symbol of the voyage into infinity, it poses the problem and sets up the opposed answers to humanity's central question: Is life ended by death, or is it eternal?

(*The Barbarian Invasions* won awards for Marie Josee Croze for Best Actress and significantly for Arcand himself, Best Screenplay. It then went on to win the Academy Award for Best Foreign Language Film of 2003.)

Reviewing the Chapter

1. Arcand, when interviewed about *Jésus de Montréal*, said that it was impossible to make a Jesus movie because we really don't know anything about him. Does his film bear this out? How successful a Jesus movie has he made?

2.   While Arcand had a traditional Catholic upbringing, he declares that he does not believe in the church. *Jésus de Montréal* is about faith, about search, a critique of the church while making an appeal to Gospel teachings and an outreach to other religions. Is it true to say that *Jésus de Montréal* is a religious film?

3.   Arcand's cultural and religious background is French Canadian Catholic. From the 1960s, the Quebecois reacted strongly against their Catholicism, many abandoning it. Does *Jésus de Montréal* give insights into this Canadian reaction against the tradition?

Part 6

Catholic–Jewish Relationships

Relationships between Christians and Jews have been tense since the deeper separation and parting of the ways between the two groups at the end of the first century. While acknowledging the roots of Christianity in the history of God's dealing with Israel, the Catholic Church took harsh stances against the Jews in succeeding centuries. The shameful persecution of Jews, the deep-seated anti-Semitism that has tainted the behavior of many Catholics in recent decades, manifested themselves in nineteenth-century pogroms in Eastern Europe. This played its part in the culmination of anti-Semitism in "the final solution" of the Holocaust and the millions of deaths in the concentration camps.

It was only in the immediate postwar years that Hollywood began to portray anti-Semitism in such films as *Gentlemen's Agreement*, which won the Oscar for Best Film in 1947.

The Second Vatican Council explicitly acknowledged the sins of its anti-Semitic past and took a stand against the religious reason given for anti-Semitic attitudes and behavior: "True, the Jewish authorities and those who followed their lead pressed for the death of Christ; still, what happened in His passion cannot be charged against all the Jews, without distinction, then alive, nor against the Jews of today." This has been the official position of the Catholic Church, confirmed symbolically by John Paul II's visit to Israel in the Christian Jubilee year, 2000, and his gesture of inserting his written prayer into the crevice of the Wailing Wall.

Two directors with Catholic backgrounds have dramatized the plight of the Jews during World War II and the action of Catholics. Louis Malle experienced a strict French Catholic upbringing, which he later abandoned. Claire Openshaw shows how he drew on it to remember his schooldays during the war, the sheltering of Jewish students in a Catholic school and both kindness and betrayal.

Roberto Benigni's Oscar-winning *La Vita è bella* also took audiences back to World War II, focusing again on a child who shares the experience of his Jewish father in Auschwitz. Benigni dares to combine presentation of the terrible regime in the camp with the tender comedy of a father trying to shield his son from the horror. Dario Vigano places *La Vita è bella* in the context of Benigni's other films and his faith.

Auschwitz is located in Poland, and Poland has a tradition of anti-Semitism. The three major directors from Poland in the later decades of the twentieth century are Andrzej Wajda, Krzysztof Kieslowski, and Krzysztof Zanussi. Zanussi is the forcefully Catholic director, making a biography of the young John Paul II and filming one of his plays, *God's Brother*. Kieslowski professed himself agnostic while exploring transcendent values in his *Decalogue*, *The Double Life of Veronique*, and his Three Colors series. For almost fifty years Wajda has dramatized Polish history and society. He comes from the complex Polish background of traditional Catholicism but a more secular experience of filmmaking during the Communist regime.

Jan Epstein is an Australian Jewish author who has worked with Catholic organizations in reviewing and serving on festival juries for the Catholic Church. Attentive to Jewish themes in Wajda's work, she looks at his film, *Land of Promise*, Wajda's portrait of industrialists at the beginning of the twentieth century, and asks whether Wajda (who critiqued the Communist regime just before the Solidarity movement in *Man of Marble* and later, in *Man of Iron*) reflects some of this Polish anti-Semitism.

15

Memory's Progress:
Ambiguity in Louis Malle's
Au Revoir Les Enfants

Claire Openshaw

In 1944 the Gestapo captured three Jewish schoolboys and the Catholic priest who had hidden them, sending them to their death in concentration camps. This happened in full view of their young classmates.

Film director Louis Malle was in that class. The words "*Au Revoir les Enfants*" were the last Malle heard his teacher say, and the first he wrote. Beginning with this ending he constructed a screenplay that revisits the country, community, and Catholicism of his childhood—not merely a reconstruction but characterization and narrative that debates truth and humanity at this remarkable time in his life.

Reading Malle as a Catholic film director raises a number of questions. Is it the issues and imagery of a religious childhood that influence his films or did his childhood awaken a will to look at moral themes? This chapter argues it is not his rejection of the church that puts him at odds with his religion. He idealizes the dignity of the priest's sacrifice and through this embraces a dimension of his Catholicism beyond imagery and discourse. However, he consciously remains an outsider and spectator, as he does not have faith.

Au Revoir les Enfants is clearly his most personal film. The voice-over in the final sequence is Malle. This final scene is so quiet, so dignified. There's no struggle, no outrage, just horror. And in this silence Malle tells his audience this is the defining moment of his life, and it has been with him every day since he stood in the schoolyard and watched these people being taken.

It took Malle twenty-five years to even consider putting the haunting events of his childhood on screen and another thirteen years passed before he began to write the screenplay. The extraordinary events portrayed were all too common-place in his childhood. When he had the first draft of the screenplay Malle checked its factual accuracy with other witnesses. Sections of the film are his interpretation of events, and witnesses disagreed about the details, particularly who had actually betrayed the children. Malle believed the narrative effectively portrayed the memory that he lived with over the subsequent years. "Memory is not frozen, it's very much alive, it moves, it changes."[1] The truth for him was not rigid details but an expression of the devastating effects of people's casual choices.

Pontifical Council Selection

Au Revoir les Enfants was included in the list of films compiled by the Pontifical Council for Social Communications as having special artistic and religious merit. This list was put together to mark the one hundredth anniversary of cinema and sent out as part of an information pack on discernment in film appreciation. However, like many of his other films, the Catholic clergy in *Au Revoir les Enfants* are presented ambiguously. Malle is always unwilling to present a one-dimensional ethical framework or a clear-cut battle between good and evil. He prefers to challenge the audience to appraise a 360-degree view of what is happening. The dynamics and actions present complex characters and situations.

This philosophical approach is at the heart of his films and certainly true of the characters in *Au Revoir les Enfants*. His portrayal of the occupying German soldiers, teaching priests, and French adults and children does not give us clear heroes and devils, although he does show us heroic and evil actions. Just as the audience is appalled by these evil actions, they are also made all too aware that the atrocities are the result of casually taken decisions. As in life, his characters are rarely aware of the implications of their actions until after the event if, at times, at all.

Malle, who rejected the rigid Catholicism of his education, explores a spiritual quest in most of his films. And it is usually the quest of an individual. Individual choice is much more part of Catholic life today. The post-Vatican II congregation is made up of individuals with diverse ethical beliefs that often conflict with the official teaching of the institutional church. Although this ambiguity will always have been present, it has now really found its voice. Both clergy and lay individuals explore their ethical position and do not necessarily have the guilt that is characteristic of earlier generations. The non-Catholic community often perceives these liberal beliefs and behavior as hypocrisy.

Louis Malle

Louis Malle was born in Thumeries near Lille, northern France, in 1932. He grew up in a mansion and was brought up in a strict Catholic faith by middle-class parents.

During the occupation his family moved to Paris. Educated initially by Jesuits, he was later moved to a boarding school in Fontainebleau. The head of the school, a Carmelite priest, provided a hiding place for Jewish schoolboys.

Malle worked on over thirty films before his death from cancer in 1995. The range of subjects covered is extraordinary. He first worked as a highly praised underwater cameraman with Jacques Cousteau and continued to make documentary films throughout his career, including his personal travelogues of India, as well as films commissioned by French and American governments.

David Cronenberg, director of *Videodrome* and *Crash*, talking[2] about his own films, claimed that genre is merely a critics' problem, at best an effective tool to sell a film rather than having any creative value for filmmakers. For Malle this certainly seems to be the case. He is rarely interested in genre's cinematic conventions to explore his themes. Although his work is not easy to categorize in terms of genre, he manages to thread questions about truth and experience in his films as he takes you across continents and centuries through historical or imagined environments. Working with inexperienced actors and non-actors as well as Hollywood stars, like Burt Lancaster, or French cinema icons, such as Brigitte Bardot, he explores the spirit of the individual as it is tested by life. The extremes of family relationships, community tensions mobilized by economic pressure, and the often dire consequences of a person's arbitrary choices provide the context for many of his films. Even in his studio films, Malle explored ethically challenging situations involving child prostitution and racial tension.[3] This ambiguity challenges anyone in the audience who sees the world from a narrow, rigid perspective.

Au Revoir les Enfants begins with boys boarding a train to return to school after spending Christmas with their families. The story focuses on Julien Quentin, an intelligent and outwardly popular boy, who misses his family life, particularly his mother. This scene at the station establishes Julien's sense of isolation and detachment. When a group of new boys arrives at the school one of them, Jean Bonnet, challenges Julien's position as top of the class. As the story unfolds Julien becomes suspicious of Jean's real identity, questioning his background and behavior. When Julien searches Jean's belongings, he finds a book with Jean's real family name, Kippelstein. Eventually he confronts him about his Jewish identity. As the friendship between Jean and Julien develops, Julien perceives similarities in their circumstances, as both are lonely, detached from their families because of the war. Both boys cling to letters from their mothers, but the young unworldly-wise Julien does not realize the enormity of Jean's situation in hiding. His father is a prisoner of war, and he is unsure whether his mother is safe. It is only in the final scenes when the Gestapo take the Jewish boys that Julien's horror forces his understanding of the war to move from the abstract to the personal.

Although acknowledging the success of *Au Revoir les Enfants*, Malle resented[4] audiences who saw the film as a simple holocaust story portraying the premature end of this friendship between Jew and Gentile children. For him the portrayal of the closeted world of the school and surrounding occupied France is critical to an understanding of the film. Likewise in considering Malle as a Catholic director, it is essential to consider the France of Malle's childhood, where he received his Catholic education.

Collapse of Vichy France

The film is set at a time of breakdown for France in the Second World War. The French nation had not recovered from its losses during the First World War, and life for ordinary people was extraordinarily difficult. Marshal Petain had established the Vichy government as part of the armistice between Germany and France in July 1941. Petain, the hero of Verdun in World War I, was eighty years old by this time. The mythology that surrounded him created his identity as a caring and responsible leader in war. With power equivalent to both president and prime minister he led a deeply authoritarian government. It aimed to establish a moral order around ideals of *Travail, Famille,* and *Patrie* (Work, Family, and Homeland) based on respect for hierarchy and authority that echoed the propaganda of its Nazi occupiers. This was generally accepted at first as people sought stability, even of this kind. Also anti-Semitism had an established history in France with Jewish property being seized as far back as the early fourteenth century.[5] The recent Popular Front government, headed by Leon Blum, had ended in the 1930s, leaving devaluation of the franc and increased social tension. The resulting right-wing backlash was anti-Semitic as well as anti-communist. In *Au Revoir les Enfants* we hear Julien's mother saying

> Mind you, I have nothing against Jews. On the contrary. Except for that Socialist Blum, of course. He deserves hanging.

This is Malle quoting his own mother, a member of the bourgeois Beghin family who were descended from French nobility and owned the sugar processing factory that Malle's father managed. Anti-Semitic legislation introduced in 1940 was led by the French rather than by the German occupying forces. It meant that French Jews could not be employed in politics, as civil servants, teachers, or journalists, and introduced quotas for other professions. Of course it also meant Jews were allowed no place in the French film industry. René Clair and Jean Renoir went to the United States, and Jewish distribution companies, such as Siriztky, were seized.[6] The Vichy government also supported the seizure of Jewish property and deportation of foreign Jews.

Malle refused to believe a postwar version of events that claimed the French population was largely unaware of what was happening.

> When I hear or read that most people in France didn't know anything about the fate of the Jews—that's an incredible lie. If they didn't know, it was because they didn't want to know. As I said, my parents knew and told us about it. I remember how shocking it was when the yellow stars first appeared.[7]

Anti-Semitism

Scenes within the film show passive anti-Semitism, small betrayals and careless-ness as well as small acts of bravery showing defiance and courage.

When the boys visit the bathhouse a sign is displayed prominently outside saying "No Jews allowed." As they leave a young man pulls on his coat with its yellow Star of David as he strides down the steps. The audience has seen German soldiers inside. One of the boys comments in surprise that a Jew would dare to flout this rule. Throughout the film the boys are shown as naïve, with little under-standing of the courage that even this small act of defiance must take. They are spectators, protected from what is happening around them by the walls of the school. They adopt the political stance of their parents on trust rather than under-standing. Even Francois, Julien's brother, who makes fun of Julien for talking of having a vocation, is light-hearted in comments about joining the resistance. Malle wanted the structure of the film to reflect this: "We were surrounded by walls, somewhat pretending the war was not taking place, feeling protected. . . . I thought it was important, little by little to show the war breaking in."[8]

Later in the film Julien, his mother, Francois, and Jean visit a restaurant, also forbidden to Jewish customers. The sequence begins with a waiter lighting a cus-tomer's cigarette. It is a respectful gesture. The customer, Mr. Meyer, is Jewish. The French militia arrive and after asking for identity papers, he is made to leave. The waiter will not do this, as Meyer has been a customer for twenty years. After this considered action by the waiter, Francois recklessly calls the militia collabo-rators. His self-perception as a hero quickly dissolves as the restaurant breaks out in uproar. Malle is all too conscious of his privileged upbringing with its safe position. The resulting argument involves all the restaurant's patrons.

Through this restaurant scene Malle illustrates the conflicting political views held within France at that time. As one table shouts for Meyer to be left alone, another shouts that "all Jews should be sent to Russia." During this exchange Meyer sits in dignified silence with a resigned half smile. Ultimately it's German Luftwaffe officers who defuse the situation telling the militia to leave. As Francois points out, their actions are more to impress his mother than to spare Meyer. They even dismiss the situation saying in German, "The French and their politics."

In a previous film, *Alamo Bay* (1985), Malle had explored the way that latent racism can be mobilized by economic pressure. The film is based on another true incident, this time in Texas. Catholic Vietnamese fishermen had left their homes with their priest after the fall of Saigon and settled in the southern Texan fishing town of Port Alamo. The Ku Klux Klan exploited the resulting tension. Malle was interested in depicting the ordinary Texan fishermen who were not fascists but could be mobilized to violent actions by the Klan.

By 1944, when *Au Revoir* begins, large-scale resistance had begun in occu-pied France. Germany had used France to maintain its own economy. Shortages and a fast deteriorating quality of life encouraged more people to militate against

German occupation and the authoritarian Vichy regime. In the film, the audience learns that Petain is no longer in favor as the boys say that he is no longer to be trusted. Again they accept their parents' political stance, unchallenged.

The scene when the Gestapo take Jean has Julien betray him with a glance. Malle was surprised that audiences picked this up as his demonstrating his own guilt about events;[9] his conscious intention had been to heighten the emotion for Julien in the scene. More striking, though, is the way that Jean behaves as he leaves the classroom. He calmly replaces the cap on his pen and shakes hands with his classmates, bidding them farewell. This dignified resignation is incredibly moving and contrasts with the reckless youth of the playground.

The Vatican and World War II

Pius XII, pope from 1939 to 1958, led a deeply authoritarian, anti-communist church that mirrored the values promoted by the Vichy government. Malle's Catholic upbringing would have confirmed these Vichy values as the institutional church supported the Vichy government, denouncing resistance as terrorism as late as February 1944. It was not until Pope John XXIII and the Second Vatican Council in 1959 that Catholic collusion in anti-Semitism was acknowledged.

The book *Malle on Malle* is an edited version of conversations between himself and Philip French, the *Observer* newspaper film critic. Malle's thoughts, edited by French, cover his complete works and were recorded over a number of days in France and England in 1990 and 1991. Throughout the book French perceives anti-clericalism as a central theme in Malle's films. Malle does talk of how he was expelled from the school in 1946 for writing notes that saying he hated God. But looking back he sees this as a childish act of rebellion against the rigidity of his Catholic education. His portrayal of the priests in *Au Revoir les Enfants* shows this rigidity that is in direct opposition to Malle's flexible approach to life. But Malle's portrayal of clergy is as individuals rather than a caricature of the institutional church.

The challenging dimension of many of Malle's films is included in Père Jean's (the priest's) challenge of the haute-bourgeois parents during the mass sequence. Here Malle seems to be showing the church's influence to the good. And it is here, through Père Jean, that Malle expresses his adult opinion. The priest confronts the parents initially, saying that "more than ever we must be aware of selfishness and indifference" and that "it is easier for a camel to pass through the eye of a needle than for a rich man to enter the kingdom of heaven." But it is his final prayer that "We shall pray for the victims and their executioners" that reflects Malle's viewpoint.

Malle may not intend us the audience to pray for those executioners, but he does require us to look closely at how easily and arbitrarily people may become executioners. Although probably unintentionally, Malle is echoing the message of John's Gospel, "Let he who is without sin cast the first stone,"[10] with this speech.

The tension point for Père Jean is when Jean goes up to the altar rail to receive communion with the other children. Here he freezes, as he cannot give communion to this Jewish child, because for him it would be so grave a sin, although he is prepared to risk and ultimately give up his life to protect this child.

This mass sequence is also one of the most visually striking in the film. Malle remembered the occupation as a time without color. And the world of this film is somber and lackluster. As a viewer you are starved of color. This lack of color in a color film creates a different atmosphere than if it were filmed in black and white. Malle talked of wanting to have the only red be the mother's lipstick,[11] a similar use of the color red in a small child's dress is later found in Spielberg's holocaust set, black-and-white film *Schindler's List*. However, the visual style of the two films is strikingly different. Watching Spielberg's film, the black-and-white photography creates a striking beauty even at its most poignant moments. Whereas in Malle's film watching it you perceive an oppressive grim world. And it brings the everyday limitations of this world closer.

Dressed in ordinary vestments, not a festival such as Easter or Christmas, the priest stands addressing the parents with a vivid green radiating from his vestments in the center of the screen. It is one of the rare occasions that any color is on screen. Although the parents in the scene are expensively and warmly dressed, some in furs, these brown tones do not radiate back to the priest. Here Malle clearly remembers the spectacle of the mass in his often grey childhood, but more than this emphasizes the importance of the priest's homily as a shining light to the audience. This scene and the character of Pere Jean are the true heart of the film. The boys are part way to becoming the men they will be, making the impact of the events a major part of their formation, and in Pere Jean, Malle pays tribute to the man he knew in his childhood who gave his humanity and ultimately his life to support his beliefs.

Collaborators and Betrayal

As in the portrayal of most of his characters, Malle does not make him a saint. In one of the fictional actions of the film, it is Père Jean's rigidity that ultimately leads to the denunciation of the Jewish children. Joseph, an orphan working in the school's kitchen, denounces them to the Gestapo, as revenge for the way Pere Jean has treated him. He has been trading on the black market with provisions the boys have bartered as well as some stolen from the school. When the priest discovers this, he sees the pupils involved to punish them, but tells them he cannot expel them because of their parents. His punishment of Joseph, however, is severe. He must leave the school although he has nowhere else to go. He tells Julien and the other boys that "I have to fire Joseph, though it's unfair." It is this action that makes Joseph vulnerable and ultimately leads him to the Gestapo. Although Pere Jean has challenged others to reflect on their privileged position earlier in the film, it is his own inequity that has fatal consequences. His sincerity is never in doubt, but his actions are both heroic and flawed and maybe for Malle this flaw somehow makes him more courageous.

Malle says his rebellion at school came from the inconsistency of the message he was being taught with the actions in the world that surrounded him. We see this in the sequence when the nun in the infirmary betrays the final boy in hiding. After the priest and other teachers' heroism, she would clearly rather have the boy taken than take any personal risk.

Malle describes the scene when Julien discovers that it is Joseph who has betrayed the boys as:

> the discovery of evil. But Joseph doesn't seem to realize the importance of what he's done. . . . That was enormously disturbing for Julien . . . that it all started with the petty story of the black market and the priest being so rigid about it.[12]

When a shocked Julien speaks to him in the courtyard, before the boys are taken away, Joseph dismisses Julien's horror with "Don't act so pious. There's a war on kid." This dismissal of scruples by Joseph is uncomfortable to watch. His mocking tone is uninformed rather than actively motivated. His actions are part of a complex situation that is personally rather than politically driven.

This example of collaboration echoes that in Malle's earlier film *Lacombe Lucien* (1974). Here he wanted to confront "the banality of evil." The film tells the story of a French peasant, an outsider, who has attempted to join the resistance but been rejected. A circumstance as arbitrary as a bicycle puncture causes him to be out after the curfew. French militia working with the Gestapo arrest him, and because they act in a friendly manner toward him he becomes a collaborator.

Unlike Max Ophul's collaboration themed documentary *The Sorrow and the Pity* (1971) that Malle had distributed, *Lacombe Lucien* became surrounded in controversy. Although initially well received, the ambivalent behavior of its characters was soon heavily criticized as it was thought it was not critical enough of collaborators. Malle saw the intellectuals' rejection of the Lacombe as refusing to look at collaboration in the way it happened and preferring to intellectualize the truth in a way that supported their own political standpoint. He felt they accused him of "putting on screen a character who was complex and ambiguous fictionalized 'to the point where his behavior is acceptable.' For them it justified collaboration."[13] Malle's experience of growing up in occupied France and continuing reflection on these themes, whether in France or abroad, meant there was no other way he could present it.

> I wanted to explore a complex character in all his contradictions. At the same time, in no way did I try to excuse or justify him. His behavior in many situations is objectively ugly, and described as such. At the same time I wanted to

make clear that he was accidentally transported into a situation he was not prepared for.[14]

The Occupying Forces

Significantly, Malle introduces the audience to the occupying German forces as Catholics. The first sight of a German soldier is not the kind of Nazi aggressor often found in films, but a man seen through the schoolroom window asking Pere Jean to hear his confession. Later when Julien and Jean are lost in the woods after curfew, it is soldiers who return them to the school. They identify themselves as Bavarian Catholics. Initially they appear an unthreatening force. Malle had spent twenty-four hours in a fortress in Algeria in 1962, accompanying a journalist from *Paris Match*. He met an accountant who was completing his military service there. This apparently mild-mannered man who wrote to his fiancé every day was actually in charge of torturing their prisoners.[15] For Malle this appearance of normality is the true terror and so it begins in the film. In life, unlike the films of our childhood, the villains are too often not obvious, their public façade and manner not warning us of the actions they are capable of committing.

It is only in the final sequence with the plain-clothed Gestapo officer that the full horror of the occupying force is identified. As he lines up the Jewish boys to be transported he states, "The boy is not French. He is a Jew. You must help us rid France of foreigners, of Jews." These chilling words are after he has questioned the three young girls that have been found in the chapel. They are spared as they respond that they have come for confession and this satisfies him. He responds by brushing the child's cheek with his hand. This gentle action is a distortion of Père Jean's final farewell.

Malle grew up in an extraordinary time. This occupied world where people were transported never to return was the only world he knew as a child. Throughout the rest of his life he searched out other extraordinary places both on and off screen. He celebrated life with all its flaws and in *Au Revoir les Enfants* drew his audience close to share his memory's warning. Events leading to the priest's and children's deaths happened not just because of the identifiable enemy but also because of ambiguity and carelessness that is part of all society.

Reviewing the Chapter

1. How do *Au Revoir les Enfants* and other Malle films use coincidence rather than identifiable enemies to explore moral themes within the narrative?

2. Considering *Au Revoir les Enfants*, is it the issues and imagery of a religious childhood or his childhood experience of events that awakened a will to look at religious themes?

3.   How meaningful is it to position *Au Revoir les Enfants* as the work of a director brought up in the Catholic tradition?

Notes

1.   Philip French, ed., *Malle on Malle* (London: Faber and Faber 1993), 167.
2.   David Cronenberg talking to Paul McGrath, *Front Row*, BBC Radio 4, January 3, 2003.
3.   *Pretty Baby*, Paramount, 1978; *Alamo Bay*, TriStar, 1985.
4.   French, *Malle on Malle*, 170.
5.   Roger Price, *A Concise History of France* (Cambridge: Cambridge University Press, 1993), 32.
6.   Susan Hayward, *French National Cinema* (London: Routledge, 1993), 155.
7.   Hayward, *French National Cinema*, 155.
8.   French, *Malle on Malle*, 181.
9.   French, *Malle on Malle*, 170.
10. French, *Malle on Malle*, 179.
11. King James Bible, John 8:3–11.
12. French, *Malle on Malle*, 174.
13. French, *Malle on Malle*, 170.
14. French, *Malle on Malle*, 100–104.
15. French, *Malle on Malle*, 96.
16. French, *Malle on Malle*, 90.

Roberto Benigni as Director:
Toward an Analysis of Values

Dario Vigano

Is there a thread of recurrent themes and ideas in the films of Roberto Benigni? Can we identify a common denominator for the several works he has directed and the far more numerous ones in which he has appeared as an actor?

Roberto Benigni was born in 1952 at Misericordia in the province of Arezzo some years after the end of World War II. He spent his formative years near Prato and attended a Jesuit college in Florence but had to leave after the disastrous flood of 1966 and went to the institute of economics in Prato. By age twenty, his vocation to be an actor seemed so irresistible that with three friends, Silvani Ambrogi, Carlo Monni, and Aldo Buti, he left Tuscany for Rome, and they made their theatrical debut at the Teatro dei Satiri with the play, *I Burosauri*. He had his first film role in 1977 with Guiseppe Bertolucci. This gave notice of his successful career in both acting and directing. While we can trace a chronological order, it is definitely more complex, even dangerous, to try to discover the connections through all his work.

In their study on Benigni,[1] Giorgio Simonelli and Gaetano Tramontana describe dealing with the subject as being "like writing with a gun at your head and a time bomb placed beneath your desk, with that ghost, that derisive imp, appearing in front of you at every word"; it is no easy task to attempt to confine him to a limited number of thematic patterns.

Despite such difficulties, it does seem possible to detect an orientation that over time has assumed a definite ethical value in Benigni's artistic output which, of course, ranges beyond the recently preeminent field of the cinema. That ethical value is the exaltation of love, in its every component but with special humanist attention being paid to the "others" of society, especially the weak, the losers. Some critics have gone so far as to see in the trend a deliberate apology for those who are different.[2] There is a constant tension, perhaps not uniform but nonetheless present, above all else filtered through a gaze which always, without exception, is clear, sunny, movingly intense, and enthusiastic.

This has been shrewdly noted by Giorgio Cremonini in a detailed and perceptive essay in which he describes Roberto Benigni as an eternal boy, endowed with "a childlike gaze that is chiefly expressed through the permanent, intoxicating discovery of a world metaphorically bent towards the dimension of sexuality."[3] The observation seems especially apt for Benigni's early films as director or actor (the latter much more numerous) but also with regard to his work for television, often astonishingly bold in its attacks on conventional sacred cows. Everything that Benigni did in the entertainment world—at least until the early 1990s—placed on center stage the exuberant, irreverent youth who blithely carried on the playful side of life. In reality that vision has altered little in substance since; if anything, it has matured and broadened, opening up from physical and carnal love to a conscious orientation toward total love in the Augustinian sense. The change may be noted more clearly in his films than in his work for television or the infrequent but unforgettable live performances, where the need for spontaneity and immediate impact on the audience led Benigni to blend his more profound reflections with a sometimes scurrilous approach.

Cremonini also underlines how the adult dimension, for the Tuscan filmmaker, is "a mask trying to hide childhood with its aggressions and freedoms; the comedian removes it in the name of the freedom with which we can regain the world, the freedom of the body and of language."[4] So far as values are concerned, it is this which seems to be the main hermeneutic key to understanding his work: the sometimes evident but more often hidden thread that runs through films apparently so diverse and scandalously irreverent.

Benigni's early television work, on the *Televacca* series in the unlikely shape of a film critic (improbably fake, caricatured and ostentatiously ignorant) and in his off-the-cuff, over-the-top contributions to the *L'altra domenica programme* fronted by Renzo Arbore, was soon followed by an equally egregious big screen debut in *Berlinguer ti voglio bene*, directed by Bertolucci. Benigni played the "obscene" Cioni Mario, a young dropout and victim of the ideological crisis of the 1970s, incapable of finding any purpose in life beyond his obsessive "genital scurrility" and the creation of his own world, midway between dream and madness. After a walk-on part in Bernardo Bertolucci's *La Luna*, his next role was the lead in *Chiedo asilo* (*Seeking Asylum*) by Marco Ferreri. Once again Benigni related to the world of childhood that always attracted him so strongly, playing a teacher with sentimental concern for the children in his care.

Then came a return to pure comedy in one of his most controversial films, *Il Pap'occhio* (*In the Pope's Eye*), directed by Renzo Arbore as was the follow-up *F.F.S.S.*; Benigni was beginning to find the definitive outlines of a persona that "combines the ingenuousness, physical agility and visual gags of Buster Keaton with the ranting monologues of Groucho Marx."[5] Benigni made his own directing debut in just such a setting, his own comic character now firmly established; *Tu mi turbi (You Upset Me)* was a rather ordinary film in terms of directing skills, a series of episodes, which included Benigni, as babysitter for the Virgin Mary, failing in the task of bathing the baby Jesus. Via the exaltation of carnal love and good living found in *Non ci resta che piangere* (*Nothing Left to Do But Cry*), a box office hit in Italy in 1984, Benigni found himself combining Pinocchio and Pierrot in Fellini's *La voce della luna* (*The Voice of the Moon*), exploring the theme of the double in *Johnny Stecchino* (*Johnny Toothpick*) and taking a close-up look at the "different" in *Il mostro* (*The Monster*).

The culmination, before dedicating himself entirely to the recreation of Carlo Collodi's dream of Pinocchio, came with *La vita è bella* (*Life is Beautiful*), his masterpiece to date. In this extravagant, unbalanced film, Benigni managed to pull off the feat of singing his love for mankind in a combination of two absolutely antithetical narrative registers, expressing the self-contradictory value of desperate optimism against the barbarity of history. Once again the dimension of childish play, ever-present in his filmography, is to the fore; now, however, it is also firmly tied to a hierarchy of values that make it both productive and ethical. Guido, the main character, uses play not only to deride authority and unmask its contradictions but also to preserve the children and their innocence from the horror.

With *La vita è bella*, Benigni extended his fame across the Atlantic, winning a degree of mainstream popularity far beyond the notoriety gained for his previous work in the United States with Jim Jarmusch, an independent director closer in spirit to the European than the Hollywood mode of filmmaking, in his films *Down by Law* and *Night on Earth*.

With gross receipts of some $58 million in U.S. theaters alone, *La vita è bella* became the Italian cinema's greatest ever international hit—despite being shown in a dubbed version because of American audiences' dislike of subtitled films. Its success was even more remarkable in the light of the comic approach to a controversial subject, such as the Shoah. This was a delicate operation that did not fail to attract criticism at the time of the film's release, mostly from those who detected a danger (albeit to my mind nonexistent) of treating the Holocaust as a laughing matter. Indeed the film represented the highest form of Benigni's poetic inspiration as a filmmaker (due in part to the contribution of his loyal cowriter Vincenzo Cerami): the ability to speak to people's hearts simply and directly, in the manner of the Gospel parables. Guido, the main character of the film, follows a Christological path in sacrificing his own life to save his son's and thus that of generations to come, to preserve his purity, remote from the horror of the Nazi death camps. It is a powerful but also a perfectly intelligible metaphor, one that hits home by the immediacy of its gaze, irreverent humor but also the profundity of its analysis and condemnation of so infamous and unfathomable an event in history.

La vita è bella marked a watershed in the personal and professional life of an artist who had previously been thought of as just another comedian—bitingly brilliant perhaps, but still just a comedian. Henceforward Benigni became a kind of emblem of the man who can do and say what he pleases because, like the innocent child in the fairy tale, he is the only one to notice that the emperor wears no clothes. This newfound omnipotence, which might have led others to rest on their laurels, induced him to reveal his most intimate thoughts, the objectives dearest to his heart, almost as if the persona of court jester, tendentious and irreverent, unpredictably comic, was one that had been forced on him up to then. After *La vita è bella*, Benigni dwelt more than ever before on the subject of religion, especially during his television appearances, making a lasting impact by his original contributions.

At the 2002 Sanremo Festival of Italian music, a quintessentially popular event in the nation's television calendar, Benigni made an inspired and overwhelming guest appearance. In front of a television audience of over 12 million he was carried away by a stream of thought-provoking theological reflections, expressed in direct, colorful language: "What I say is, if Our Lord were to return today, what would he think of us? Just imagine, all of a sudden God comes back and he finds the Earth in the mess it's in now, a living hell, wars everywhere, people hurting each other, the forest burning, the gap in the ozone layer. . . . Oh mother—hey, Peter, take a look down here, mother what a mess these wars . . . all in my name, too, seeing as how I'm the same everywhere, look what a mess, the amount of genetic transfigurations. . . . What's that, a mandarin orange? That wasn't me! They made a mandarin and an orange make love and the result was a mandarin orange. And what's that, a wolf hound? A wolf and a hound made love and the result was a wolf hound. And what's that: the tiger mosquito. Is that really a mosquito?"

In the auditorium the audience was fascinated, laughter punctuating Benigni's outbursts, with the comic prancing back and forth across the huge stage. In a few crystal clear words, up-to-date today as ever, he touched on war, environmental disasters, and genetic interference. He was telling jokes, but beneath the surface he was also revealing the evils of the world.

He went on: " 'I gave you all kinds of teachings,' says God, 'but there's one which sums the rest up and it's the one by St. Augustine: love, and do what you will. When you love you can commit sin, you can jump on someone, look at this [at Belvedere, one of the San Remo showgirls], at the delights of the world that when they smile the air around us is scented with violets. Look at her: a blazing quietude, a shining salvation. . . . When you love you can do what you want because love is the hand of God on man's shoulder. When they love, even dogs bark in rhyme. And you mustn't just love here and there, but the whole time: love that ignites and dies down burns out. You have to love large. Love that scrapes along bit by bit is love that dies. Love is the Neptune of the blood. And when you're lost for words, that's love. Love is the only constraint upon freedom that makes us more free. It's a marvelous thing, love with a capital L.' "

It was a direct hymn to the universal, greatest value of all, quoting from St. Augustine as if he were a household name, and spreading his profound teachings in new and original words.

This indeed is the secret of Benigni, his innate ability to speak of profound issues with a child's enthusiasm and fascination with his subject, in speeches that touch the heart.

He had this to say, for example, regarding the existence of God: "The brain is not the right tool to prove the existence of God with. It's like trying to smell the taste of salt through your nose. He didn't manage to do it himself when He sent His own son down to earth, so we are hardly likely to succeed—we're not even close relatives!"

In another instance, he tells of his own early curiosity as a child to know who created the world: "In short, the ontological argument collapsed, the scholastics and the mystics failed to convince. The Theory of the Immovable Mover is a load of nonsense. What can I do but go back and ask my Dad? I must have been four years old, it was coming back from the fields one night. I asked him:

Dad, who made the world?
—God.
And who made God?
—His Mum and Dad.

" 'Of course,' I thought, 'how stupid of me.' I went to bed happy, but quite convinced my Dad wouldn't think much of my intelligence. I should have worked it out on my own."

On December 23, 2002, Benigni adjusted his aim even higher. Going beyond his occasional, albeit protracted, guest appearances on regular mainstream guest shows, he presented a one-man show on the premiere State network Rai Uno. It ran over two hours, without commercial breaks. Divided into two parts—the first, a long, inspired monologue of political and social satire, and the second, a recital and commentary on the last canto of Paradise from Dante's *Divine Comedy*—the show attracted a record audience with peak ratings of over 15 million; moreover, against all expectations the audience peaks occurred mostly in the second part of the program.

Critics and commentators were lavish in their praise. Maurizio Costanzo gave perhaps the best summary the next day: "Wonderful. The people in the film industry who love to lash out at him will have to get used to the idea that he's the only winning brand in Italy apart from Ferrari." Costanzo saw Benigni's formula as "following his own diversity, a winning alchemic mixture. It's not true that he always does the same things, either. He knows how to blend difficult concepts, like an academic. His political satire is elegant, not the work of a vulgar person but of a poet."

Benigni's reading of Dante was so heartfelt and inspired and his commentary so skillful in bringing home the verse, even to the majority of listeners who were unfamiliar with thirteenth-century Italian, that the program led over subsequent days to an unprecedented boom in sales of the *Divine Comedy*, which topped that month's best-seller lists.

It takes a lot of courage to do Dante in prime time. Benigni apparently knows the entire *Divine Comedy* by heart, often quoting extensive passages in his speeches. The choice of the final canto was anything but a coincidence. It contains the most complex and inexpressible vision, which the poet fulfills at the end of his journey: the vision of God. Benigni is a fine interpreter of Dante's verse, still as rich and vivid as ever today.

The career of this great artist, after the transgressive, irreverent early comedy, in the "Little Devil" as in the mouthpiece of Beauty and the Word, which he chose to be at the height of his success, has thus revealed the maturity of the man who made a virtue of his boyishness.

Reviewing the Chapter

1.   *La vita è bella* was screened, with Benigni present, for Pope John Paul II. Does the film show Benigni's "Catholic sensibility"?

2.   One critic described Benigni's perspective in *La vita è bella* as both Catholic and humanistic. He also includes a sympathetic Jewish perspective. Do these factors help explain the worldwide acclaim for and popularity of the film?

3.   Some commentators criticized the film for associating humor with the Holocaust. Is this criticism apt or a misunderstanding of the film's humanism?

Notes

1.   Giorgio Simonelli and Gaetano Tramontana, *Datemi un Nobel! L'opera comica di Roberto Benigni* (Alessandria: Falsopiano Edizioni, 1998).

2.   Cristina Borsatti, *Roberto Benigni* (Milan: Editrice Il Castoro, 2001), 82.

3.   Giorgio Cremonini, *Viaggio non organizzato nel cinema comico* (Turin: Lindau, 2000), 109.

4.   Cremonini, *Viaggio*, 110.

5.   Gianni Canova, ed., *Cinema* (Milan: Garzanti, 2002), 95.

17

Land of Promise:
A Reflection on Andrzej Wajda's
Merchants of Lodz

Jan Epstein

My love affair with cinema began with the heady mixture of poetry and politics that I experienced in European films while a student at Melbourne University in the early 1960s. During this time I discovered Andrzej Wajda's great trilogy *A Generation* (1954), *Kanal* (1956), and *Ashes and Diamonds* (1958). These films excited me intellectually and aesthetically. They seemed to me revolutionary, opening windows into the way cinema can illuminate life and make commentary on the past.

It seemed self-evident that Wajda ranked alongside such masters as Federico Fellini, Ingmar Bergman, Vittorio De Sica, and Francois Truffaut. When *Man of Marble* (1975) was released in Australia, I was filled with admiration. I saw the film as courageous, the work of a defiant, humanist director driven to expose betrayal and political deceit.

It was therefore with great anticipation that some months later I attended a screening of *Land of Promise* (*Ziemia Obiecana*, 1974), which in 1975 had won an Oscar nomination for Best Foreign Film. What I saw on the screen, however, shocked me. I felt betrayed.

Set in Lodz at the turn of the century, the film was stylistically baroque and lurid in content. It was 180 minutes long, with several scenes depicting at gratuitous length the wheels of industry literally grinding into mincemeat the hapless workers who operated them.[1] I was aghast at the relentless depiction of Jews as parasites and bloodsuckers, hypocrites in prayer shawls, whose lascivious wives had gluttonous appetites.

Twenty-five years later, I am revisiting *Land of Promise* in this chapter in an attempt to understand better both the film and my response to it as a film critic and a Jew.

Land of Promise was adapted for the screen by Wajda from the 1898 novel *Ziemia Obiecana* (*The Promised Land*). Written by Wladyslaw Stanislaw Reymont, who won the Nobel Prize for literature in 1924, *The Promised Land* is written in the exaggerated, hyperbolic style of Charles Dickens and Émile Zola and is an account of the rapid transformation of Lodz—a small town still using hand looms to manufacture cloth in the 1860s—into the "Manchester of Poland" in the 1890s.

Reymont has also been called "a rich, realistic writer . . . whose characters were colorful, vivid, and true to life,"[2] and Wajda tells the story of capitalism coming to Lodz through the novel's three main characters: a Pole, a German, and a Jew. Almost all synopses of the film, and Wajda himself, describe the protagonists this way.[3] This reduction of character to national type is an indicator of the way the film makes use of stereotyping to portray Polish history in broad strokes. Yet to describe the protagonists in this fashion is to make a category mistake.

Avoiding this category mistake would require the description of the characters to be "a Protestant, a Catholic, and a Jew," or alternately "a Polish Catholic, a German Protestant, and a Polish Jew." I will expand on this later. However, notwithstanding this denial of a nationality for the Jewish protagonist, these three characters serve as a convenient shorthand for Wajda's depiction of Lodz's ethnic heterogeneity.

Polish lands had always incorporated many people, but Lodz's multiculturalism had its origin in the several partitions of Poland. These occurred between 1772 and 1795 and saw the kingdom of Poland divided between the empires of Tsarist Russia, Hapsburg Austria, and Hohenzollern Prussia. After the Congress of Vienna in 1815, some of this territory was annexed to Russia as the semiautonomous kingdom of Poland. Also known as Congress Poland, this area (which included Warsaw and Lodz) was the core of ethnic Poland, the heart of its culture and politics, and the region that would give birth to swift industrial economic growth.[4]

Industrialization came late to Poland,[5] but when it did it came first to a small town on the eastern rim of the Russian Empire, which had its face toward Prussia and other industrialized nations in western Europe. Lodz was designated an industrial town by the local municipal authority in 1820,[6] but its transformation into a major manufacturing center was initially slow. The year 1823 saw the start of a flow of textile workers from abroad (mainly Germany), and in 1835 the first steam engine was set up in Ludwig Geyer's spinning mill.[7] In 1842 the ban on the export of spinning machines from England was lifted, and customs duties between Poland and Russia were removed in 1850.[8]

When mechanical weaving machines replaced handlooms, and new factories were built to accommodate them, capitalism took off. From the 1880s to the end of the century, Lodz saw an explosion of economic energy as well as a huge jump in population. The majority of those flocking to the promised land, as Lodz was commonly perceived to be, were peasants and others from the surrounding countryside and elsewhere, mainly Germany and Russia. A sizable number of these were entrepreneurs and businessmen, some of them Jews.[9]

Jews had come to Poland as early as the tenth century,[10] but migration began in earnest in the fifteenth century when a tide of anti-Jewish agitation swept through Europe from Portugal to Brandenberg and from the Netherlands to Sicily.[11] By 1570, the majority of German Jewish exiles had migrated to Poland-Lithuania, which emerged as one of the twin centers of a newly constituted Jewish world, along with the Ottoman Balkans.[12]

Despite the upheavals to the Jewish people caused by the Chmielnicki massacres of 1648–1649 and Partition, Jewish culture and social life generally flourished in Poland. A mainly urban people, census figures show that by 1816, Jews constituted 8.7% of the total population of Poland. Following the lifting of restrictions on Jewish migration from Russia by Tsarist decree in 1862, they constituted 13.5 percent in 1865 and by 1897, 14 percent (this was despite massive emigration to the United States and England).[13]

By the time Reymont was writing his book in 1898, the Jewish community of Lodz, over a period of sixty years, had become the second largest Jewish community in Poland after Warsaw and one of the largest in the world.[14]

Thus, there is an intentional aptness to the nationalities of the three dramatis personae of Wajda's *Land of Promise*, and the proportions they represent in the exploitative cutthroat world of turn-of-the-century Polish capitalism depicted in the film.

Karol Borowiecki (Daniel Olbrychski) is an urbane but ruthlessly ambitious young Polish nobleman, working as a managing engineer for a brutish German textile manufacturer called Bucholz (Andrzej Szalawski). Maks Baum (Andrzej Seweryn) is a handsome, seemingly bland young German with a temperamental streak, whose father faces bankruptcy because he refuses to mechanize his factory out of old-fashioned scruples. Moryc Welt (Wojciech Pszoniak) is a Polish-Jewish broker and middleman. He plays the buffoon but is fervently devoted to both making money and maintaining his friendship with Karol, whom he admires unreservedly.

All three have been friends since university and are dedicated to greed and hence to each other, because alone they cannot raise the capital they desperately need to build their own factory.

Karol is penniless despite his nobility, and through his fiancée Anka (Anna Nehrebecka), whom he has known since childhood, he persuades his father (Tadeusz Bialoszczynski) to sell the family estate to a local racketeer. But when Karol learns through his mistress Lucy Zuckerowa (Kalina Jedrusik), the wife of a wealthy Jewish industrialist, that the duty on American cotton is about to rise, the three friends are beside themselves with glee.

Moryc obtains a loan to purchase cotton through Grünspan (Stanislaw Igar), one of his Jewish financial contacts, and armed with this insider knowledge the friends make enough money on the Hamburg futures market to begin building their dream. Maks contributes his share by bullying his father into selling their factory, but Karol continues to have credit problems. Grünspan fears that honest Poles will inhibit corruption in the sweatshops, but Moryc, no longer abject after having made a killing on the market, confronts Grünspan and forces his own business rules on the greedy financier.

Karol brings his ailing father and Anka to Lodz after the estate is sold, and in due course the factory is built. However, on the day of the factory opening, Zucker (Jerzy Nowak) accuses Karol of making Lucy pregnant and forces the younger man to swear on a religious icon that the baby she is expecting is not his. When Zucker discovers that Karol has lied and is accompanying Lucy on the train to Berlin where he has sent her to have her baby, he exacts his revenge by burning down Karol's uninsured factory.

Karol makes good his losses by marrying Mada, the simple-minded daughter of a German textile millionaire, Müller. The film ends with Karol in his palace, his son held ceremoniously in his arms like a young Tsar. Gathered around him in their finery are Lodz's industrial barons and their wives, including Moryc, Maks, and in the background, Zucker (a sign that losing money is ultimately more important than being cuckolded). On the streets, workers are protesting in support of a strike that threatens to bring manufacture in Lodz to a halt. Karol gives orders for the military to open fire on the crowds, and as a worker falls in the street, a red flag tumbles from his hand.

This synopsis, while it may not do justice to the flamboyancy of Wajda's larger-than-life slice of Polish history, nonetheless outlines the prominence of Jewish characters in the story in addition to Moryc. I have done this because in many synopses of the film the importance of these secondary Jewish characters is either glossed over or so blended into the plot that they become merely background characters.

This is not the case at all. The role played by Jews is pivotal to the story, and one of the reasons why the film has been tainted by the slur of anti-Semitism.

In their chapter on Wajda in *The Modern Cinema of Poland*, Boleslaw Michalek and Frank Turaj have deemphasized the role of Jewish characters, such as Lucy Zuckerowa, her husband, and Grünspan, for fear—I will argue—of giving credence to those who accuse the film of anti-Semitism. In fact, they give short shrift to details generally. After categorizing the main characters as "a Pole, a German, and a Jew who decide to start a factory together," Michalek and Turaj write: "The film deals with their separate and joint interests. They do manage to open the factory and eventually end up destroying it. Apart from that subject there is also the depiction of life in a country house, a picture of a world that was dying out."[15]

The writers then commend Wajda for his narrative clarity and originality notwithstanding the film's conventional structure and make the point that "it is not at all a simple costume work with a touch of history." The film, they write, was a huge success and had been nominated for an Academy Award when out of the blue, "something happened that no one expected, least of all Wajda. After showings in Scandinavia and the United States in 1976, *Land of Promise* was charged with containing anti-Semitism by its negative portrayal of the Jews in Lodz."[16] The two writers finish their review by mounting a spirited justification of the film, which deserves close examination.

Michalek and Turaj admit that there are elements in the original novel which can be considered "suggestively anti-Semitic," but argue that Wajda had gone to considerable lengths to change this:

> He makes the personality of Moryc, the Jew, the most likeable of the three main roles. In the final scenes, it is the Polish nobleman who is portrayed as perfidious and despicable. To be sure, each ethnic representation in the film comes in for some negative treatment—the film is after all about the negative aspects of laissez-faire development. But since there are Jewish characters among the rest of those who are satirized, the argument was advanced that that kind of portrayal, a negative depiction of characters who are Jewish, constitutes, ipso facto, anti-Semitism. The real conflict in the film has nothing to do with nationalities; it has to do with capital and labor. All this was obscured by the allegations. The writers express bewilderment as to how, *to this day, against any sensible interpretation of the reality of the thing,*[17] the film is thought to be anti-Semitic in Scandinavia and the United States.

The remainder of this chapter will focus on explaining how the film can indeed be read as having anti-Semitic overtones despite Wajda's sincere efforts to expunge them.

Land of Promise is based on historical events. However, Wajda's interpretation of the role of Jews in the development of Polish capitalism seems to be driven by two imperatives. The first is the director's wish to portray the inherently exploitative nature of the relationship between capital and labor.[18] The second, despite his philo-Semitic intentions, is his inability to escape all of the baggage of Polish anti-Semitism, which seems to be almost inextricably woven into the fabric of Polish political culture.

Wajda's depiction of the inherently exploitative relationship between capital and labor is unashamedly Marxist. Regardless of the arguments that can be mounted against Marxism, this is still a worthy value position from which to interpret Polish history. Yet it would seem that Wajda's Marxist viewpoint has been distorted by anti-Semitism, for nowhere does the film recognize that the majority of Jews in Lodz (as in Congress Poland generally), "constituted an urban, middle-class and proletarian element within the great mass of the Polish peasantry."[19]

Although Jews were disproportionately represented in the capitalist class in Lodz (the 1880s saw the rise of a group of powerful Jewish industrialists who employed hundreds and even thousands of workers), most of the Jewish-owned textile and other factories (ceramics, glass, metal products, food-stuffs, haberdashery, etc.) were small and nonmechanized.[20] Moreover, throughout the second half of the nineteenth century, Jews continued without change to engage in traditional Jewish occupations, such as tailoring, fringe-weaving, hat-making, butcher shops, and the like.[21] Noteworthy, too, is that by the end of the century a numerically small but highly influential Jewish professional class had emerged, especially in Warsaw.[22]

Seen in this light, any analysis of the role of Jews in the political economy of Lodz or Congress Poland demonstrates the inadequacy of a simplistic Marxist bipolar class model. Jews may indeed have been disproportionately represented among factory owners, but they were also disproportionately represented in the other strata of the Polish middle class and petty bourgeoisie.

Wajda's thesis on the participation of Jews in the evils of capitalism, and his contemporary perspective on the inherent right of workers to rise up against exploitation,[23] is disturbingly prejudicial to Jews and dependent on a false syllogism: "All capitalists are evil. All Jews are capitalists. Therefore all Jews are evil." This invalid syllogism permeates the film and is driven by Wajda's unmitigated use of Reymont's anti-Semitic stereotype. This cannot be denied, no matter how he, or the film's defenders, may try. In fact, a powerful argument can be made that it is anti-Semitism that gives the film its energy and momentum.[24]

It is true that Wajda, when translating *Land of Promise* to the screen, was aware of the anti-Semitism in the book and sought to avoid it. Michalek and Turaj attempt to minimize the anti-Semitism in the book by calling it *suggestively anti-[S]emitic*.[25] Yet a few lines later they write that it is the Pole whom Wajda depicts as "perfidious and despicable," the implication being that this disapprobation was used (correctly) in the novel to characterize the Jew, and not the Pole, who was drawn as virtuous.

In fact, this transfer of the anti-Semitic stereotype from Jew to Pole created indignation among many Poles who saw Wajda's film. This is apparent in a contemporary review by Michael Schwarze,[26] who wrote: "*Land of Promise* was received in Poland with many reservations. The main accusation against the director was that he equipped Borowiecki, a Pole, with the most disgusting features of the three. Such an interpretation was not faithful to the original, since Reymont's novel was at times very anti-[S]emitic."

Wajda's attempt to ameliorate the book's anti-Semitism is confirmed by Polish director Krzysztof Zanussi, who together with Wajda and the late Krzysztof Kieslowski, form a triumvirate of Poland's most important postwar directors. Zanussi told me that *Land of Promise* was most severely attacked in France.[27] He believes that Wajda's relationship with Jewish culture is particularly painful because Wajda, he says, "is very much a philo-[S]emite."

For instance, the carousel erected by Nazis outside the smoldering ruins of the Warsaw Ghetto, first seen in Wajda's film *A Generation* (1955) and later in *Holy Week* (1995), has since become part of Poland's collective mythology. Says Zanussi, "The image was seized upon by poets. Very few people remember there was a carousel close to the wall of the Ghetto when the uprising was crushed. Wajda used it as a metaphor for indifference [to the fate of the Jews], and he used it again in *Holy Week* because he felt that he must remind people again. He also made *Korczak* [1990].[28] He has been rejected so many times," he adds, "somehow reflecting the fate of so many Jews rejected by gentiles."

Zanussi makes the point that at the time of Wajda's translation of the book to the screen, Jewish culture and all references to Poland's Jewish past had been totally erased by the Polish Communists. "They simply denied that there were ever any Jews in Poland. It was forgotten, forbidden, never spoken about. So when Wajda brought these characters back [in *Land of Promise*] it was a novelty for the public to learn that there were Jews amongst us. He was reminding us that we were a multicultural society."

Before World War II, there were 3,351,000 Jews in Poland. The number of Polish Jews saved by fleeing to the Soviet Union in 1939 is estimated at 250,000, while the sum total of Polish Jews who survived the war is thought to be 370,000, just 11 percent of the prewar population.[29]

In addition to the 80,000 Jews who returned or were already in Poland after the war, over 154,000 Polish Jews were repatriated from the Soviet Union in 1946. This brought the total Jewish population of Poland at that time close to 250,000. However, the majority chose to emigrate, both because of a reluctance to remain in a land where millions of Jews had perished and because of assaults on Jews which resulted in two pogroms, one in Krakow in 1945 and the other in Kielce in 1946.[30]

Migrations continued to deplete Polish Jewry, as Poland became more and more a satellite state under the Soviet Union. In 1948, Jewish political parties were disbanded under the guise of unification, and Jewish cultural life was severely restricted. By 1956, the number of Jews in Poland was reduced to 30,000.[31]

Poles and Jews alike identified those Jews who stayed in Poland with the Communist regime. But in the aftermath of the student riots in 1968 that led to resurgent state-sponsored anti-Semitism and the repression of Polish intellectuals, even Jewish Communists were subjected to anti-Semitic purges.[32] Most of the remaining Jews emigrated, and when Wajda made *Land of Promise* in 1974, only 6,000 Jews remained in Poland.[33]

If Wajda wished to bring Jews back to the foreground and rehabilitate their role in Polish culture in a positive way, as Zanussi suggests, then one can only ask why he chose to do this through *Land of Promise*. What was he thinking when he refashioned Moryc, Lucy, Zucker, and Grünspan from Reymont's novel?

Tomasz Kitlinski and Joe Lockard have called Reymont a "dreck-writer."[34] By this they mean that Reymont uses *dreck* (German-Yiddish for complete crap or rubbish) as a metaphor for the corrupt and immoral system of early capitalism in Lodz. The book opens, they write, with thousands of workers "crawling out of side streets, which resembled canals full of mud, from the houses which stood on the outskirts of the city not unlike huge refuse heaps."

Images such as these from the book are given an astonishing force in Wajda's film, as well as those which show Lodz's "human garbage" (the industrial proletariat) being literally ground like grist in the mills of greedy capitalists to feed their insatiable hunger for profit. This sense of an obscene and rotting biological process at work in the system pervades *Land of Promise*, and it is the way this metaphor clings more to the Jews than to other nationalities in the film, that makes the film in this regard so offensive.[35]

Wajda sought to restore the Jews in Polish history by substituting the perfidious and despicable Moryc of the book with a more likeable version. In doing so, however, he exchanged one stereotype for another. Of the three friends, Moryc may well be the most likeable, but he achieves this at the expense of him being presented in the film as a buffoon, playing the clown to the aristocratic Karol in much the same way as the fool plays the faithful subordinate to King Lear.

Moryc's entry in the film is classic buffoonery: From riding tandem with Karol through the bucolic Polish countryside, he is shown as struggling to preserve his dignity in the presence of Karol's father after running in fear from a playful dog.[36] He is then hailed with jocularity by the elderly nobleman who explains to his friend the priest: "It's no Shylock; it's our Karol's friend!"

Several points can be made about this introduction. First, Wajda is playing knowingly on anti-Semitism and the ambivalent relationship Poles have with Jews. There is at once the open recognition that they are seen as Shylocks (bloodsuckers), and the sly acknowledgement that this Jew is different; he is one of us ("our Karol's friend"). Next, there is the interdependent nature of the friendship between the Pole and the Jew. However, this is a relationship based on inequality, which engenders sycophancy in the Jew.

"You're an aristocrat, a Lodzermensch; me, I just want to make money!" Moryc tells Karol in an early scene. His tone is admiring, and his loyalty to Karol unstinting, even though it costs him money. Yet despite the pains taken by Wajda to show this quality as laudable, and his success in making Moryc a more three-dimensional character than his friends, this attribute is undermined by the sense of Moryc being an opportunistic Jew who knows which side his bread is buttered, and by whom. An illustration of this is the sly wink of collusion Moryc gives to the camera at having got the better of Grünspan, thus abetting Karol whose goodwill he is dependent on to further his own ends.

Moryc's sycophancy runs deep. Unaccountably (or so it seems) he always carries a photograph of Karol in his pocket and is mortified when it is discovered with malicious glee by Maks. Here Wajda's portrait of the Jew is almost poignant. Moryc, it would seem, envies Karol's ontological security despite the Pole's poverty and sees this stemming from Karol being at home in the world and not being an outsider. It is the Jew's shame at not belonging, and his doubting of his own legitimacy while envying Karol his, which causes his adulation of the Pole and his need for symbiotic attachment.

Seen from this perspective, the category error of ascribing nationalities to the Pole and the German, and only religious affiliation to the Jew, appears to make sense. In reality, this denial of a nationality to the Jew (it would be contrary to the intentions of the film to call Moryc a Polish-Jew) is a result of prejudice (anti-Semitism).

In the hyperreal biological metaphor that constitutes reality in *Land of Promise*, the steps leading from homeless and outsider to foreigner, rootless cosmopolitan,[37] parasite, bloodsucker, and Shylock are short. It is a route traveled swiftly through the power of stereotype; and even if Wajda intended to spare Moryc the stigma of being seen as Shylock, this is certainly not the case with Zucker.

Moryc is portrayed as an assimilated Jew, and something of a fop, who dons a yamalka only when groveling to Grünspan. Zucker, on the other hand, wears his black silk skullcap and Jewish side-curls proudly, the latter in the dignified fashion of Disraeli. We know little about his financial dealings, only that he is an inside trader. Hence Zucker's importance to the plot. It is through Zucker that Karol and his friends make their killing on the stock market. This enables them to build their factory. And it is Karol's affair with Zucker's lewd and voluptuous wife Lucy that provokes Zucker into burning down Karol's factory and exacting his pound of flesh.

Like Shakespeare's merchant of Venice, Wajda's industrialist from Lodz is a proud man. When informed that Karol is the father of Lucy's unborn child, he confronts Karol with the intention of preserving his dignity. "I'm not made of wood, and I have my honor," Zucker tells Karol in a paraphrase of Shylock's best-known speech. "I'm a simple Jew. I can't challenge you to a duel. I've waited fourteen years for this [a child]. You must tell me the truth!"

As with Moryc, there is poignancy in Zucker's speech. He fears that he has been duped. Despite being a Jew, he is a man with feelings who will bleed if he is pricked. He belongs to a peaceable people who have no skill in wielding arms. Faith is sacred to him; when Karol swears on a religious icon, Zucker believes him. But when Karol is revealed as having deceived him, then like Shylock the suppressed vindictiveness of his "race" erupts.

The temptation to continue interpreting the Jewish characters in this way is strong but depressing. I am convinced that my own argument holds, but I am mindful, too, that any interpretation of an event, book, or film, is constrained by the worldview in which we operate. It is impossible, however, to conclude an overview of *Land of Promise* without reference to the portrait Wajda paints of the "Jewess" Lucy Zuckerowa.

Tomasz Kitlinski and Joe Lockard[38] draw attention to a strand in eastern European literature in which gentry are shown as being both sexually attracted and repelled by peasants and Jews. "Where humans are [considered to be] 'filth,' social systems of degradation inevitably emerge to maintain the barrier between purity and contamination," they write. Thus the allure of these socially inferior groups is their "impurity," and any sexual liaison with either group amounts to "dirty sex." Without any shadow of a doubt, this is the bond that attaches Karol to Lucy ("Miss Piggy") and becomes his obsession.

The "lascivious Jewess" has appeared in literature in several incarnations, most notably in Balzac's *Of Harlots High and Low*, where Esther (who is redeemed by conversion to Christianity) can be taken as emblematic of the complex love-hate relationship many nations and individuals have with Jews. Nevertheless, it must be said that of the many representations of this anti-Semitic stereotype in either literature or film, Lucy as she is seen in the original version of *Land of Promise*, is one of the most offensive.

This chapter has been difficult to write, because I do not believe that Wajda is anti-Semitic in the sense that he set out consciously to denigrate Jews in his film. There is much evidence that his intentions were sincere, and that he was, alongside his mentor, the Polish-Jewish director Aleksander Ford, among the first Polish directors to bring to public cognizance the terrible fate of Polish Jews. More than most Polish directors, he has sought both before and after *Land of Promise* to give Polish-Jews their place in Polish history.

However, I continue to question his judgment in choosing Reymont's *The Promised Land* as an appropriate vehicle for philo-Semitism and conclude this chapter with a quote from the British-Jewish actor Jason Isaacs.[39] When asked how he would play Shylock if he were invited to do so by the Royal Shakespeare Theatre, Isaacs replied:

> I wouldn't do it. I think it's an anti-Semitic play. I wouldn't dream of doing it. Jews were the stage villains, and the play is constructed around that.[40] God knows, I've seen people strain against the construction of the play by setting it in different contexts. I've even seen people wearing yellow stars, and I know that famous Jews have played the part many times.
>
> But I think the construction of the play is such that you're meant to cheer when Shylock has his money taken away, and his daughter taken away, and finally his religion. You're meant to be thrilled. I think that no matter how much people with the right conscience try to work against it, you can't ever work against the [anti-Semitic] structure of the play.

Reviewing the Chapter

1. What are the arguments for maintaining that *Land of Promise*, in the final analysis, is an anti-Semitic film?

2. Is the portrayal of Jews in *Land of Promise* historically accurate?

3. Why is this chapter on *Land of Promise* subtitled Wajda's Merchants of Lodz?

Notes

1. This horrific scene appears to have been shortened and other scenes of machine mutilations substantially edited, in subsequent screenings I have seen of this film, notably on SBS television (Australia) in the 1980s and in a VHS purchased in 2002.

2. Boleslaw Michalek and Frank Turaj, *The Modern Cinema of Poland* (Bloomington: Indiana University Press, 1988), 153. This notion of realism and "true-to-life-ness" is questionable, in Reymont's fiction as in Dickens's and Zola's. Realism is a narrative device congruent with a particular view of history.

3. Andrzej Wajda, Official Website, www.wajda.pl (accessed on November 27, 2002).

4. Ezra Mendelsohn, *Jewish History of Poland: After Partition*, www.heritagefilms .com (accessed December 4, 2002).

5. England used steam-powered machines to manufacture cotton as early as 1800. The Industrial Revolution occurred in Great Britain between 1750 and 1830. See John Lord, *Capital and Steam Power*, chapter 8 (London: P S King & Son Ltd, 1923), available at: www.history.rochester.edu/steam/lord.

6. Pinkas Hakehillot Polin, *Encyclopedia of Jewish communities, Poland*, volume 1 (Jerusalem: Yad Vashem, 1976) 1:1–41.

7. Polin, *Encyclopedia*, 1–41.

8. Polin, *Encyclopedia*, 1–41.

9. Michalek and Turaj, *The Modern Cinema*, 153.

10. Mendelsohn, *Jewish History*.

11. Jonathan I. Israel, *European Jewry in the Age of Mercantilism 1550–1750* (Oxford: Clarendon Press, 1985), 6.

12. Israel, *European Jewry*, 26.

13. Israel, *European Jewry*, 26.

14. Polin, *Encyclopedia*, 1–41. Population figures for nineteenth-century Lodz: 1808, 434 (58 Jews); 1827, 2,837 (397 Jews); 1857, 24,655 (2,886 Jews); 1897, 309,853 (98,386 Jews).

15. Michalek and Turaj, *The Modern Cinema*, 153.

16. Michalek and Turaj, *The Modern Cinema*, 154.

17. My italics.

18. Acknowledged by Michalek and Turaj, *The Modern Cinema*, 154.

19. Mendelsohn, *Jewish History*. According to Mendelsohn, by the end of the nineteenth century, Jews were gradually losing ground to non-Jews in trade. Thus the typical Polish Jew was far from wealthy. For instance: in 1857, 44.7 percent of all Jews in Congress Poland lived from commerce and 25 percent from crafts and industry, while in 1897, 42.6 percent were engaged in commerce and 34.3 percent in crafts and industry.

20. Polin, *Encyclopedia*, 1:1–41.

21. Polin, *Encyclopedia*, 1:1–41.

22. Mendelsohn, *Jewish History*.

23. A reference to the Solidarity movement, and the betrayal of workers by the Communist regime, both of which form the subject of Wajda's subsequent films *Man of Marble* and *Man of Iron*.

24. According to film director Krzysztof Zanussi, Wajda's decision to reissue the film in a new format, with offending material deleted, has detracted from the original. Born in 1939, Zanussi is a film and theatre director, and the author of several books. His

most important films include *Illumination* (1972), *The Constant Factor* (Best Director, Cannes, 1980), *Year of the Quiet Sun* (Golden Lion, Venice, 1984), *Our God's Brother* (1997), and *Life as a Fatally Transmitted Disease* (2000).

25. My italics.

26. Michael Schwarze, reviewer, *Frankfurter Allgemeine Zeitung* (GmbH Frankfurt, January 12, 1976); Wajda Website, available at www.wajda.pl/en/filmy/film/8.htm (accessed on November 27, 2002).

27. Epstein interview with Zanussi in Melbourne, Australia, on December 1, 2002.

28. In response to my suggestion that Wajda had de-judaized the Polish Jewish doctor, Janusz Korczak, who accompanied Jewish children into Auschwitz rather than escape with his own life, Zanussi replied: "He's Christianized him. Korczak was very much a layman, reacting against traditional Judaism. He was an emblematic layman who rejected Zionism. He was a very mysterious character. His legend is very strong, and this final apotheosis is part of mythology based on Christian sensitivity. I totally agree with it. I think it is legitimate in art to use such a kind of trick. But definitely, his Jewishness in the film is not related to his historical roots, because (his) character was like that." Epstein interview with Zanussi.

29. Isaiah Trunk, *History of Poland, Holocaust Period*, www. heritagefilms.com (accessed on December 4, 2002).

30. David Sfarad, *History of Poland, Renewal of Jewish Life*, www.heritagefilms .com (accessed on December 6, 2002).

31. Sfarad, *Renewal*.

32. Cecil Roth, ed., *The Concise Jewish Encyclopedia* (Colchester: Signet, 1980), 431.

33. Roth, *The Concise Jewish Encyclopedia*, 431.

34. Tomasz Kitlinski and Joe Lockard, "Polish Garbage and Dreck Heroes," *Bad Subjects* 55 (May 2001), available at eserver.org/bs/55/kitlinski-lockard.html (accessed on January 24, 2003).

35. In *Illness as Metaphor* author Susan Sontag refers to the close links between biological metaphors and racism. One of the most memorable examples of the use of biological metaphor in film is Constantin Costa-Gavras's *Z* (1969) in which the Junta General likens the opposition to a cancer that needs to be eradicated from the body politic, thereby justifying violence for political ends. The most egregious example of this usage in Nazi cinema was Joseph Goebbels's infamous *Der Ewige Jude* (*The Eternal Jew*, 1940).

36. This scene in the countryside begins *Land of Promise* in the original version released theatrically in 1974.

37. "Rootless cosmopolitan" was a phrase coined during Stalin's Doctor's Plot conspiracy of 1948 to 1953, and referred to Jews in the USSR.

38. Kitlinski and Lockard, "Polish Garbage," 10.

39. Epstein interview with Jason Isaacs in Melbourne, Australia, in December 2002. The talented actor was promoting *Harry Potter and the Chamber of Secrets*, in which he plays Draco's father, Lucius Malfoy.

40. Isaacs is referring here not only to Shakespeare's *Merchant of Venice*, written between 1594 and 1597, but also Christopher Marlowe's *The Jew of Malta*, which was written in 1589 or 1590.

Part 7

Catholicism: Past and Future

Mel Gibson is the Catholic past, clinging like his screen characters to their principles, to a traditionalist heritage that should not be changed. The difficulty with this stance is that it often makes an arbitrary choice of what century of the Catholic past is to be the exemplar of that tradition. For Mel Gibson, his word is *Tridentine*, placing him firmly in the sixteenth century, within the counter Reformation theology and practice, liturgy and spirituality. It has been deepened by his discovery of eighteenth-century mystics and a predilection for the Passion of Christ. Cinema commentators point out how regularly his characters suffer torture, whether it is his William Wallace in *Braveheart* or his Martin Riggs in *Lethal Weapon*, or his Mayan hero, Jaguar Paw, in *Apocalypto*. His extraordinary success with *The Passion of the Christ* and his comments about his personal conversion, experiencing his wounds being healed by the wounds of Jesus, show him to be a man of faith, a proud Catholic.

Kevin Smith, on the other hand, was born in 1971, about fifteen years after Gibson (and in the same general region of the United States). They were a crucial fifteen years in the Catholic Church's twentieth-century history. Smith was born half a decade after the close of the Second Vatican Council in 1965. He is a postmodern, pop culture Catholic not burdened by overreverence. His Catholic upbringing, parish life, and parochial school were different from the traditional ways. And many say that it shows: an eclectic choice of doctrines and interpretation, clever but sometimes ignorant approaches to the history of the church, a Catholic who believes that the church's hold over his soul and conscience should be light.

Neither is he puritanical nor Jansenist. Where Gibson can be eschatological, Smith is scatological. *Dogma*, his millennial comedy, puts all this up there on the screen; though with *Jersey Girl* (2003), and its celebration of family and children and the loving dedication to his father, he has had a (momentary?) move toward a calm and quiet approach.

Gibson and Smith are contrasting faces of Catholicism, looking back and looking forward.

18

Following His True Passion:
Mel Gibson and
The Passion of the Christ

James Abbott

A new church sits in a sixteen-acre plot in a mountain valley near Malibu, Los Angeles. This pre-Vatican II Catholic Church, built by the Holy Family religious group, has attracted much controversy. However, this has not stemmed from their refusal to recognize Rome, nor indeed, because Sunday Mass will be conducted in Latin alone but rather from the fact that the church's principal ally and $2.8 million sole benefactor is Mel Gibson.

The sixth of eleven children, Gibson was born in Peekskill, New York, in January 1956 to Hutton Gibson, a railroad brakeman, and Australian Ann Gibson. His formative years were spent in Australia after his father won the U.S. game show *Jeopardy!* and moved his family to Sydney, where Mel attended an all-boys Catholic high school before securing a place at the University of New South Wales. He sidestepped university to join the National Institute of Dramatic Arts at the same time as Geoffrey Rush and Judy Davis. In 1977, Gibson did well enough on his low budget feature debut—*Summer City*—to serve notice of his talent, and two years later won the Australian Film Institute's (AFI) best actor award for his portrayal of a young man with below average intelligence in *Tim* (1979). In the same year came *Mad Max* (1979), a film that catapulted Gibson into the global arena and sparked a career that would see him become synonymous with the heroic, tough-guy persona. He won another AFI best actor gong in 1981, impressing as Frank Dunne in *Gallipoli* and followed that with a second outing as Mad Max Rockatansky as well as *The Year of Living Dangerously* (1982) before breaking into America with *The Bounty* and *The River* in 1984.

In 1987, he took the lead in a film that exploited American cinemagoers' love of an all-action, unorthodox cop with a dark sense of humor—*Lethal Weapon*. Martin Riggs remains one of Gibson's most popular characters and the film, unsurprisingly, spawned three sequels. In the late 1980s and early 1990s,

he made a series of films combining romance with the now obligatory sprin-
kling of action—*Tequila Sunrise* (1988), *Bird on a Wire* (1990), and *Forever
Young* (1992)—punctuated intermittently by another *Lethal Weapon* (1989) and
a brave decision to take on Shakespeare in Franco Zeffirelli's *Hamlet* (1990;
Zeffirelli had famously directed Robert Powell in the Gospel adaptation *Jesus
of Nazareth* in 1977).

The year 1989 saw the formation of Icon Productions with business partner
Bruce Davey and in 1993, Gibson debuted behind the camera, acting in and
directing *The Man without a Face*. This encouraging directorial debut proved the
precursor to a career-defining moment when he won a Best Director Oscar for
Braveheart (1995). His emotive film portraying Sir William Wallace's battles
with the tyrannical English not only moved cinema audiences worldwide, it
reputedly swelled support for the Scottish National Party by more than a third. As
well as action films *Ransom* (1996), *Conspiracy Theory* (1997), and *Payback*
(1999), Gibson could not resist fighting the English again in another battlefield
epic—*The Patriot* (2000) —and even enjoyed a reasonably successful foray into
mainstream comedy alongside Helen Hunt in *What Women Want* (2001). More
recent projects include *We Were Soldiers* (2002; in which he played a Catholic
Lieutenant Colonel) and the crop circle conspiracy thriller *Signs* (2002).
However, it was the third film under his direction that commanded global media
attention. *The Passion of the Christ* (2004) is the culmination of Gibson's decade-
long desire to chronicle the crucifixion. Who could have predicted a near billion-
dollar turnover (including DVD sales)? It certainly disproved the theory Jewish-
run studios would end the Australian's long career in the movies. However,
directing projects since have been few and far between. Gibson appears only
capable of taking on projects that stir his passion. *Apocalypto* is his long-awaited
winter 2006 release. It may not be a "religious" film (set in Mexico five hundred
years before the sixteenth-century Spanish conquest of Central America), but the
imprint of *The Passion of the Christ* is there for cinemagoers to see—or hear at
least. With a newfound fastidiousness approach to historical accuracy, Gibson is
filming the Mayan epic in an authentic dialect with a cast of indigenous actors.
Come back subtitles, all is forgiven.

Traditional Catholicism

Despite confessing that, "from about the age of 15 to age 35, I kind of did my
own thing as it were, not that I didn't believe in God, I just didn't practice faith
or give it much consideration,"[1] Gibson is regularly pigeon-holed as a Catholic
traditionalist. His father, Hutton, espoused and educated his children in accordance with his own pre-Vatican II Catholic beliefs. Traditional Catholicism is a
grey area as most Catholics would consider themselves traditional insofar as they
simply practice what the Church teaches morally and theologically. The common-

ly held definition of Gibson's traditional Catholicism (in secular circles at any rate) is a staunch, pious, defensive adherence to anything pre-Vatican II and the rejection of the papacy and magisterial amendments thereafter. In an article on the EWTN Website, Colin B. Donovan, STL, discusses traditionalism and assesses pre-1962 Catholicism:

> A spiritually more dangerous variety is the intellectualized traditionalism of those who have rejected Vatican II, or some portion of it (such as liturgical renewal or ecumenism). This rejection is rationalized as obedience to "Tradition" as they understand it. The bishops and even the Pope are seen as being unfaithful to the deposit of the faith (at least in practical matters), with only the traditionalist remnant upholding true Catholicism. Pope John Paul II has referred to this error as Integralism. This name was first used earlier in the century by the popes to describe certain super-orthodox persons who rejected any accommodation with intellectual movements outside the Church and who took it upon themselves to ferret out heresy and heretics within it.[2]

Despite describing pre-Vatican II Catholicism as "dangerous," Donovan does then point out that, in the area of liturgy, the Holy See has recognized those who follow the rites of the Roman Catholic Church prior to the Second Vatican Council:

> This was manifested by the apostolic letter Ecclesia Dei granting the privilege of using the Missal of 1962 to those who desired it and who accepted the Vatican Council and the authority of the Holy See over the Liturgy.[3]

In an interview with Italian newspaper *Il Giornale*, Gibson affirms his religious views, referring to himself as an "old fashioned Catholic" and reveals: "My love for religion was transmitted to me by my father. But I do not believe in the Church as an institution."[4] Hutton Gibson has clearly had a strong influence on his son's beliefs although he is far more outspoken when it comes to his contempt for the Vatican. A former national general secretary of the Australian Latin Mass Society, Hutton has written a number of books on the subject including *Is the Pope Catholic?* and *The Enemy Is Here*. The cover sleeve for the latter has an arrow pointing to Rome. He also publishes a quarterly newsletter *The War Is Now!* Although father and son clearly share traditionalist theological beliefs, Mel has suffered at the hands of the mainstream press, who regularly apply a guilt by association policy and use Hutton's controversial views on subjects like September 11 and the Holocaust to criticize the filmmaker, branding him anything from a homophobe to an anti-Semite. However, as an elder of the Holy Family puts it: "He doesn't go along with a lot his father says."[5]

It must be said that Mel Gibson seems every inch the good Catholic family man. Married to Robyn Moore since 1980, he has seven children. His Catholicism has clearly had an impact on his kids—daughter Hannah has reportedly decided against following her father into the entertainment industry and was reported as wanting to become a nun.[6] However, she married guitarist Kenny Wayne Shepherd in a traditionalist Latin Catholic ceremony in September 2006.

A Truly Catholic Film Director?

Now that we know a little of the man and his beliefs, we can examine how Gibson's Catholicism manifests itself in his work. By his own admission, he started taking his faith seriously only in his mid-30s; this indicates we should look at his work post-1989 to assess any conscious expressions of faith. However, we should not rule out the possibility that his Catholic upbringing had a more subconscious impact prior to this.

Jim Caviezel, the actor chosen by Gibson to play Christ in *The Passion of the Christ*, has said his Catholicism is so important that he only accepts roles in films that hold a morally redeemable value. Without instigating a debate of titanic proportions, we can apply this rationale to Gibson's filmography. Despite the fact that the results are rather mixed, an identifiable trend does establish itself in his films under the umbrella of Icon Productions. We can comfortably argue that *Hamlet*, *The Man without a Face*, *Braveheart*, *The Patriot*, *We Were Soldiers*, *Signs*, and *The Passion of the Christ* hold morally redeemable value in their plots, notwithstanding the fact that these films are still interspersed with comedy and action movies like *What Women Want* and *Payback*.

There are a few caveats that help explain why we do not see a pattern prior to Icon. One, Gibson has been branded with a macho image born out of his early success playing Mad Max in 1979. Two, his religious convictions would not necessarily come to bear in the formative years of his career when breaking through is often the primary concern over picking and choosing films; and three, Gibson has worked for other studios and production companies since 1989, not exclusively Icon. It is for these reasons that we see sensitive portrayals like Tim alongside the bullish Mad Max—likewise, a few years later playing Mac McKussic, a drug-dealer-going-straight in *Tequila Sunrise* alongside tough cop Martin Riggs in *Lethal Weapon*.

Direct references to Catholicism in any dialogue are scarce, although the comical opening rant in *Conspiracy Theory* stands out. Gibson plays New York taxi driver Jerry Fletcher and slates the papacy to two nuns in his cab:

Don't get me wrong Sister, I'm sure your heart's in the right place, OK, but, you know, someone has to lift the scab—the festering scab that is the Vatican.[7]

However, suggesting that lines in films represent the personal beliefs of the reciting actor in any case makes for a flimsy argument. First, a screenwriter detached from the cast usually writes the script—the above example is by Brian Helgeland. Helgeland studied at Loyola Marymount University (the only Jesuit and Marymount Catholic university in Los Angeles). This line is used in early character formation and if anything, is a jovial dig by Helgeland rather than antipapist sentiment from Gibson. (It is an interesting aside that the character Fletcher is a paranoid conspiracy theorist who publishes a newsletter called *Conspiracy Theory*. Gibson's father publishes a similar newsletter.)

If we are struggling to find Gibson's Catholicism permeating his pre-Icon acting roles, we have no trouble locating it in films where he's occupied the director's chair. The acceptance or rejection of a film role can constitute an expression of faith—as Jim Caviezel proves—but from that moment on, the picture is in the hands of the director with minimal input from the cast. When Gibson has directed, the morality of the subject matter is abundantly clear: *The Man without a Face* (society's cruelty toward a disfigured recluse), *Braveheart* (the epic struggle of a man who ultimately allows himself to be martyred to inspire his people to rise up against a tyrannical monarchy), and *The Passion of the Christ* (how God's son died for the salvation of all). We will examine these films in more detail later.

Icon Productions

Success in Hollywood usually comes from toeing the line. Hollywood longevity of Gibson-like proportions means avoiding studio-unfriendly decisions or those that counter commercial common sense (in the early years at any rate). The only way to mass market a more personal viewpoint is to have a reputation, a lot of money, and your own production company complete with distribution arm.

The last utterance of William Wallace in *Braveheart* is one of the most memorable moments in modern cinema—"Freedom." This encapsulates exactly what Gibson has sought, creatively at least, since founding Icon Productions in 1989. Icon has given him the platform to make and star in films where aspects of his faith have become increasingly visible. His directorial debut, *The Man without a Face*, is based on a book written in 1972 by Isabelle Holland and follows the life of Chuck Norstadt, a thirteen-year-old boy who desperately wants to attend the same military boarding school as his (deceased) father but needs a tutor to help him pass the entrance exams. He turns to Justin McLeod, a recluse cruelly branded "hamburger head" by local youths after a car accident leaves him permanently disfigured. Gibson plays the suspicious and reluctant ex-teacher who builds a relationship with Chuck but sees it threatened by persistent rumors that he is a child molester. The film covers several moral themes and suggests that, as a society, we are quick to judge people and place a superficial emphasis on appearance. It is apt that *People Magazine*'s inaugural "sexiest man alive" (1985) should choose to make a film about a disfigured man who rejects society and is, in turn, rejected himself. But why pick this film as his first behind the camera? By 1993, Gibson had been looking for a project to direct for a few years and jumped at Malcolm McRury's screenplay. He had served his apprenticeship by paying close attention to the directors he had already worked under, and in an interview with Rachel Abramowitz, he confessed to

> pillaging off everyone I've ever worked with: George Miller? Shock tactics, making people jump out of their seats—very specific, by-the-numbers thing. Dick Donner? Sort of that light, touchy edge. Try to get a little artsy? Peter Weir. And I picked a lot of stuff up off *Forever Young*'s Steve Miner, because when we were working, I knew I'd be directing soon, so I used to ask him all sorts of questions, just basic things that you need to know.[8]

In the same interview, he reveals he was looking for a character-driven piece, and that to a certain extent, he identified with the lead character:

> I was his age in 1968, which is when the film is set, so . . . there's a bit of me in there . . . just being unsure. I came from a very secure family, where this kid doesn't. But people are people, you know, and it's, like, a lot of the same things can torment them. They all have their devils at age twelve and thirteen, fourteen. There's a little bit of biography, but it's very light.[9]

In all his directorial projects to date, Gibson has desperately tried to avoid taking a starring role. William Hurt and Jeff Bridges were approached for the part of McLeod in *The Man without a Face*, and *Braveheart*'s backers insisted that Gibson take top billing in front of the camera as well as behind before agreeing to finance the film. Searching for evidence of his religious beliefs surfacing in *Braveheart* is a difficult task. By their own admittance, Gibson and Davey took on *Braveheart* for its surefire commercial appeal, and the plot does not really facilitate too many religious moral statements (with the exception of the final scene where Wallace allows himself to be martyred for his people).

The Passion of the Christ

Gibson's film *The Passion of the Christ* offers the clearest example yet of how his Catholicism has influenced his filmmaking. It is a graphic account of the final hours of Christ's life and his suffering on the Cross. Gibson has been a slave to accuracy and detail, and if remarks attributed to the pope are correct, it would appear he has been successful. The pontiff reportedly said: "It is as it was."[10]

The Passion of the Christ has become one of the most talked-about films in cinematic history. Gibson conceded that tackling such a project could have proven a career killer and bravely strayed from commercial filmmaking conventions. For a start, overtly religious films are either ridiculed or treated with great skepticism by modern secular audiences who are more interested in films that challenge the Gospels or sensationalize reverent themes. *The Passion of the Christ* is presented in Latin and Aramaic so viewers can hear Christ speak in his native tongue, although Gibson backtracked on his original desire to show the film without subtitles (his thinking being that subtitles should be superfluous considering the powerful and compelling story—visual artistry over the spoken word).

Source material for the film extends beyond the Bible. Gibson studied the life of a nineteenth-century Augustinian nun and mystic, Anne Catherine Emmerich. Her visions are documented in a book by the poet Klemens Brentano called *The Dolorous Passion of Our Lord Jesus Christ according to the Meditations of Anne Catherine Emmerich*, published in 1833.[11] The venerable sister, despite never leaving Germany, carried the wounds of the stigmata and witnessed many events from biblical times, not least the birth, life, crucifixion, and resurrection of Christ. The Gospels, enhanced by Emmerich's detailed visions and Gibson's self-confessed gift for imagery, have resulted in one of the most unbridled, vivid, accurate, and inspiring accounts of Christ's Passion to date.

However, there were drawbacks to using such material. Emmerich's association with the film fueled the frenzied and initially preemptive charges of anti-Semitism against the director.[12] Not wishing to give the accusations too much credence, Gibson has gone on record stating: "To be certain, neither I nor my film are anti-Semitic." Objective criticism discussed in a fully informed environment should be encouraged, but Gibson appears to have suffered greatly at the hands of critics who passed judgment on the film without having seen it for themselves. A year before the film's release, the controversy started in earnest when a stolen script attracted attention from a group allegedly attached to the American Bishops' Conference and the Jewish Anti-Defamation League (ADL). Abraham Foxman of the ADL even sent an open letter to Gibson seeking assurances that the film would neither give rise to anti-Semitism nor charge the Jews with deicide. Others who had actually seen an early cut reacted more positively to *The Passion of the Christ*. The *Denver National Catholic Register* reported that Father Willy Raymond (who is director of the Catholic production company, Family Theater) "noted that viewed 'with a proper Catholic theological background' there should be little problem with the film."[13] Michael Medved, an orthodox Jew and prominent American film reviewer, has spoken glowingly of Gibson, saying his film was by far the best adaptation of the Bible in Hollywood history, and writer David Horowitz described it as "an awesome artifact and an overpowering work."[14]

Unfortunately the anti-Semitism accusations were not dispelled by the film's release. Leading Jewish figures, like Rabbi Eugene Korn, have pointed out that Gibson's own pre-Vatican II beliefs must result in his rejecting the *Nostra Aetate* (1965) that, in Korn's opinion, repudiates the deicide charge against Jews. In fact, a closer look reveals that the document actually states that Jews of today and the Jewish people collectively at the time of Christ should in no way be held accountable for His death:

True, the Jewish authorities and those who followed their lead pressed for the death of Christ; still, what happened in His passion cannot be charged against all the Jews, without distinction, then alive, nor against the Jews of today.[15]

Gibson goes further and, in his interview with EWTN, points out that his film does not lay the blame on any one group: "We're all culpable with no exceptions . . . that's my hand in there [in the movie] pounding the nail in."[16]

Such sustained criticism of *The Passion of the Christ* has seen a few edits in postproduction to soften the way that Jews are depicted. We see dissenters among the Pharisees when they condemn Jesus without convening a full council, and we also witness many sympathetic Jewish characters objecting to the crucifixion. Paul Lauer, Icon's marketing director, is at pains to highlight the places where the film departs from the Gospels. Referring to Matthew 27:25 where the Jewish mob calls for the blood of Christ to be "on us and on our children," Lauer states: "that's in the Gospel, it's not in our film."[17] He goes on to point out that during the consultation process, Gibson was always forthcoming in discussing the film with both Jewish and Christian leaders.

Gibson's most insightful interviews on the film were given to Raymond Arroyo of EWTN's *The World Over* program. Gibson talked about his desire for accuracy, his opinion of earlier Gospel films (and their depiction of the crucifixion), and how his own faith helped in the making of the film. As a defining point in the history of mankind, Gibson has made the crucifixion centric to the film. Powerful and emotive flashbacks are used to place Jesus's sacrifice in context, show the bond between mother and son, and reveal Christ's relationship with his disciples. In one scene, when John is at the foot of the cross, his eyes are used to pan back to the Last Supper juxtaposing the physical sacrifice on the cross with the sacrifice of the altar. Gibson justifies the importance of accurately document-ing the crucifixion by pointing out that "it has affected every possible part of everyone's life, whether they know it or not."[18]

With the criticism flowing, Gibson had to answer charges that *The Passion of the Christ* is bloodthirsty. However, he explains the graphic and extreme vio-lence by insisting "the audience has to suffer in order to understand it more."[19] No expense has been spared in producing a film of meticulous detail with the direc-tor financing the film with $25 million of his own money. Although his use of ancient languages like Aramaic and Latin stole the headlines, several other meas-ures were taken to safeguard the film's authenticity. For instance, Gibson exam-ined the eating customs and clothing styles of Christ's time to ensure he repre-sented the people in a historically accurate fashion.

Accuracy is again paramount in the casting of Jim Caviezel as Jesus. In his interview with Arroyo, Gibson laments that Hollywood Christs are often too effeminate, pointing out that Caviezel is appropriately masculine and in the film, actually looks like a man who has been working with wood for several years. He also refers to the part technology has played in making *The Passion of the Christ* the most accurate film of its genre. As well as making the action more brutal and realistic, digital editing enabled Gibson to change the color of Caviezel's eyes from their natural blue to brown.

The role Gibson allows the Virgin Mary is another good indication of his Catholicism. Mary, played by Romanian actress Maia Morgenstern, is present in a large proportion of scenes, contrasting greatly with other films of Jesus's life where she takes more of a backseat (only appearing at textbook moments as at the foot of the cross). Gibson offers a theologically accurate Mary—namely Mary as Theotokos.[20] Mary's suffering is an important theme; not only do we see her suffer but we also watch her bear her suffering. As Gibson puts it:

> She suffered as much almost. She didn't have to bear the wounds but imagine if that was your child. And not only that, your child who you know is a deity. Imagine what that's doing to you.[21]

We have to conclude that Gibson's motivations for making this film are centered on his Catholicism. He has talked of his disappointment that previous attempts to tell the story of Christ's passion have been inaccurate and influenced by the politics of the time. He has exposed himself to a great deal of criticism for no personal financial gain (giving over the equivalent of his paycheck for *Signs* to make the film), claiming his principle aim is "to profoundly change people with it."[22] It should also be recognized that during production expressions of Catholicism went beyond what was actually committed to film. Gibson ensured the team had a priest on set to offer daily Latin Mass and also to hear confessions. As for the actors, devout Catholic Jim Caviezel prayed the rosary to help him through his grueling fifteen days of recreated torture on the cross. Of his experience, he says

> I'm interested in letting God work through me to play this role. I believe the Holy Spirit has been leading me in the right direction and to get away from my own physical flesh and allow the character of Jesus to be played out the way God wants it—that's all I can do.[23]

It can now be seen just how profound and widespread the positive response has been to *The Passion of the Christ* from Christian audiences and beyond. I certainly found the film deeply moving and, at times, immensely uncomfortable viewing—just as Gibson intended. Mary's prominence is striking in comparison with other Gospel films, as is the emphasis placed on the bond between mother and son. Juxtaposing Jesus falling under the weight of the cross with a slow-motion flashback where he falls as a child (with a panicking Mary rushing to his side) pulls hard at the heart strings and will make parents reflect instantly on the responsibilities and vulnerabilities of parenthood. It also helps convey the magnitude of Christ's sacrifice for the salvation of humankind.

The Resurrection

The emphasis Gibson places on the resurrection has brought about further debate. John Hartl, a film critic for Microsoft Website MSNBC, describes the film's depiction as perfunctory and compares it unfavorably with Zeffirelli's more classical interpretation in *Jesus of Nazareth* where Christ quietly appears among his disciples.[24] Gibson simply shows Christ sitting in the cave with a cleansed hole in his hand to confirm the crucifixion. The stone rolls back dramatically and he stands and walks away, leaving the shroud behind. Although this is an undeniably short scene, we should not jump to the conclusion that the director has treated the resurrection with flippancy. First, this is the film's final scene and as such contains the inspiring image of Christ people take from the auditorium. Second, its powerful imagery holds true to Gibson's desire that the visual story negates the use of words.

But is it enough to cover such a crucial part of Christ's story? The importance of making a strong point of the resurrection, particularly to nonreligious members of the audience, is to show that Christ is divine and therefore could have prevented his suffering. However his death may be interpreted dramatically, we must at least witness that Jesus, son of God, through his love for us all, allowed himself to be subjected to the most abject humiliation and degradation by those his father created. In my opinion, Gibson succeeds in communicating this in his brief finale.

Many secular friends of mine have asked questions like: What's the point? Why two hours of such vicious brutality? Why do we not see the Passion in context with the rest of Christ's life? To which I point out that the use of flashbacks sparingly shows both his humanity and divinity and although we do not see sermons and miracles, they weave critical lead-up events like the Last Supper into the plot. Gibson prioritizes the brutality to ensure people understand the gravity of the sacrifice to the point that we do not necessarily need to see a Christ who walks on water, multiplies loaves and fishes, cures blindness, and turns water into wine. He reasons, with some justification, that a majority of people, non-Christians included, know the Gospel story, whereas few have seen a nonsanitized version of the Passion.

As for the point of the film, Daniel Johnson made a speculative comment in an article written for the *London Daily Telegraph* (online) prior to the film's U.K. release. It now carries some weight:

> [A] great rabbi once told me that all religions have their difficult texts; the answer, he said, was not to censor them, but to wrestle with them, just as Jacob wrestled with the angel. If *The Passion* succeeds in encouraging Christians to read the Gospels, wrestle with them, and ultimately attain a deeper insight into their faith, then Mel Gibson's crusade will not have been a wasted effort.[25]

Conclusion

Keeping his Catholicism at the forefront of our minds, dissecting and analyzing Gibson the director (while also examining his rise to prominence as one of Hollywood's leading actors) is not a straightforward task. His films cannot be compartmentalized into those in which he has acted and those he has directed. To date, he has directed three feature films with *Apocalypto* the fourth. The first two, *The Man without a Face* and *Braveheart*, additionally saw him take the part of lead actor. The third, *The Passion of the Christ*, is singularly the most important for our purposes, not merely, and obviously, because it gives us a window on his personal religious beliefs, but crucially, by not acting in the film he was able to implement his vision without distraction. It is also important to recognize that post-1989 and the formation of Icon Productions, Gibson's creative input would be greater in films made by Icon than in those he worked on for other studios and hence, it should follow that his Icon films display more of his personality and beliefs.

In terms of religion, Gibson has followed a well-trodden path, starting life as a cradle Catholic, attending a Catholic high school, losing touch with his faith before exploring it further and reaffirming his beliefs in his mid-30s. His filmography also reflects a roller-coaster ride where he has played sensitive characters alongside macho all-action heroes. On more than one occasion, EWTN's Arroyo has pushed Gibson to agree with his assertion that his films are becoming increasingly centered on the fight between good and evil and the inner spiritual struggle citing *Braveheart*, *We Were Soldiers*, and *Signs* as examples. The latter is particularly interesting as he plays Graham Hess, an Episcopalian minister who nearly loses his faith when tested. Arroyo asks whether this trend will continue, to which Gibson responds cautiously, "Probably. You have to talk about what you know about. . . . I'm no expert. But you can only put your own experience in your work. How that manifests itself I have no way of knowing in the future. I don't know if I'll work again."[26]

After completing *The Man without a Face*, Gibson made a profound statement that certainly holds true to the films he has made since: "All movies are about moral transgressions. Life is about the battle between the spirit and the flesh."[27] If we set aside what is said and written about Gibson and instead examine what he himself has put on record in interviews, we form a picture of a successful, contented family man who is in the enviable position of only making films that are important to him. These days, financial recompense does not appear so important to Gibson. If he considers *The Passion of the Christ* an expression of faith—part of the learning curve—then he would probably consider it $25 million well spent. Add to this the $2.8 million donated to the Holy Family to start a pre-Vatican II Catholic Church in Malibu, and we see a man who takes his Christianity seriously.

Having completed filming on *The Passion of the Christ*, does Gibson now consider himself a Catholic film director? He admits to Arroyo that *The Passion*

of the Christ has focused his faith but is still tentative when it comes to categorizing himself as a Catholic director: "It's going more in that direction . . . if
you're raised in that way, you use what you are."[28] The film gives us a glimpse of
his strength of faith although he is guarded when it comes to discussing the finer
points of his Catholicism. He confirms: "It reflects my beliefs and I've never
done that before . . . because I haven't had the opportunity." He goes further:
"When you're focused on something like this for five months solid, you're looking at it all the time. It's going to work its way in, in a way that you don't even
first perceive but the effects are going to stay with you—the marks."[29] His admission that the film represents the first and only time he has been able to commit
his own beliefs to celluloid aptly demonstrates why we must examine *The
Passion of the Christ* in detail to examine Gibson's Catholicism.

The fact that he judges previous attempts to tell Christ's story as sanitized
and unrealistic and that Christ's ultimate sacrifice is of such paramount importance that he had to make a film to bring it to a mass audience—risking his career
and reputation—shows what the crucifixion means to Gibson. He tells EWTN: "I
was focused on the Passion for a long time—it was my own personal meditation.
I focused on that because I found it healing for me because, like most of us, you
get to a point in your life where you're pretty wounded by everything that goes
on around you . . . by your own transgressions . . . by other people's. Life is kind
of a scarring thing. So I used the Passion as a meditation of healing myself."[30]

Box office figures in the United States show a record-breaking return on the
$30 million budget ($170 million in the first three weeks alone) so any fears of
career suicide can be put to one side. If Gibson wants people to sit up and take
notice of Christ's Passion, reams of column inches and mountains of box office
dollars would suggest he's succeeded admirably. One thing cannot be disputed;
Mel Gibson followed his true passion.

Reviewing the Chapter

1.   Having used the medium of film to spread knowledge of Christ's profound sacrifice globally, is Gibson a new type of evangelist or is this an easier
option than the street corner?

2.   In a bloodthirsty age where little makes the censors blush, is the success
of *The Passion of the Christ* based more on its graphic content and aesthetically
pleasing cast than its message of salvation? Given the fact it spreads the story of
Christ, does it matter?

3.   Just how much of a career gamble was making *The Passion of the
Christ*? Did Gibson time the release to cash in on the religious dollar in a way that
some may suggest *Brokeback Mountain* harnessed the pink pound?

Notes

1.   Holly McClure, "A Very Violent 'Passion,'" *New York Daily News*, January 26, 2003, available at: www.nydailynews.com/front/story/54288p-50909c.html (accessed on June 18, 2003).

2.   Colin B. Donovan, EWTN Website, www.ewtn.com/expert/answers/traditionalism.htm (accessed June 12, 2003).

3.   Donovan, EWTN.

4.   Taken from an interview with Mel Gibson in *Il Giornale*, quoted by Richard Owen in "Mel Gibson Launches Scathing Attack on the Vatican," *The Times*, September 13, 2002.

5.   Christopher Noxon, "Is the Pope Catholic . . . Enough?" *New York Times* magazine, March 9, 2003, available at: www.nytimes.com/2003/03/09/magazine/09GIBSON.html?ex=1163394000&en=4fb945948c64278c&ei=5070.

6.   Sydney Morning Herald (Australia) Website quoting Gibson's interview with *Il Giornale* (Sept. 2002), available at: www.smh.com.au/articles/2002/09/14/1031608343843.html (accessed June 2003).

7.   *Conspiracy Theory* (1997), Warner Bros Pictures, Silver Pictures Production, directed by Richard Donner.

8.   Rachel Abramowitz, Interview with Mel Gibson, *Premiere*, September 1993.

9.   Abramowitz, Interview.

10.   This is contested by Archbishop Dziwisz, the pope's personal secretary, who later claimed the pontiff had not passed judgment on the film at all.

11.   Emmerich's piety had a profound effect on Brentano, who sought the inspiration to reaffirm his Catholic faith when he met the stigmatic in 1818.

12.   One critic, Rabbi Marvin Hier, dean and founder of the Simon Wiesenthal Center in Los Angeles, referred to how Emmerich described Jews with "hooked noses" in her visions.

13.   Andrew Walther in the *National Catholic Register*.

14.   Hugh Davies, "Mel Gibson Christ Film Is Branded Anti-Jewish," *The Daily Telegraph*, August 6, 2003, available at: www.telegraph.co.uk/news/main.jhtml?xml=/news/2003/08/06/wmel06.xml.

15.   Pope Paul VI, *Nostra Aetate*, October 28, 1965, footnote 13 within the extract refers to John 19:6.

16.   Raymond Arroyo, Interview with Mel Gibson, *The World Over*, EWTN, February 2004.

17.   Paul Lauer quoted by Kevin Eckstrom of the Religion News Service published in "Gibson Says He Has 'Softened' Crucifixion Story in New Jesus Movie" available at: http://www.beliefnet.com/story/131/story_13109_1.html (accessed June 2003).

18.   Raymond Arroyo, Interview with Mel Gibson, *The World Over*, EWTN, March 2003.

19.   Arroyo, Interview, March 2003.

20.   God-bearer.

21.   Arroyo, Interview, March 2003.

22.   Arroyo, Interview, March 2003.

23.   McClure, "A Very Violent 'Passion.'"

24.   John Hartl, "Review of *The Passion of the Christ*," MSN's MSNBC Website,

www.msnbc.msn.com/id/4360578 (accessed March 2, 2004).

25. Daniel Johnson, "Will Mel Gibson's Passion of Christ Help Save Christianity?" available at: www.telegraph.co.uk/opinion/main.jhtml?xml=/opinion/2004/02/11/do1101 .xml&sSheet=/opinion/2004/02/11/ixopi nion.html (February 11, 2004).

26. Arroyo, Interview, February 2004.

27. Abramowitz, Interview.

28. Arroyo, Interview, March 2003.

29. Arroyo, Interview, February 2004.

30. Arroyo, Interview, February 2004.

19

View Askewed in *Dogma*: Kevin Smith—A Funny Guy?

Rose Pacatte

Kevin Smith is a funny guy. According to one young woman who recently introduced him to a group of students at a university, Kevin has given new meaning to "spirituality, sexuality and human relationships" through his movies. And if I were one of the nuns or teachers who taught Kevin during his eight years of Catholic education in New Jersey, I would probably want to kill myself. I will use those categories to explore the work of Kevin Smith, especially in his 1999 film, *Dogma*.

As of this writing, Smith is in his thirty-third year, and he has been on the filmmaking radar since 1994. He's written, directed, and acted in six feature films, *Clerks* (1994), *Mallrats* (1995), *Chasing Amy* (1997), *Dogma* (1999), *Jay and Silent Bob Strike Back* (2001), and *Jersey Girl* (2004; the only one of his films in which he does not appear). Smith was one of the executive coproducers for the Academy Award–winning film *Good Will Hunting* (1997), written by and starring pals Ben Affleck and Matt Damon. So far Smith has been involved in about thirty projects for the screen or television. For a film school dropout (he spent four months at the Vancouver Film School in British Columbia), Smith is making a serious mark in the world of college students and Hollywood.

Here are some basic facts that can be gleaned from his wacky Website,[1] the DVD set *An Evening with Kevin Smith*,[2] and *A View Askew: The Films of Kevin Smith*.[3] Smith grew up fat, and this is the source of his comedy; making movies with his friends is the whole point of his career; there has to be a God because he has a career; he's self-conscious; writes his films in a world of comic books, pop culture, and monologues; he plays "Silent Bob" in his movies because he cannot act. This is what he says about himself. What comes through his sessions with university students is that he is smart, funny, educated, and kind.

> I do what I do because I grew up fat . . . a heavy kid. It made me want to be funny because a fat kid can't get by on "looks."
>
> Making movies with my friends is the whole point of my career.
> I believe in faith, God and Christ. I am a spiritual person . . .

I appreciate who Christ is and what he did, but I wanted to have sex before marriage.

Smith's 2004 release *Jersey Girl* presents a more mature filmmaker. It is constructed in the classic film mode, a major change in Smith's cinematic style, so to speak, and the way he sees the world. It is the story of a high-powered Manhattan publicist, Ollie (Ben Affleck) who gets married only to have his wife die in childbirth. He gets fired when he loses it at a press event for the actor Will Smith and has to move back to Jersey to live with his dad. There is a good deal of Catholic imagery that seems to be used as props, and there are innumerous Catholic culture references and the typical bathroom, body parts, and porn humor—after all, Smith is the writer. Then there is wonderful conversation between Will Smith (as himself) and Ollie about children, family, and what really matters. *Jersey Girl* is more Catholic than meets the eye. *Jersey Girl* is not the focus of this chapter however; it will focus on *Dogma* as a journey toward Smith's understanding of what he has been taught as a Catholic.

The Story: Leave it to the Catholics to Destroy Existence

Dogma is a story about God, looking like an old man, who one day goes for a stroll along the boardwalk in Asbury Park, New Jersey, and gets mugged by minions of a demon, Azrael (Jason Lee), and ends up on life support at the local hospital.

Meanwhile, a *fallen* woman named Bethany (Linda Fiorentino) who has had an abortion, is now sterile, divorced, and works in an abortion clinic outside Chicago as a counselor. But she is still a believer and even tithes her salary. An angel named Metatron (Greek for "instrument of transformation"[4] played by Alan Rickman) appears to her with a message that she has been called by God for a special mission. She must leave for New Jersey on a journey (which film critic Richard A. Blake, S.J., said could compare to a pilgrimage of conversion[5] if some audiences were not so distracted by other elements of the film).

On the way, Bethany encounters a host of characters with whom her destiny is bound. First there are the fallen angels, Loki and Bartleby (Damon and Affleck), who have divined a way to get back into heaven via a loophole in Catholic doctrine. Loki was an efficient and violent avenging angel at the height of his career, when—through a misunderstanding—he and Bartleby were banished to Wisconsin. They must get to New Jersey by a certain date so they can get back into God's good graces. They have heard about a plenary indulgence that is available only there, because Cardinal Ignatius Glick (George Carlin), the Archbishop of Red Bank, has declared an amnesty. He is promoting a *Wow* Jesus, instead of the one who was crucified, so more people will come to church.

Bethany also meets a couple of prophets, Jay and Silent Bob (Jason Mewes and Smith), a fallen muse named Serendipity (Salma Hayek) who works as a stripper, and Rufus (Chris Rock), the Thirteenth Apostle who, in passing, is black—like

God. The characters have their moments along the way, from annihilating a room full of television executives to combating a poop monster. Once in New Jersey, the angels pass through the doors for their indulgence, but annihilate more people, Bethany takes God off life support, and *He* then appears as a *She* (Alanis Morrisette) and cleans up the mess Bartleby and Loki have made (they lose their wings). Bethany then finds out she is pregnant through divine intervention.

The Aftermath

There was a tremendous hue and cry in the United States against *Dogma* that began when it was in postproduction and continued through the first weeks of its release. The Catholic League for Religious and Civil Rights, founded in 1973 to combat anti-Catholic bias in the media, started a campaign to stop Disney from distributing the film. William Donahue, the president of the Catholic League, roundly and loudly condemned the film—even though he had never seen it. Ultimately Miramax distributed *Dogma* internationally, and Lions Gate covered the domestic market. Once this distribution change was accomplished, the Catholic League was heard from no more, and *Dogma* grossed $30 million at the box office.[6]

The film, however, was still greeted by picket lines. It carries a disclaimer that identifies the film as a "comedic fantasy," but this did not seem to quell the storm. Smith and his wife received three hundred thousand pieces of hate mail and at least three death threats. Miramax hired bodyguards for the couple when they were at the film festival in Cannes. In typical Smith fashion, he, wife Jennifer Schwalbach, and a friend made their own picket signs, joined some picketers at a local theater, and fooled a television reporter into thinking he was just another disgruntled moviegoer. When he tells this story, Smith continues to repeat the question: This is a rubber poop monster; how much damage can it do?

Kevin Smith as a Director

Smith is candid about his skills as a director, writer, and actor. There's no mystery here. His visual style, at least until the more conventional *Jersey Girl*, is that he has no visual style.[7] However, Smith's films are interesting because of the simple framing of scenes—they often seem as if they are taken right out of a comic book. His approach to visual composition works, because it is tried and true—not because he is offering the art of cinema anything new. The only perspective is straight on and what binds the scenes together is the dialogue. Smith's films do not create an emotional atmosphere unless the viewer is on the same wavelength as he is. If this is the case, as the testimonials toward the end of this chapter reveal, then he achieves his goal to entertain and explore Catholicism as he perceives it, through a film about dogma.

Smith cannot really write, except for monologues, and he admits that he cannot act. That is how he became an actor in the first place. Further, this is why he has almost no lines—he cannot act. I would agree with this except for his role in *Chasing Amy*. He had decided to act in *Clerks*,[8] because he figured that if he never made another film, at least he would have been in one. *Clerks*, however, started a cinematic cult and the rest is history in the making. (It should be noted, however, that Chicago film critic Roger Ebert wrote about *Jersey Girl* on March 26, 2004, and called Smith "a gifted writer.")

As a writer, Smith's ideas often seem better than their execution. In *Dogma*, however, he got to work with special effects for the first time. Thus we have the desexualized angel, Metatron, the mechanical rubber poop, and Loki and Bartleby's wings. *Mallrats* had some great lines, such as "I love the smell of commerce in the morning"—a reference of course to Coppola's Vietnam 1979 epic, *Apocalypse Now*. *Jersey Girl* will not be remembered for great dialogue, either, but it does the job—it conveys a lot of heart.

The gift shop at the Los Angeles County Museum of Art sells note cards that say, "Fear no art." Given the negative reaction to Smith's movies from the grown-up establishment that might be construed as fear that Catholic beliefs are being deconstructed and attacked, we may ask: Did people fear Kevin Smith's *Dogma* because it is art or because it is not? Georgia O'Keefe once said, "True art irritates." If this is the standard for art, then on some level, *Dogma* must qualify.

Smith's knowledge of popular culture is exhaustive, and he milks it for all it's worth. And why not? His moviemaking is completely consistent with the experience and values of his world. What Smith does have is an unspecified talent for storytelling combined with the gifts of comedy and empathy. These elements make him a credible and authentic communicator, and in this day and age, this is what makes him a notable director.

Dogma: Catholic and Postmodern

By the end of *Dogma*, the lost have been found, order is created out of chaos, and the fallen have risen, but the meaning of the film is ultimately up to the viewer. *Dogma*, however unsubtle its premise, begs to be seen more than once, simply because there is so much going on and so much being said. Smith creates this religious, spiritual, and philosophical journey for his characters so they can probe the meaning of the Catholic faith and ask all the questions Smith can think of. That their journey follows a skewed path with such skewed characters is the fun part.

Smith signals his Catholicism in every movie he makes, even if it is only using the names of Catholic colleges (*Mallrats*.) In *Dogma*, however, he gets serious even though he obviously does not have a good grip on Catholic doctrine. It is as if everything he has ever learned or heard about what Catholics believe and practice has gone into a processor and been spewed out in this doctrinal hodgepodge of a movie. But is Smith to be blamed for this? Has he done something wrong by asking questions about the creed and culture that surrounds the Catholic faith or its beliefs? I do not think so. To me, Smith is trying to make sense out of what he, personally, has heard, seen, been taught, and experienced to test its veracity and relevance.

Perhaps, like many of us, he has seen too many little old Italian ladies race across the sanctuary of a church in front of the blessed sacrament, the body, blood, soul, and divinity of Jesus Christ, without even a nod, to genuflect, prostrate themselves, and light numerous candles to St. Anthony.

In a real sense, *dogma* has lost its meaning for Smith's generation, because the young have the perception that the essentials of faith have been replaced by nonessentials and man-made laws. For them, there is no logical connection between dogma and God, but they want to check it out anyway. Hence the film's title.

In one of the early episodes of the controversial hit comedy cartoon series about perpetual anti-Canadian fourth graders, *South Park*, creators Trey Parker and Matt Stone have the teacher join with the parents in telling the children not to watch certain television programs that ruin their minds, because they are about bathroom humor and not based in reality. Meanwhile, Kenny, who has explosive diarrhea, pollutes the classroom with smell and sound. Then Stan asks if it is okay to kill someone if they ask you to, like Dr. Kevorkian. The teacher tells the children: "I am not touching that one with a ten-foot pole." In other words, poop is not part of the real world so we do not talk about it, and physician-assisted suicide is about life and death issues but controversial, so we do not talk about that either. So what do we talk about, parents, teachers, and clergy?[9]

Dogma is the Catholic live action version of *South Park* (the series and the 1999 film, *South Park: Bigger, Longer & Uncut*). Both question the inconsistencies of adult behavior and beliefs, and both pursue religious, spiritual, and moral questions that irritate the parent, church, school, and civil establishment to no end. They use the same means: smart and insightful dialogue, crude language, gross-out scatological humor, and perceived irreverence to time-honored beliefs and customs—all within the context of self-referent pop culture. Thus, both are entertainment productions consistent with the era in which they exist, offend, and delight. In these ways they are entirely postmodern. Ultimately *Dogma* confirms the filmmaker's belief in a transcendent God—even if truth is still unclear, and doctrine, dogma, and the behavior of believers seldom seem to match.

Says Smith about *Dogma*: "It was just a kind of offering up of what I consider myself to be, a contemporary Catholic. I'm Catholic, I go to church, but I am not one of these people who condemn others for not believing in the same thing that I do. So isn't it possible for a guy who makes a movie chock-a-block full of dick and fart jokes and still have faith in God?"[10]

Spirituality

According to Thomas P. Rausch, S.J., "Spirituality is a term used to describe a particular vision of the Christian life and the manner of living it. A spirituality is a discipline for discipleship. There are many different spiritualities in the Church, monastic, Franciscan, Ignatian, social justice, feminist, and so on."[11]

If we are to apply this definition to Smith's idea of spirituality in *Dogma*, it would yield a split-level view of his way of relating to the Christian life or actually Christ. Although Smith touches on issues of human dignity in *Dogma* (racism and feminism for starters), his vision does not go far beyond his personal viewpoint. We do not get a big picture of the world. This is Smith's personal journey. Perhaps we could categorize Smith's spirituality as one of hope that is searching for a more transcendent and existential expression but which in fact then questions the relevance of the premise for traditional spiritualities.

In *Dogma*, Smith's vision of the Christian life is that it is absurd—yet there might be some basis for belief and morality if we can only dig through all the excrement in which humans have buried essential Christianity along with the person of Christ. Smith seems to know that the kindness he communicates to others is rooted in something beyond himself.[12] In his conversations with university students he talks about religion and spirituality as evenly as he does other subjects, because he assumes everyone in the audience is on the same page he is in life. This probably is not true, but the respect and reverence they have for Smith supersedes any assumptions on his part. He is like a guru. He is kind, he listens, he empathizes, he is a master storyteller, he is self-deprecating and funny and for this young, Gen X and Gen Y postmodern self-referent world of the United States today, it is enough.

Smith is familiar with the scriptures and the many negative aspects of Church history. In *Dogma* he identifies a matrix made up of faith, doctrine, dogma, belief, and Christian morality and uses it to ask: "Did someone create God?"[13] Are we dealing here with ideas or doctrine?

If Smith has a spirituality, a "discipline for discipleship," it is that of loyalty to his friends. His movies bear this out. Not unlike classical directors of film, such as John Ford or Alfred Hitchcock, Smith uses the same actors—and characters—over and over. If there is a way to find God in these relationships, then perhaps Christianity will work for him. Smith admits that he had a crisis of faith when he was eighteen or nineteen and that writing and making *Dogma* was a way for him to work through it. He believes in God, in Christ, and admits openly that he is a spiritual person. In *Jersey Girl* we find out that Smith is no longer so dependent on friends, because he now has a family of his own to use as material for his films.

Sexuality

When the angel Metatron appears to Bethany early in the film, she asks what God is like. Metatron answers, "Lonely, but funny. He's got a great sense of humor. Take sex, for example—there's nothing funnier than the ridiculous faces you people make, mid-coitus." She replies, "Sex is a joke in heaven?" And he says, "The way I understand it, it's mostly a joke down here, too."

By the third or fourth viewing of this scene, it is possible to recognize a certain pathos to Bethany's question and regret in Metatron's voice—not because as an angel he cannot have sex, but maybe because it is so important that it is sad when sexuality is reduced to a joke. Smith talks and jokes a lot about sexual activities in *Dogma* (and his sessions with college students) but one senses that while he says one thing, he means something else.

Smith and Schwalbach were married while *Dogma* was in postproduction and Schwalbach was eight months pregnant. "Kevin and I had a special moment that I hope everyone who gets married goes through. We had thrown our lives together, we were having a child, and we didn't think we could become any closer. It was more than I ever expected or hoped for, and he feels the same. We just love being married."[14] Jennifer's words seem to mark a certain maturity in Smith's personal growth and development. One can never be too sure with Smith, though. Despite moments of brilliance (the scene in *Chasing Amy* when Silent Bob finally talks about Amy), he easily goes where he has gone before, to the land where genitalia and passing gas inform all of life and offer people the most entertaining insights sotto-culture. *Jersey Girl* has these elements as well, but Smith uses them more like gags to connect you to his past films and therefore reassure his audience that he is still here.

Smith outed his brother as a homosexual in the DVD *An Evening with Kevin Smith*, if not before. Kevin is clear that he is a heterosexual male, but he makes gay jokes and talks about gays and lesbians without ambiguity—case in point, *Chasing Amy*. Even Gay and Lesbian Alliance against Defamation (GLAAD) was upset with him for the way he represented gays and lesbians, although this must surely depend on the subjective interpretation of the audience. Smith actually has great empathy for what others must endure to survive, and this is what he is really showing when he has his characters talk about issues such as homosexuality. His jokes are meant to be cool, not cruel. Smith seems to consider sexuality only on the physical level, and he must take responsibility for giving this impression. Only Smith knows where he is on the scale of psycho-spiritual development now that he is a husband and father. In *Jersey Girl* Smith treats us to the whole issue of psycho-sexual development; parenthood must be giving him a whole new awareness.

I wrote this chapter before *Jersey Girl* was released and as I did so I wondered if he would make it for his Gen X audience or if he would be capable of retaining this fan base and acquire new ones, older and younger. Would he forever be an adolescent or will he just play well to them? I cannot predict the future of Kevin Smith's filmmaking, but *Jersey Girl* played to positive reviews and a solid box office.

The thoughtful viewer, especially one who looks at all Smith's films, might concede that there's more going on in his films than meets the eye. They are a work in progress. They are Smith in progress, like a chronicle of his journey to adulthood.

Dogma makes the unsuspecting viewer ask if Smith knows the difference between sexuality and scatology. Oh, he knows. He also knows how to play an audience and to tap into human insecurities about growing up and relationships. Human sexuality is another item on the excrement-covered church agenda that Smith is trying to wade through. If Smith has offered the world a new (or better yet, confusing) way to look at sexuality, perhaps it is because he is willing to look—and talk—about it, at all. If this is what Smith thinks, should we blame him for making a film that expresses and explores the way he sees how Christianity and the church teach about and witness to sexuality, or should we ask ourselves why he has a different perspective from that of Catholics of twenty, thirty, forty, or fifty years ago? How well has the church communicated itself to the modern world?

The more important question to ask when considering how Smith has given us new ways of looking at sexuality is for the viewer to reintegrate sexuality with the concept of the human person and explore what Smith's idea of the human person actually is. *Dogma* at first seems more concerned about an image of God, the relevance of Christ, and the human dimension of the church than the human person. Smith seems to sublimate friendship as the ultimate relationship over the bond between man and woman, husband and wife. On the face of it, Smith also seems to fail to realize that while he questions spirituality, sexuality, human relationships, God, Christ, and the church by using humor and irony, he seems to trivialize the themes and issues he calls into question. This is the complex nature of comedy, however. Smith's humor may just be a mask that covers the deepest yearnings of the human heart for connectedness, transcendence, and intimacy.

The year 1999 must have been good for philosophers about the culture. Not only did Smith's *Dogma* arrive on the scene, but so did a thoughtful book called *Shows about Nothing: Nihilism in Popular Culture from Seinfeld to the Exorcist* by Thomas S. Hibbs.[15] In it, Hibbs says that nihilism means that pizza and abortion have the same moral value. A couple of years later, in an episode of *Dawson's Creek*, Jack tells Joey that having sex is no big deal, because there is no right choice; life is just a bunch of choices. Does Smith really believe this, too? Or does he struggle to recognize that this kind of ideology is not enough to give a person a reason to get up in the morning?

On one level in *Dogma*, Smith's adolescent approach objectifies sexuality by reducing it to talking about functions and fun. Another way to express this

would be to say that he does not seem to understand the balance between freedom and responsibility, even when talking about sexuality. Yes, he *gets* the
pragmatic side to using birth control in the sermonizing conversation between
Bethany and a girl in the Planned Parenthood office at the beginning of the film.
The conversation is confused about abortion, guilt, and consequences, but it
gives me hope that the writer is grappling with issues that go beyond entertainment value. Smith is a product of his culture. He reports what he sees. The fact
that he even folds these issues into a film that explores a crisis of faith means
one thing to me—he is a seeker.

Human Relationships: Friends and Family

As noted previously, Smith's friendships are what motivate him and give meaning to his life and career. Mewes, who plays Jay to Smith's Silent Bob, seems
omnipresent, and Smith speaks continually of partner Scott Mosier, wife
Jennifer, and friends Affleck and Damon. He is faithful to them, and they to him.
"He doesn't write about fictional characters," says Jennifer. "He writes about
himself and his friends."16

Dogma is a kind of road trip where different people—and creatures—join
together on a common quest. For the most part, they respect one another. Even
though Loki and Bartleby's relationship ultimately suffers, the message that
Dogma offers is one that celebrates the bond between fellow travelers, and this
commonality makes them friends. The film is not as skeptical as it may seem,
because God is present in and to those relationships. God is not obscure to Smith,
who may ultimately be asking why those who call ourselves believers want to
obscure God with a lot of nonessentials. Perhaps life is as simple as Smith would
have us believe, or it is so complex that the only way to understand what's going
on is to return to the bare bones of human culture: relationships.

Smith's loyalty to his friends is admirable, but perhaps it also limits his
vision of the natural universe that provides the context for our existence. The
audience gets a good look at New Jersey and life at the mall and on television as
he experienced it there, but what difference does the life of a lonely fat boy and
the lives of a few Jerseyites make to the world—and the world to them? Does
anyone or anything matter?

Comic books, a major factor in the creative life of Smith and friends, give us
superheroes, and some would say that these kinds of characters epitomize the
nihilism of our age. Perhaps they do. On the other hand, if nihilism is the message younger generations are getting or the meaning they are making from the
culture, to whom or what shall we accredit this?

It was hard for me to get a sense of Smith's view of family as I researched
this chapter. I only found mention of his brother and wife at the release of *Jersey
Girl* in 2004. He dedicated this film to his recently deceased father and told his

wife it was his valentine to her (even though the mother dies in the first fifteen
minutes of the film). Smith wants to keep his friends indeed, but in all honesty,
his love for his family is all over this film in his own too-imitable style.

A film is at the crossroad between the meaning intended by the filmmaker
and the meaning that the audience makes from it. At times, the struggle for meaning pits audience against filmmaker—and filmmaker against the audience. For
Kevin Smith's audience, the apex of meaning appears to be in the relationships
he creates on screen, behind the screen, and out there in the front row. This relationship is dynamic and spiritual because of its transcendent qualities of loyalty,
respect, kindness, and love. *Jersey Girl*, coming along four years after *Dogma* (its
release was delayed for several months), embraces these qualities and lets us see
just how important they are to Smith now that he is a husband and father.

Religious educators and catechists know that the best way to lead students to
a relationship with Jesus is to begin in the life experience of the child: the world
they know, their families and friends. Smith has let us experience the world the
way he sees and experiences it. He has borne witness to the mall as a playground,
rather than nature, as the great masters have done. In all his films he has forced
the audience to consider another perspective of the world—his world.

What Think Thee of Smith?

To prepare for writing this chapter I saw all the films of Smith, saw *Dogma* in the
theater when it came out plus two more times on video, read two of the screenplays, and screened the entire two-disk DVD of *An Evening with Kevin Smith* (it
was more like five evenings but at least it was not repetitious) and tried (unsuccessfully) to get an interview with Smith when he was in Los Angeles. I also post-
ed a brief survey on a Smith/Dogma bulletin board out there in cyberspace. I
especially wanted to know what females thought of Smith, given that his form of
humor is so adolescent and so male. Here are some of the answers that contribute
to a more universal look at Smith as a filmmaker:

> I am female, 20 years old, non-Catholic from Arizona. I absolutely loved
> *Dogma*; it was intelligent, surprisingly well delivered; gave organized religion a
> reaffirming, humbling kick in the mouth in an incredibly delightful, witty way.
> Even being atheist, this delivered some tiny shred of mythical hope not often
> found in film.

> I am a 20 year old female from Florida, non-Catholic. Yes, I liked *Dogma*
> because it has a great plot, and it poked fun at the way religion has just become
> one big pissing contest (pardon my French) about what religion does what,
> which religion is better, etc.

I am a female, I was born and raised Catholic for 18 years and am currently an agnostic (as so many of us are). Hell yes (no pun intended), I liked *Dogma*. Why? Because the storyline was brilliant and hilarious. Anything I could write sounds trite when I compare it to the way the movie made/makes me feel—my feeble words won't do it justice. But I don't like Ben Affleck. I liked him in this movie except for the part in the train where he says "do I look gay to you" and smiles in that Affleck-y way. It really bugs me. What did *Dogma* mean for me? I tend to think—if this movie had only come about earlier, it could have kept me on the path to God and saved my soul from eternal damnation.

I am a female, 30 years old, a non-Catholic from Washington, D.C. No, I did not like *Dogma*. Just because Kevin Smith created it, doesn't make it good. It's scary when Kevin Smith waxes philosophical. I'm not interested in his opinions. I'm not offended on religious grounds, I'm offended on artistic ones. The movie was gory and confusing, the dialogue was ludicrous, the acting was awful (Salma Hayek wore a "why the hell am I here?" expression the whole film).

I think Kevin Smith is very talented, but I also think he takes a lot of artistic shortcuts—he goes for the gross-out joke when he can't think of anything better to do. He also does a lot of gay jokes, not because he's homophobic, but because they're cheap and easy. *Clerks* is legitimately a good movie, although a lot of the jokes seemed lifted from Lenny Bruce. *Mallrats* was underrated—I thought that was actually the funniest one in the series. I thought *Chasing Amy* was good the first time I saw it, now I find it strident and preachy. Plus Joey Lauren Adams is a poor man's Renee Zellweger with an extra dose of whininess. *Dogma* is a black hole (it sucks the life out of everything). *Jay and Silent Bob Strike Back* was actually very funny, but it didn't really take off until everyone got to Hollywood.

I'm actually a huge Kevin Smith fan. I am a Presbyterian in training for ministry, but I go to a pretty liberal church (liberal for Presbyterians). I think Kevin is brilliant. *Chasing Amy* is definitely my favorite. But I loved *Dogma*, which was shot in my hometown of Pittsburgh, P.A., and *Clerks*. The other two are okay. I think he does well to represent the young male Catholic. It's a stereotypical opinion, but my ex-roommate is Catholic, and he was pretty similar to the characters of the film. He did wild party stuff, yet he never missed Mass. I've also read some on Kevin Smith, and it seems he is more into comedy—being funny—than anything. What I thought was most significant about *Dogma*, what I took from it anyway, was the notion of having ideas instead of beliefs. I thought it was pretty profound. I get the impression there's a great deal about the faith he wishes would change, but he still loves it. In the scene between Loki and Bartleby in the parking lot, I think he was able to crystallize all the celestial hierarchy stuff—the pageantry and cosmology of faith pretty well and that's how he deals with spirituality. When it comes down to it, God loves humans more. Grace is given to humans only—none of the celestial beings. What is hardest is doing what God commands, but doing it anyway. Even though the characters of the film are cynical and question God, I don't think they really question their faith. The only ones are the two angels, and they both die. I think his main message is that God is with everyone, and he seems to want people to know that. I think it's what I really appreciate. God loves first and corrects/judges later, but that doesn't mean there's no judging going on. I think his films are relevant and say more about God to a young audience than any other—certainly more than the *Omega Code* films and the *Left Behind* series. I would think *Dogma* would get people into church, rather than away from it. He's certainly got a following on the [I]nternet. He also speaks to the over-intelligent, under-social comic book/sci-fi fantasy crowd better than any church people I know. Ultimately, I think his story is great. It is one guy, who decided to make movies, and went about doing that. There also isn't any arrogance in his work. And most people don't realize Smith produced *Good Will Hunting*, which was a phenomenal film about coming to terms with life—choosing to live.

Conclusion

Smith's films are controversial, because they are crude, they challenge religious, societal, and cultural mores, and they are crude again. Many viewers that I met did not like the film *Angela's Ashes* or the book on which it was based, because, as one Irish priest told me, "There are certain things you don't talk about." Smith persists in talking about a lot of things in *Dogma* and his other films, and asking "Why not?" Others disliked *Angela's Ashes* because they felt it criticized the church. I think author Frank McCourt was doing for the older Catholic generation what Smith is doing for his—they are questioning and challenging the culture that has grown up around the essentials of Catholicism in a search for Christ and meaning.

Until we—who believe ourselves to be the guardians of a Catholic culture and the cross that in the West seems to have been emptied of its meaning—can explain the hope that is within us, the Smiths of the world will persist. They will ask us to walk the talk. We can shoot the messenger or we can enter into a process of theological reflection so we can hear the questions the modern world is asking. Is there such a thing as objective truth? Is there a still point in the changing world?

Is someone hiding in the rubber poop monster?

Kevin Smith is a funny guy.

Reviewing the Chapter

1.   Smith is a new generation Catholic who received little religious education in the post-Vatican II Church. How is this evident in *Dogma*? How does his

commentary on hierarchy, doctrines, and moral issues reflect a disconnection with an understanding of Catholic beliefs, worship, and practices?

2. Smith has made many comedies. He also enjoys genre pictures and their conventions as well as spoofs. How valid is his satire on religion and the religious ideas or practices of the church itself and the beliefs of others?

3. In a New Age era, many audiences are fascinated by angels and demons. How was Smith playing on this popular trend with his imagining of the recalcitrant angels and the strange demons? What does this representation mean for believers? For nonbelievers?

Notes

1. As of April 2003, Smith's Website, www.viewaskew, had 69,723 registered users on message boards and 250,000 hits a day or more when Smith is online.
2. *An Evening with Kevin Smith* (2002), DVD, Columbia TriStar.
3. John Kenneth Muir, *A View Askew: The Films of Kevin Smith* (New York: Applause Theater & Cinema Books, 2002).
4. Muir, *A View Askew*, 127.
5. Richard A. Blake, "Fallen Angels," *America*, December 4, 1999.
6. To put this in perspective, Martin Scorsese's religious-themed drama *Bringing Out the Dead* made $19 million.
7. *Evening*, DVD.
8. *Evening*, DVD.
9. Trey Parker and Matt Stone, "South Park: Death," Comedy Central, September 17, 1997.
10. *Evening*, DVD.
11. Thomas R. Rausch, *The College Student's Introduction to Theology* (Collegeville, MN: Liturgical Press, 1993), 16.
12. *Evening*, DVD.
13. *Evening*, DVD.
14. Muir, *A Askew View*, 132–33.
15. Thomas S. Hibbs, *Shows about Nothing: Nihilism in Popular Culture from Seinfeld to the Exorcist* (Dallas: Spence Publishing, 1999).
16. Hibbs, *Shows about Nothing*.

Index

vocation. *See The Devil's Playground*
vocational crisis. *See The Priest*
La voce della luna (*The Voice of the Moon*), 205
The Voice of the Moon. See La voce della luna
La Voie lactée (*The Milky Way*), 153–54

Wajda, Andrzej, 2, 4, 103, 192, 209–20
Walker, Stuart, 20
wandering. *See* Subiela, Eliseo
Wanted: Perfect Mother, 135
The War Is Now!, 227
Watling, Leonor, 82
We Were Soldiers, 228, 235
Weight, but Found Wanting. See Tinimbang Ka, Ngunit Kulang
Weir, Peter, 35, 230
Welles, Orson, 29, 154
Wemba, Papa, 124
Wend Kuuni (*The Gift of God*), 121–25; children, 124–25
Wenders, Wim, 173
Wharton, Edith, 12
What Have I Done to Deserve This?, 77, 81
What Women Want, 226, 228
Williams, Niall, 25

Without Sender. See Sin remitente
women, in Catholic directors' films, 50. *See also* Africa; *All About My Mother*; Almodóvar, Pedro; *Household Saints*
Women on the Edge of a Nervous Breakdown, 78
Wong Kar Wai, 1
Wootton, Adrian, 26

Yaaba (*Grandmother*), 123, 125–26
The Year of Living Dangerously, 225
Year of the Quiet Sun, 220n24
Yeelen, 122–23
You Upset Me. See Tu mi turbi
The Young and the Damned. See Los Olvidados
Young at Heart, 18
You're the Mother of Your Child. See Ina Ka ng Anak Mo

Z, 137, 220n35
Zan Boko, 121, 124
Zanussi, Krzysztof, 103, 192, 214–15, 219n24, 220n28
Zeffirelli, Franco, 226, 234
Zero and Counting Four. See Cero y van cuatro
Ziemia Obiecana (*The Promised Land*), 210, 218

About the Contributors

James Abbott is a British journalist who has reviewed films for the Catholic Herald and other papers. He was manager of the online Christian radio state XT3 and is a journalist and on air reporter for Premier Christian radio in the United Kingdom.

Tom Aitken was born and educated in New Zealand but has lived in England since 1967. He was film critic for *The Tablet* for eight years and has served on film juries in Berlin, Venice, and Setubal. He is a frequent contributor to the *Times Literary Supplement*. His book *Blood and Fire, Tsar and Commissar, The Salvation Army in Russia 1907–1923* will be published in 2007.

Lloyd Baugh is a Jesuit priest born and raised in Canada, and he did his doctorate in Fundamental Theology and Cinema at the Pontifical Gregorian University in Rome. Now a full professor at the Gregorian, he has published widely and has taught in the United States, Canada, Philippines, and Madagascar. His main areas of research and writing are the films of Krzysztof Kieslowski and the Jesus and Christlike figure films.

Guido Convents is a Belgian film scholar who has researched the early years of silent film in Europe. He has also written extensively on African cinema including a recent history of cinema in the Congo. He works at the General Secretariat of SIGNIS (The World Catholic Association for Communication), organizes SIGNIS juries at international film festivals, and edits SIGNIS Media.

Nicasio Cruz is a Jesuit from the Philippines. He has lectured on film in universities in Manila and written extensively on cinema subjects. He has contributed to an awareness of Filipino cinema, especially because of his personal knowledge of the filmmakers.

Jan Epstein writes for several Jewish newspapers and magazines in Australia. Her movie reviews also appear on the Australian Bishops Conference Website, and she is an associate member of the Australian Catholic Film Office. She is working on a documentary on images of migration and race in Australian cinema.

Greg Friedman is a Franciscan priest and producer of video for religious education. He hosts a national Catholic radio program in the United States and is also a pastor in an inner-city neighborhood in Cincinnati, Ohio, the setting for a number of major American films, including two by director John Sayles.

Michael Paul Gallagher is an Irish Jesuit priest who lectured on English literature at University College, Dublin for twenty years, has served as a member of the Pontifical Council for Culture, and is the author of many books and articles, including *Struggles of Faith*, *Free to Believe*, *Letters on Prayer*, and *What are they saying about unbelief?* He is currently the dean of theology at the Gregorian University in Rome.

Marc Gervais is a Canadian Jesuit. He has been writing on cinema and its religious dimensions for many years. He has also been a lecturer on cinema at Concordia University in Montreal. A particular focus of his writing and lecturing has been the cinema of Ingmar Bergman, including *Ingmar Bergman: Magician and Prophet* and an audio commentary on a DVD collection of Bergman's films of the mid-1960s.

Peter Malone, an Australian Missionary of the Sacred Heart, has been reviewing films since 1968 and taught theology and media studies. After serving as president of The International Catholic Organization for Cinema (OCIC) during the 1990s, he was elected world president in 1998. He was then president of SIGNIS (The World Catholic Association for Communication), 2001–2005. He has published a number of books and articles on cinema, theology, and spirituality.

Claire Openshaw is a senior teaching fellow in the Institute of Communications Studies at Leeds University. Her professional background is in new media, Web management, and system(s) accessibility. Her academic interests are in new media and film narrative, teaching and learning development, organizational management, systems, and team development. Claire is also a professional/personal development coach.

Luis García Orso, born in Tijuana, Mexico, has been a Jesuit priest since 1973. He teaches fundamental theology and is the author of numerous articles and three books on cinema and spirituality (*Imágenes del espíritu en el cine: Una guía para ver cine ¿Cómo aprovechar la espritualidad del cine?*) He is former president of the International Catholic Organization for Cinema (OCIC) and SIGNIS (The World Catholic Association for Communication) Mexico (1995–2006). He has been a SIGNIS jury member in many national and international film festivals.

Gaye Williams Ortiz teaches communication studies at Augusta State University in Georgia and is an Honorary Fellow of York St John University in York, England. She is the coeditor (with Clive Marsh) of *Explorations through Theology and Film* (1997) and (with Clara Joseph) *Theology and Literature: Rethinking Reader Responsibility* (2006). She served as vice president of SIGNIS (The World Catholic Association for Communication) from 2001 to 2005.

Rose Pacatte has her master of arts in education in media studies from the Institute of Education, University of London, is a Daughter of St. Paul, and the director of the Pauline Center for Media Studies in Los Angeles. She is coauthor with Peter Malone, MSC, of the award-winning *Lights, Camera, Faith . . . ! A Movie Lectionary* series, and the film and television columnist for *St. Anthony Messenger*, a national Catholic magazine in the United States.

Rob Rix was head of Spanish at Trinity and All Saints College Leeds until his retirement in 2004. He has published widely in the field of Spanish and Latin American cinema, literature, and culture as well as language teaching methodology, and is currently working on Latin American cyberliterature.

Maggie Roux is an associate principal lecturer at Leeds Trinity College in Yorkshire. Her professional background is in radio and television. Her academic interests are in myth and narrative, screening psychological type, screening performance, film, and spirituality. A professional/personal development coach and retreat leader, Maggie has been a regular preacher on the BBC's *Daily Service*. She reviews film weekly for BBC radio.

Jose Tavares de Barros is a retired university professor of cinema studies from Belo Horizonte, Brazil. A representative of the International Catholic Organization for Cinema (OCIC) Brazil, he was international vice president (1990–1994). He conducts media seminars for the episcopal conferences of Latin America. He has written articles and books, served on a number of international film festival juries, and commented on film in the media in such programs as Sala de Cinema on *TV Horizonte*.

Dario Vigano is an Italian priest who was born in Brazil. He belongs to the archdiocese of Milan. Rome-based, he is the director of Ente dello Spettacolo and has responsibility for cinema and entertainment for the Italian Bishops Conference (CEI). He lectures at the Pontifical Urban University in Rome and has written many articles and books, including *Il cinema delle parabole, I sentieri della comunicazione,* and *Storia e teorie, Gesu e la macchina de presa, Dizionario ragionato del cinema cristologico.*

Ricardo Yáñez, a native of Los Angeles, grew up in Buenos Aires, Argentina. He is a catechist, journalist, and media education facilitator. He was vice president of the International Catholic Organization for Cinema (OCIC) and SIGNIS (The World Catholic Association for Communication) in Argentina, from 1998 to 2003. He is the assistant to the secretary general of SIGNIS in Brussels, Belgium.

This book is a project of SIGNIS, The World Catholic Association for Communication. All the authors are members or associates of SIGNIS.